In January 1992 the Canadian Broadcasting Corporation (CBC) broadcast *The Valour and the Horror*, a three-part television series on Canada's role in World War II. The series sparked a major controversy among viewers, war veterans, and historians. Brian and Terence McKenna, the authors–producers of the series, were accused of distorting historical facts, maligning individuals such as commanders Arthur Harris and Guy Simonds, presenting a biased account of events, and overstepping the line between journalism and drama. *The Valour and the Horror Revisited* brings together source documents, original essays, and commentaries to provide an analysis of the specific accusations and of larger questions concerning responsible journalism.

Included in the collection are reports by David J. Bercuson and S.F. Wise, who were asked to assess the series: the CBC ombudsman's report; the McKennas' response to the ombudsman's report; the ombudsman's commentary on the McKennas' response; and three new essays by historians John Ferris, William McAndrew, and Scot Robertson on the incidents covered in the series – Canadian involvement in the battles in Hong Kong and Normandy, and the bombing of Germany.

The Valour and the Horror Revisited addresses such important issues as the dangers of "docudrama," the meaning of the Canadian experience in the war, and the nature of history.

DAVID J. BERCUSON is a professor in the Department of History and dean of Graduate Studies, University of Calgary.

S.F. WISE is a professor in the Department of History and former dean of Graduate Studies and Research, Carleton University.

The Valour and the Horror Revisited

Edited by
David J. Bercuson and S.F. Wise

McGill-Queen's University Press
Montreal & Kingston • London • Buffalo

© McGill-Queen's University Press 1994
ISBN 0-7735-1259-4 (cloth)
ISBN 0-7735-1271-3 (paper)

Legal deposit fourth quarter 1994
Bibliothèque nationale du Québec

Printed in Canada on acid-free paper

McGill-Queen's University Press is grateful
to the Canada Council for support of its
publishing program.

Canadian Cataloguing in Publication Data

Main entry under title:

The Valour and the horror revisited

Includes bibliographical references.
ISBN 0-7735-1259-4 (bound) –
ISBN 0-7735-1271-3 (pbk.)

1. Valour and the horror (Television program).
2. World War, 1939–1945 – Canada. 3. Journalistic
ethics. I. Bercuson, David Jay, 1945– .
II. Wise, S.F. (Sydney Francis), 1924– .

D768.15.V35 1994   791.45'72   C94-900378-6

Contents

PART THREE: HISTORIANS' COMMENTARY

APPENDIX

PART ONE

Drama or Documentary?

S.F. WISE AND DAVID J. BERCUSON

Introduction

The controversy over the CBC televised series on the Second World War, *The Valour and the Horror*, erupted almost immediately after it was broadcast in early 1992. Both the CBC and the National Film Board (which had commissioned the series from Galafilm, Inc.) had had previous experience with public controversy over their offerings, but nothing quite like this. Indeed, the public debate over *The Valour and the Horror* was without precedent, since the quarrel appeared to be over the interpretation of an aspect of Canada's immediate past. Canadians are not usually disposed to debate their history, and especially not those aspects that are military in nature. Conscription, yes; the Normandy Campaign, no.

The editors of this book were drawn into *The Valour and the Horror* controversy because they agreed, as professional military historians, to evaluate the series for the CBC ombudsman. In particular, they were asked to consider how well the three episodes depicted Canadian participation in the Second World War in terms of their fairness, balance, and accuracy. Our reports are published for the first time here and follow this introduction. They provided the basis for the report of the CBC ombudsman, William Morgan, and hence for the response of the writer-producers of the series, Brian and Terence McKenna. Both these documents are reproduced here, and are followed by two further documents that call for an explanation.

The first is a letter from S.F. Wise of 16 November 1992, published in the *Montreal Gazette* and the *Globe and Mail*. It was written in response to the slurs on the professional reputation of Wise and his predecessor, C.P. Stacey, as director of history, Department of National Defence, found in the Galafilm response to the ombudsman's report. Without it, an unwary reader, unfamiliar with the evolution of the controversy, might imagine that these slurs had gone unchallenged and unrebutted.

The second is the comments of William Morgan, the CBC ombudsman, on the response of Galafilm to his original report, carried in a CBC press release of 18 November 1992. This important document, which must be read together with the Galafilm response, was virtually ignored by the media at the time, though it contains some significant passages. One of the most telling is the demonstration by Mr Morgan that the producers of *The Valour and the Horror* concocted dialogue for the actors portraying participants, dialogue not found either in the historical record or in the transcripts of relatively recent interviews with these persons. Had we been aware of this circumstance at the time we wrote our reports, we both would have been sorely tempted to depart from the measured and dispassionate analysis we separately strove to achieve.

One further word of explanation about the documentation is necessary. The CBC ombudsman received three reports from historians, and only two are printed in this volume. The third was from Denis Richardson, a British historian who had written the introduction to Air Marshal Sir Arthur Harris's book on Bomber Command. To us, the controversy over the dramatic depiction of Harris in *The Valour and the Horror* was not a central matter, though both of us touch on it in our reports. In our opinion, the issues raised by the Galafilm production were essentially Canadian, and therefore we made the decision not to include the Richardson report, had it been available to us. We have in fact not seen Mr Richardson's report.

The reason we decided to publish our reports, together with the findings of Mr Morgan and the retort of the McKenna brothers, is because, as historians, we believe that the issues raised by *The Valour and the Horror* are important and are far from being resolved. Indeed, in certain respects, some of the issues can never be settled.

At the outset of the *Valour and the Horror* controversy, it appeared that the core of the debate was over the accuracy of the series as history. In each of the three programs the writer-producers put forward a similar and powerful thesis: they were about to tell the true story of Canadian participation in the war for the first time, a story of idealistic young men betrayed by their commanders. The McKennas seemed to be trying to condemn the war, to condemn the professional soldiers whose job it was to fight wars, and to praise those warriors who were not professional soldiers but had volunteered to fight out of the purest motives.

This thesis is provocative and surely deserves both an airing and a full debate. There is, after all, some evidence – a great deal of which the McKennas missed entirely – which might be said to support their viewpoint. And there has been little or no public discussion about either the role Canada played in the Second World War or the quality of its contribution to the Allied victory. At a time when Canadians seem to have lost their sense of their own history, and with the fiftieth anniversary of the end of the Second World War rapidly approaching, such a debate could have done much good.

That, however, was not to be. Soon after the controversy began it became apparent that very deep chords had been touched within Canadian society. Enraged veterans' groups intervened, furious that the part they had played in the war had been mocked or called into question; a subcommittee of the Senate of Canada gave notice that it intended to hold hearings on the issues raised by the series; and the embattled writer-producers were joined by journalists and media persons of every description to defend the sacred causes of freedom of speech, freedom of the press, and freedom of expression. The *Globe and Mail*, in the wake of the ombudsman's report, assaulted the Senate subcommittee as a "kangaroo court" and "a disgrace to democracy" in which "the machinery of state" was arrayed "against a free press" pursuing "free historical inquiry."[1]

The media won the first public debate. So thoroughly were the avenues of expression choked with the outpourings of journalistic indignation that contrary views were submerged. The media outcry shifted ground from the central question of just how accurate the McKenna thesis really was to the murkier ground of whether veterans' groups, the Senate, and others who became involved had any right to question how appropriate it had been for the CBC, a publicly funded network, to air the programs. That shift was unfortunate, because the *Valour and the Horror* controversy always had two dimensions: whether the CBC should have aired the programs, and just how good they were as history. For the most part, the media became obsessed with the first and ignored the second. We have always ignored the first and, as our reports show, concentrated on the second.

It is true that letters to the editor in various newspapers provided the basis for dissenting opinion, but, on the whole, media solidarity obtained. It was in vain that such commentators as Desmond Morton pointed out in the Toronto *Star* that the phenomenon of pack journalism stood in the way of any free public discussion.[2] Because the media are, of course, dominated by people who, in general, have little more knowledge of Canadian history than that of the majority of their fellow citizens, the media's agenda became *the* agenda that the rest of the nation was supposed to address. Thus the Senate hearings, whether they ultimately served the purpose of free discussion or not, were one of the few venues for professional historians to present their views. On radio and television, for example, journalists clearly preferred pitting the McKennas against veterans than professional historians. The veterans, often emotional, usually capable of drawing only upon their own personal experiences, and generally with little technical knowledge of the history of the war, tended to fare badly. What's more, they almost always approached the topic from the perspective that the McKennas had no right to question an "accepted" version of history. Virtually all the professional historians who did speak up, however, queried the McKennas' facts, not their right to express themselves.

That part of the debate is now over and the media has won. As Morton pointed out in the *Star*, A.J. Liebling, himself a revered journalist, once said that the only true freedom of press belongs to those fortunate individuals who can buy one. In this instance, the media claque cut off debate and ensured that they, and they alone, could be prosecutors, jury, and judge in *The Valour and the Horror* case.

Though journalists and other media folk may believe that the debate has been successfully concluded, it has only just begun in the opinion of the historical profession. We often hear discarded politicians appeal against the judgment of the present to that of history, with little comprehension of what that implies. The judgment of history, like it or not, is in the long run the judgment of historians. A number of historians gave their opinion during the Senate subcommittee hearings, but most Canadian historians have yet to take a public position.

Why has the historical profession in Canada been so slow off the mark, with the exception of those historians who testified before the Senate subcommittee or who have achieved some commercial or media prominence? It must be said that most members of the discipline are not particularly adept at engaging in any form of public controversy, even though the subject matter in this instance was very much up the historians' street. The profession has seen some notable controversialists, such as A.R.M. Lower and Lionel Groulx, but the nature of the discipline does not lend itself to pungent sound bites. Historians, like lawyers, are careful in assessing evidence and witnesses, and are mistrustful of generalization, particularly without sustaining detail. They see the past as complex and have a professional bias against simplification. Dispassionate analysis, the balancing of conflicting testimony, an awareness of the fallibility of witnesses, and a healthy scepticism are the marks of the historian. Such qualities do not consort readily with the doughty public fighter, unless one is Arthur Lower or Lionel Groulx.

Then, too, it is just plain difficult for professional historians to come to grips with the sometimes outlandish and even fabricated claims of amateur historians that they have suddenly discovered some new truth that historians have allegedly been hiding, especially when historians have to prove a negative to do so. As one example, take the claims advanced in the first program in the series, "Savage Christmas," that the British knew war with Japan was imminent when they asked Canada to provide defenders for Hong Kong. That is easy to state, but to challenge and reject it a historian must have a thorough knowledge of British-Japanese diplomacy, of documents residing in archives across the ocean, and of the immense secondary literature surrounding this event, and must then take the time to publish the sort of exhaustive reply that no newspaper or popular magazine will print and no radio or TV station will air. That type of rebuttal will be read primarily by other historians, most of whom will have recognized the inaccuracy of the claim in the first place. In the face of such difficulties it is the rare historian who will even be bothered to try.

We were more fortunate than most of our colleagues in the historical profession in that we were asked to analyse *The Valour and the Horror* from the perspective of professional historians, not for a popular audience but as part of an internal evaluation of the series by the CBC ombudsman. We were given a particular time frame in which to submit our reports and broad latitude in what we could address. Obviously the ombudsman did not ask us to write monograph-sized evaluations, so the space we could devote to any given issue was limited, and some aspects we chose not to address at all. Given the McKennas' use of oral evidence, however, we want to stress that current recollections of events that took place long ago must always be used with care and must be identified as current, so that readers will not be misled into thinking that the words presented were actually spoken or written at the time. What a person remembers or thinks or says can be very different from what he or she might have remembered or thought or said long ago.

During the controversy that followed the publication of the CBC ombudsman's report and the reply by the McKennas, we received a number of letters from colleagues, students, and other interested persons asking for copies of our reports or for publication of them. We assume that CBC management decided not to publish the reports, though we had thought they would be appended to the ombudsman's report. On 15 November 1992 we wrote to the president of the CBC requesting the publication of our reports, in part to counter the attacks made upon our professional integrity and competence by the writer-producers of *The Valour and the Horror*. More important, we hoped that publication would enable the public, as we wrote to Mr

Veilleux, "to read what we said, and why we said it," so that debate would be refocused "where it ought to be: on the programs themselves." Mr Veilleux did not acknowledge our letter.

Most of our correspondence was more productive. We were particularly impressed by letters from fellow historians and students of history pointing out that our reports, together with the films of the series, the report of the ombudsman, and the response of the McKennas, would be useful as discussion materials illustrating the problems of historical interpretation.

This book is an attempt to meet that need and to assist a wider public in forming a judgment on what we believe are the important questions raised by the series. We, as editors, are already committed; we watched the films, reviewed the evidence, and took our stand when we wrote our reports. These reports are printed as they were written for the ombudsman; second thoughts and felicitous revisions have not been allowed to creep in, though a few typographical errors have been corrected. No one who reads them will be in any doubt about our position on the series or why we took the stance we did.

Our contributors, however, are not so committed. Each of them was asked to review the historical literature surrounding the issues raised by the three episodes of *The Valour and the Horror* and to comment on the relationship of that literature to the content of the series. Beyond those general guidelines, they received no further direction from us. The essays by John Ferris on Hong Kong, by William McAndrew on the Normandy campaign, and by Scot Robertson on the strategic bombing campaign are intended to provide expert guidance to anyone wishing to pursue these subjects further. Each historian is a specialist in the field in which he writes, and we think readers will find their essays of considerable help in understanding the issues raised by the series. The careful reader will observe that in some particulars our contributors differ from the views we have expressed. So be it; unanimity is not a characteristic of historical study.

As for us, we have not changed the opinions recorded in our reports – reports written independently of each other, since we had no knowledge at the time of the identity of the ombudsman's consultants. Our long silence has had its frustrations. Both of us, for example, were pilloried by the writer-producers of *The Valour and the Horror* for sins and shortcomings of which we were innocent. As frustrating, but infinitely more interesting, were the conversations with various members of the media. One of the most intriguing was a lengthy telephone conversation with the late Stephen Godfrey, whose able arts criticism is now much missed. In the course of that conversation Mr Godfrey asked, somewhat rhetorically, "Well, who owns our history?"[3]

This question has some importance in terms of the controversy surrounding the series, and certainly it was raised often by the McKennas. Let us look again at their assertion in each of the episodes of *The Valour and the Horror* that what was to come exposed the truth for the first time. Here they claimed, in short, that there had been a conspiracy of silence on the part of the historical establishment to suppress the truth and to propagate an official version of what Canadians had endured during the Second World War. In this sense it was the historical profession itself that was on trial, having furnished Canadians with a false picture of the past.

Any professional historian has difficulty with the concept of historical truth and is aware of the philosophical pitfalls in store for those who claim to have achieved it. No professional historian believes he or she owns history; on the contrary, historians are only too aware that their findings are subject to criticism from their colleagues. But unless one is a postmodern deconstructionist, permitted by this curious ideology to treat history and historical evidence as a species of fiction, professional historians believe in the merits of sound scholarship, criticism of evidence, the importance of context, and the cumulative weight of rational analysis carried out as dispassionately as can be managed. The assertions of the McKennas in *The Valour and the Horror* that they were in exclusive possession of an absolute truth, long hidden by some form of collective plot, savour more of mysticism than history and should have been warning signals to the journalists who leaped so enthusiastically on the bandwagon.

We strongly believe that just as no one owns history, there can be no official version of the truth, especially if democracy is to be sustained. We have no quarrel with the McKennas venturing upon historical ground and no argument with any attempt – by them or others – to demythologize history. A careful reading of our reports will show that our objections were based not on indignation that the series was aired, but on our assessment that it was badly flawed, especially in the critical area of lack of context. That is worth stressing because some of the defenders of the series asked, "How much context will these historians ever be satisfied with?" The answer is surely "as much as is needed to allow viewers to arrive at a reasonable conclusion about what actually happened."

We have found it more than ironic, however, that in claiming to demythologize the history of Canada's role in the Second World War, the McKennas came up with no better answer than to replace the myths they alleged to have existed by a new myth of their own – the myth of betrayal by commanders who were either incompetent or downright evil. And we are disturbed that in an era when the schools have failed to teach young Canadians the history of their own country, and especially their country at war, the students will now learn about the Second World War from this series.

There is much the McKennas could have told a wide audience about Canada in the Second World War that *is* new and that would have changed Canadians' conceptions of their own history. They might have told the story of how the Canadian government's insistence that Canada have its own bomber formation (6 Group) caused heavy casualties among Canadian aircrew. They might have told Canadians that the country's disgraceful unpreparedness for war in 1939 hamstrung the Royal Canadian Navy and relegated the RCN to a lesser role in the war to destroy Hitler's U-boat packs. They could have depicted the bloody and waterlogged struggle of Canada's Cinderella army to clear the Scheldt Estuary in the fall of 1944 – Canada's greatest victory in the Second World War – and the blunder by Montgomery that made that battle necessary. But to have done any of that, they would have had to dispense with the mythmaking task they had set themselves. And they would have had to be far more knowledgeable about the Second World War, and Canada's part in it, than their unhappy performance in this series proved them to be.

We are aware that, for many, there is no special expertise required to write history. The kinds of rigorous criticism and analysis demanded of the honours and graduate students in history are unknown to the public and, it seems, to many journalists. Most of our fellow citizens believe that anyone with motivation and assiduity can write good history. Unlike physics or medicine, the practice of history has no central mystery. Of course, while we recognize that much good history has been written by amateurs, we contend that the real response to Stephen Godfrey's question is that it does not matter so much *who* writes history; what matters is *how* history is written. We believe that *The Valour and the Horror* is bad history, even though some of the issues raised in it are worthy of debate. But the verdict lies with our readers.

NOTES

1 *Globe and Mail* editorial, 12 Nov. 1992.
2 Desmond Morton, "Hell hath no fury like the media scorned," Toronto *Star*, 19 Nov. 1992.

3 It was also clear from that conversation that Mr Godfrey, in attacking
   the Senate subcommittee and the report of the ombudsman, believed he
   was upholding, not the freedom of the press or "free historical enquiry," but freedom of artistic expression. To him, the "creative" use of
   history was the central issue, a position he laid out in a Spectator
   column in the *Globe and Mail*, 21 Nov. 1992, "Doctoring the line between docu and drama."

S.F. WISE

The Valour and the Horror:
A Report for the CBC Ombudsman

INTRODUCTION

In a letter to me of 24 June 1992 enclosing VHS cassettes of the three episodes of *The Valour and the Horror*, as well as transcripts of the post-production scripts, the Ombudsman expressed the hope that I would "be able to form [my] main impressions and judgments as far as possible from viewing what was actually broadcast before turning to the transcripts for ease of reference." That is the procedure I have followed, viewing each of the episodes in turn, beginning with "Savage Christmas: Hong Kong 1941," and concluding with "Death by Moonlight: Bomber Command," before checking my impressions against the transcripts.

As I had mentioned to the Ombudsman, this was my first viewing of the series, since at the time it was broadcast I was engaged in research at the Library of the British Museum in London. Prior to viewing the series, I had of course read a number of press reports on it, but I do not believe that any of them coloured my perspective one way or another. For me, it was a fresh experience, and the views and judgments expressed in this report are very much my own.

When I discussed with the Ombudsman the possibility that I might review these programs for his office, I asked what he expected from me in the way of a report. His response, as accurately as I can recall, was that he wished my judgment on them as a professional historian, particularly because my area of research and writing has included Canadian military history. What I have to say is based essentially upon that directive. I have no expertise as a critic of television drama, or of the technical modes of production of television programs. My concern has been solely with the validity of these presentations as history.

Nor have I seen it as part of my responsibility to check for accuracy every statement or presentation of an event occurring in the series. Indeed, to do so, particularly with respect to the engagements dealt with in the Battle of Normandy episode, would involve considerable research. At various points, however, I have queried the historical accuracy of statements forming part of the narration of each of the programs.

Finally, I have assumed that what was wanted was *not* a scholarly paper, studded with the usual paraphernalia of references and footnotes, though from time to time I have cited certain sources which appear to me to bear directly upon the burden of argument developed in one episode or another. Rather, I have assumed that what was called for in each case, and overall, was an assessment of whether these presentations embodied a fair and balanced assessment, in historical terms, of three important aspects of Canadian participation in the Second World War.

SAVAGE CHRISTMAS: HONG KONG 1941

The treatment of the dispatch of the Royal Rifles and the Winnipeg Grenadiers to Hong Kong in November 1941, the Japanese assault upon the Crown Colony, the operations in which the Canadians were involved, the conduct of the Japanese, both militarily and as captors, and the sufferings of the Canadians appears to me to be generally sound. The story is both a tragic and a puzzling one, and lent itself to the mode of presentation adopted admirably.

Nevertheless, a number of questions were raised by it, and by the transcript. It is stated early in the presentation (Transcript, p. 4) that "the details of what happened to these soldiers were for a long time suppressed by the Canadian government. The terrible story is known to very few Canadians. Many Japanese would also prefer that it be forgotten." While I have no doubt that the last sentence in this statement is absolutely correct, the rest of it is problematic. The first documented historical account of what happened to these two Canadian battalions was published in 1948, in C.P. Stacey's *The Canadian Army, 1939–1945*, pp. 273–88. An expanded version was published by Col. Stacey in 1955, in volume I of the official history of the Canadian Army in the Second World War, *Six Years of War*, pp. 437–91. The television presentation differed in no significant particular from the Stacey account of 1955, both in terms of military operations and what Stacey called "the numerous acts of wanton barbarism" and the "particularly revolting atrocities" committed by the Japanese. The only other Canadian monographic account of these events is Carl Vincent's *No Reason Why*, published in 1980.

There were two government inquiries into the Hong Kong affair, a Royal Commission in 1942 and a parliamentary enquiry in 1948. In each case reports were subsequently published, and documents used by each enquiry, including those having a wartime security classification, have been open to researchers for about twenty-five years. That the government of the time was deeply embarrassed by the Hong Kong episode goes without saying, but I do not find any pattern of deliberate suppression of details that departs from the long-standing archival practice for government records.

It may be, however, that the writers of this episode are referring to details of the cruel and inhumane treatment suffered by Canadian soldiers during their long period of imprisonment at Hong Kong and their subsequent employment as a form of slave labour in the Japanese home islands. If that is so, that is certainly generally correct, although, through press and radio, Canadians very rapidly became acquainted after the end of the war with the fate of their compatriots and of their brutal treatment at the hands of the Japanese – public knowledge which was reinforced by the vivid American accounts of similar episodes. I was left with the impression, however, that the writers intended to plant the idea that there had been a conspiracy of silence about Hong Kong. It has not been my experience that "the terrible story is known to very few Canadians"; most Canadians, at least of my generation, know it all too well, even if they cannot trace actual operations from the Gin Drinkers' Line to the Stanley Peninsula.

The central contention of the broadcast presentation is that the two Canadian battalions were not trained to engage in the defence of Hong Kong against an experienced and battle-hardened enemy. This is certainly correct; both units had seen previous garrison service in Newfoundland and the West Indies, and do not appear to have had rigorous training prior to their dispatch. They contained as well a number of soldiers who had had virtually no training whatsoever. Though opinions may differ, in terms of the historical record, about the proportion of well-trained officers and men in these battalions, no one who has written on the episode would argue that these troops were combat ready, either in terms of training or scale of equipment.

But the real historical problem about Hong Kong is barely touched upon by this program. What were Canadians doing in Hong Kong anyway? How had it come about that a government headed by W.L.M. King, a man notably reluctant to commit Canadian forces in overseas ventures, especially those savouring of empire, had dispatched these men to an outpost of that empire, in which Canada had no conceivable interest?

We are told in the narration that the request came from Britain, and "incredibly, Canada answered England's call without making an independent assessment of the peril, accepting the mother country's assurances that the men would not be in harm's way." Here indeed is the core of the matter historically: that is, the context which gives meaning to everything that followed. But all the audience is given on this crucial point is a set of assertions, which, I believe, required some elaboration if one was to understand how this bizarre affair had come about.

The writers say that in early 1941 Winston Churchill "said privately that there was not the slightest chance of holding Hong Kong or of relieving it if the Japanese attacked." He didn't say it "privately"; he stated it repeatedly in War Cabinet memoranda and in memoranda to his Chiefs of Staff. The combination of pressures that led him to change his mind, and agree to a small reinforcement of the garrison, depended in part on American and British intelligence of Japanese intentions, and in part on representations from the British theatre commander in Malaya (the overly optimistic Air Marshal Brooke-Popham) and of General A.E. Grasett, who had just finished a tour as base commander at Hong Kong. Grasett was a Canadian, a graduate of RMC Kingston, who stopped in Ottawa to see General Crerar on his way back to Britain. It was from Grasett that the suggestion came to ask Canada to supply the reinforcements; the Dominions Office (successor to the Colonial Office) appears to have thought it would be a good thing to get Canada committed in the Pacific region.

The British made no assurance that the Canadian troops would "be out of harm's way"; but from the Dominions Office dispatch it would be possible to form the judgment that another spell of garrison duty for Canadian units was contemplated. "We have thought hitherto that it would not serve any ultimate useful purpose to increase the existing army garrison ... Situation in the Orient however has now altered. There have been signs of a certain weakening in attitude of Japan towards United States and ourselves. Defences of Malaya have improved. Under these conditions our view is that a small reinforcement ... of Hong Kong garrison would be very fully justified. It would reassure Chiang Kai Shek as to genuineness of our intention to hold the colony and in addition would have a very great moral effect throughout the Far East."

What about the "independent assessment" the writers suggest should have taken place? The only source of intelligence as to Japanese intentions possessed by the government of Canada was Britain, plus what could be gathered from our embassy in Washington. One looks in vain at the government structure of the period for anything which might be viewed as expertise on Japan or the Far East generally. The Cabinet referred the request of the Dominions Office to the General Staff of the Army and to the Minister of National Defence, Col. Ralston. General Crerar, for the staff, merely indicated that it would be possible to provide two battalions; subsequently Ralston gave his approval. No one, at least so far as the documentary record is concerned, questioned whether Canadian troops should be dispatched to defend a British colony (Canada already having done so in two instances), or whether these troops would be in any danger.

The Hong Kong decision is full of irony, a kind of throw-back to another time and another set of constitutional arrangements, in which Prime Minister King, that apostle of autonomy, gave what amounted to a "Ready, aye, ready" response to the British call. Canadians, of course, were no more prescient than Americans in the autumn of 1941. The Japanese invasion of Hong Kong was no more dreamt of than was the Japanese attack upon Pearl Harbor. Even had an "independent check" been possible in 1941, it is doubtful whether anyone could have been found to predict such events. With our knowledge of what was to come, it is easy to condemn both the British and the Canadian governments, especially in view of the tragedy which then unfolded. But hindsight is not history.

At two points in the broadcast, a participant, Roger Cyr, or the actor representing him, says: "The thought that my government would knowingly offer a couple of thousand of its young men as lambs to the slaughter in order to meet some sort of political expedience ..." (p. 3, 53). Such a statement is utterly understandable on the part of a survivor; the fair – if unsatisfying – reply is that no member of the government, or of the military, "knowingly" sent these lambs to the slaughter. Incidentally, shortly after the end of the Hong Kong debacle, in January 1942, the British government asked whether Canada would be willing to send "one or two battalions" to, of all places, the Falkland Islands. Hong Kong was very much on the mind of Norman Robertson, a senior officer of the Department of External Affairs, when he advised that Canadian troops should not be sent "as lambs to the slaughter" in response to British requests!

On balance, then, I conclude that this presentation told a terrible story well, in terms of narrative history, but failed to give the events

it recounts the background which would render them fully meaningful to the audience.

I must confess to a considerable degree of discomfort with the use
of actors to voice excerpts from letters, diaries, or interviews with
actual participants, even despite the assurance of the writers that such
speeches are "documented." I am too acutely aware, as an historian,
of the treachery of the written word, and even more so when it is
given voice by an actor, under direction, who is remote in time and
circumstance from the original authors of the words attributed to
them.

On the other hand, I must record my heartfelt admiration for the
two veterans of Hong Kong who appeared in this episode. They were
quintessentially Canadian, wholly believable, and some of the
sequences in which they appeared were inexpressibly moving.

IN DESPERATE BATTLE: NORMANDY 1944*

This production, in my view, was much weaker than the Hong Kong
presentation. Many of the events touched on, especially the engagement of a number of units, would call for considerable research on
my part to check the broadcast account against the documentary
record. Rather than adopt this kind of detailed treatment, I have
commented below on three aspects of the presentation which gave me
pause, as an historian. Each is important in itself; taken together, they
raise questions for me about the motives of the writers and the principles which determined the selection of the operations to be dealt
with. These aspects are as follows: (1) that the Canadians were as
guilty as their German enemies in the slaughter of prisoners; (2) the
charge that Canadian manpower shortages were a result of Canadian
Army "bungling"; and (3) the general allegation that Canadian
military leadership was worse than inadequate and sacrificed Canadian troops because of incompetence.

Purported Slaughter of Prisoners

I found this section deeply offensive. It is asserted (Transcript, p. 15)
that "what happened to prisoners of war on both sides in this battle
is one of the darkest chapters in the Second World War." In this manner is a Canadian audience introduced to the murder of Canadians

---

* In the original presentation of *The Valour and the Horror*, the
program "Death by Moonlight: Bomber Command" preceded "In
Desperate Battle: Normandy 1944."

at the Abbey of Ardenne. The Abbey was the headquarters of the general commanding 12th SS Division, Kurt Meyer. He, we are told, "was preoccupied with the battle." That was certainly a contention of the defence at his War Crimes trial. This insertion is at least gratuitous. That the Canadians were murdered, in cold blood, by officers and non-commissioned officers of Meyer's headquarters staff, in the very garden outside the building where he was preoccupied with the battle, is beyond question. Witnesses were present then, and one of them appears in the production to testify to what occurred. The narrative further states that "at least 134 Canadians were executed by the SS in Normandy" (p. 17).

It is then stated that "the German side of this story is different." May I observe that the facts in the previous paragraph do not represent a "story." They are true, and sufficiently attested by the evidence presented at the trial of General Meyer. We are then given, by the Meyer actor, a statement he used at his trial, namely, that he alleged that on the body of a dead Canadian officer notes were found that "no prisoners were to be taken." For the purpose of argument, let us concede that such orders were given, either in writing or verbally. In war (not just this one) such orders are not unknown. Retaliation may occur when just cause has been given, as in the case of the Abbey of Ardenne, or, more frequently, when there is a military requirement for rapid advance unimpeded by prisoners. In the latter case, armies of all descriptions have refused to accept surrender; drastic though this is, and certainly ruthless in the extreme, it differs vastly from the shooting of prisoners who have been disarmed by the enemy and find themselves ensconced in his headquarters.

It is alleged (p. 18) that "some Canadian Generals did give orders to take no prisoners." "Alleged" is the operative word. By whom? What is the evidence for this? Is there documentation for it? I know of none. It is well understood that Normandy was a vicious and brutal battle, and particularly on the Canadian front, where Canadian units were confronted by an enemy imbued with the spirit of Nazi Germany. That there were excesses is certainly possible; such excesses have occurred at all times in all wars.

But what are we to make of the "evidence" of the single British sailor cited on page 18, who claims he found German soldiers with their throats cut? Or the statement by the writers that "similar incidents" occurred under the command of Jacques Dextraze? Any objective reading of the Dextraze testimony is that certain German prisoners, for whom, as an officer, he was responsible, were drowned when forced to swim across a river. I am confident General Dextraze had no idea that this anecdote, recounting the admittedly bloody-minded treatment of prisoners by his troops, would be depicted by the writers as an "Allied atrocity" fully comparable to the cold-blooded murder of Canadian soldiers in the garden of the Abbey of Ardenne. That the battle in Normandy was harsh and unforgiving, and that terrible incidents occurred on both sides, I have no doubt, but I – and I am sure many viewers – reject absolutely that there is any equivalence between the shocking acts which occur during the horror of battle and the deliberate murder of disarmed prisoners who are under the control and protection of an organized unit. Nor do I accept, on the basis of the unsupported allegations of this production, the statement that "the message seems clear. War crimes committed in a good cause are politically acceptable, perhaps regrettable, but such crimes are prosecuted only on the side that loses the war." The issue is essentially that which has been debated since the Nuremberg Trials. On that score, surely (with all we now know) there can be little doubt that we had most of the right people in the dock. There is some validity in the statement that only the victors judge, and their own crimes go unpunished, despite the court martials following the My Lai incident in the Vietnam War. We have only to think of the Soviet Union, prosecuting at the Nuremberg Trials, with the crime of that Katyn Forest on its hands. Unless the writers have evidence to bring forward more convincing than what they offer, what cannot be accepted – and I trust the Canadian audience has not accepted – was that there was no distinction between the treatment of prisoners by the 12th SS Hitler Jugend Division and 3rd Division Canadian Army.

The Manpower Shortage

It is stated in the narration (p. 31) that "the shortage of good reinforcements was blamed on a conscription crisis back home. In fact the shortage was caused by army bungling. From the beginning the army had enough volunteers. But four out of five were trained to do everything but fight. When casualties were higher than predicted, cooks, clerks, mechanics and brand new conscripts had to be given crash weapons training. The results were murderous."

Why should television production be regarded as a licence to engage in grand simplification? Here the writers touch upon one of the most complex issues of the war, so far as Canada was concerned. It is not clear precisely who blamed the crisis on conscription (presumably because large numbers of conscripts were serving in Canada); it is even less clear how "conscripts" got involved in the Normandy battle – this is clearly wrong. No conscripts fought in Normandy; the Cabinet crisis over the manpower issue did not occur until late

October 1944. Remustering of gunners and engineers to infantry to meet the Normandy crisis did take place during the Normandy battle, and it is true that a number of other trades were also remustered for infantry service. That many of them did not have sufficient infantry training, or familiarity with standard infantry weapons, is also true – but the bulk of the soldiers so remustered arrived in the war theatre from Britain only after the end of the Normandy battle.

Was it true that Canada had sufficient volunteers to meet the infantry shortage? There were 120,000 general service soldiers in Canada during the Normandy campaign, and another 80,000 or so in the United Kingdom. In August/September 1944 Ralston and the Canadian General Staff frantically examined these pools of apparently available infantrymen, all, as volunteers, eligible for infantry service. As might be surmised, the bulk of them were either over age, under age, or of medical categories which rendered them unfit for infantry service. Were it otherwise, the writers would be quite correct – but they are not, and this is why the country had a Cabinet, then a conscription crisis. Why? Because (1) the available general duty soldiers in the pools I have mentioned would have taken months to retrain as infantry; (2) modern armies, of the First as well as the Second World War, require a technical, logistical, and administrative tail much larger than armies of the past, and cannot function effectively without such support services; and (3) the *only* source of trained infantrymen lay with the National Resources Mobilization Act (NRMA) men at home in Canada, who, Col. Ralston insisted, would have to be persuaded to serve overseas. This was the heart of the crisis. It was at best naïve of the writers to suggest that army "bungling" had got the country into this fix – it would have made much more sense to argue that mistaken manpower policies in the early years of the war had built up a far higher reservoir of highly trained Canadian aircrew than could be used on operations in 1944.

An army did bungle, but it was not the Canadian Army. Carlo D'Este, in *Decision in Normandy* (1983), his fine book on the Normandy campaign, uses the word "bungle," but of the British Army, not the Canadian. The British War Office had in fact grossly erred in its prediction of casualties in Normandy. Its manpower requirement projections were based upon North African experience, and predicted that in periods of heavy fighting, 48 per cent of the casualties would be suffered by infantry, 15 per cent by the armoured corps, and 14 per cent by the artillery, the rest being distributed among support units. In fact, both the Canadians (who had governed their requirements by the British projections) and the British suffered approximately 80 per cent infantry casualties during periods of heavy fighting in Normandy. As D'Este points out, the British official history "whitewashes the issue"; "one has to look at the official Canadian account for the truth." Col. C.P. Stacey provided the real explanation in his *Victory Campaign* (p. 284), and in a more detailed way in *Arms, Men and Governments* (p. 425ff). As Stacey remarked in the latter publication, it was necessary "to reduce a large and complex subject to brief compass," but even the technical limits of television production should not permit over-simplifications so gross as the writers' unsophisticated "solution" to one of the major political and military crises of the twentieth century in Canada. This is not only inadequate history, it is *bad* history, and misinforms grievously the audience for this program.

The Inadequacy of Canadian Military Leadership in Normandy

As with Hong Kong, the audience is told near the outset of the Normandy production that "the true story of those battles [ie, in Normandy] has never been told" and that the war artists (their pictures now sequestered in warehouses) were "the only ones allowed to record the truth." The most obvious – and vulnerable – targets for these assertions are the war correspondents, and it is a platitude that truth is the first casualty in wartime. Among the examples of cheer-leading journalism cited (p. 8) is the "radio voice" intoning that, on the Normandy beaches, "the Canadian assault troops went almost contemptuously through minefields and curtains of machine gun fire." It is worth noting that Stacey's *Victory Campaign* dismisses such accounts as "nonsense"; as he pointed out many years ago, "the assaulting forces' casualties were heavy at every point ... except Utah Beach." Wartime journalism is an easy target; neither the Canadian official history nor the many regimental histories which have appeared since the end of the war have fudged the fact that Normandy, from the landings to Falaise, was a most desperate and bloody campaign.

The special truth held out by the writers of this production would seem to lie in the interpretation they place upon the Canadian part in the campaign. We are told repeatedly that the Canadians were poorly trained, that they were poorly equipped, and that they were badly led. Like the innocents at Hong Kong, they were lambs led to the slaughter against a superbly trained and equipped German army under magnificent leadership.

How poorly trained were Canadian troops who fought in Normandy? We know that the assault elements (3rd Division and 2nd Armoured Brigade) had begun training for the landings in the summer of 1943 and that this training went through four phases, culminating in a divisional exercise in May 1944, shortly before D-Day. Unlike many German units, however, the Canadians had no battle experience; they had been doing nothing but train during the years they spent in Britain. That shortcomings appeared under battle conditions (particularly in communications) is hardly surprising – this is normal for formations first introduced into operations. But we are in fact never told what the shortcomings of Canadian training were; instead, there are a series of assertions to that effect without a shred of evidence.

The argument that Canadian troops were poorly equipped seems to rest on the superiority of the German tanks over the Sherman. There is convincing evidence of this, both in the film and in the sources. But there is also convincing evidence, not touched on in this production, that the Germans were staggered by the sheer weight of equipment possessed by the Allies, including the Canadians. Rommel, Rundstedt, Kluge, and subordinate commanders comment upon this factor at one time or another during this campaign. And in addition to this vast superiority in *matériel*, the Allies had overwhelming air support, a factor that bedevilled German army operations throughout the Normandy battle.

The heart of the argument is that Canadian generalship was poor. Field Marshal Montgomery's well-known strictures on McNaughton and Crerar serve to condemn the higher command, but the real target is General Simonds, not to speak of General Keller and other lesser lights. In order to do this, an actor is selected to project Simonds's less engaging personality traits, and a series of engagements on and around Verrière Ridge are chosen to illuminate Simonds's heartlessness and incapacity. In my circle, this is called stacking the deck.

The assessment of the calibre of generalship is one of the most treacherous judgments a military historian can engage in. Certainly, however, no competent military historian would try to do so on the basis of two actions in which Canadian units were not successful, and in which very heavy casualties were sustained. If Grant were to be assessed on the basis of Cold Harbor alone, or Lee by Gettysburg, their reputations would hardly stand as high as they do. One of the first things the student of military affairs learns about war is that it is at least as subject as any other human activity to the frailties which beset all of us. It is an activity conducted under conditions of enormous stress for all ranks, under the most confusing and horrifying of circumstances, and mistakes and misunderstandings are frequent. There were no superman generals fighting in Normandy, on either side. Countries with long military traditions have a certain edge over countries like Canada, since they have possessed an officer class for many generations. Even so, in the First World War Canada produced a first-class general in the civilian-soldier Arthur Currie; Australia did so as well, in John Monash.

Whether General Simonds and other Canadian generals belong in such company is open to doubt, but the quality of their performance must be based on the whole record, not on one or two disastrous actions. And here, finally, is why I find this episode deeply unsatisfying as history. The German army, depicted by the writers as far superior to the Canadian forces opposing them, was defeated in Normandy. Its defeat was so overwhelming and conclusive as to presage the end of the war. No one can examine the catastrophe which overtook the German forces in the Falaise-Argentan sector without being deeply impressed by the fighting qualities of all the Allied armies. Germany suffered not a loss but a rout; its armour was drastically depleted, tens of thousands of German soldiers were made prisoner, and the remnants of German forces were compelled to use horse transport in their precipitate retreat through France.

The writers make a fleeting reference to this outcome and account for it by saying that "officers like Jacques Dextraze and Radley Walters and their men found astonishing ways to turn the tide of battle and find the path to victory" (p. 46). According to the whole thrust of the broadcast to this point, German defeat was not supposed to happen; the Canadians were overmatched and condemned to take enormous losses. The viewing audience must only conclude that somehow, despite its poor training, bad equipment, and incompetent leadership, the Canadian Army, along with its Allies, managed to snatch victory against all odds through "astonishing ways."

A more sober and balanced judgment might be that the inexperienced Canadian (and American) forces in Normandy learned a great deal about modern warfare in the crucible of Normandy. Out of that campaign came the Canadian Army which liberated the Channel ports and Holland, and was fighting on German soil when the war ended. From travail, bloodshed, and terrible reverses came a fighting force as entitled as any other to claim a share in what was, after all, a victory.

DEATH BY MOONLIGHT: BOMBER COMMAND

Of the three episodes of *The Valour and the Horror*, that on bombing is probably the most tendentious. It shares certain characteristics with the other two presentations: Canadians had a central role in Bomber Command, constituting as they did a major portion of aircrew, but at the same time they were guileless victims of ruthless leaders and their government remained on the sidelines. What sets this episode apart from the others is the moral issue raised by area bombing, and the complicity of Canadians, witting or unwitting, in the heavy burden of guilt engendered by massive raids upon the German civilian population.

Much is made by the writers of the purported "secret plan" in 1942, by which "Germany would be crushed through the deliberate annihilation of its citizens" (Transcript, p. 4). I have been a student of the evolution of aerial bombing for many years and can say two things about it with confidence. The first is that the "bomber school," whether British, American, or German, has never delivered on its apocalyptic promises, with the exception of the bombings of Hiroshima and Nagasaki with atomic weapons. The second is that "extermination," "area bombing," or striking at the will of civilian populations through bombing was not an invention of 1942, or of the Luftwaffe in 1940 or at Guernica in the Spanish Civil War. Its roots are to be found in the First World War.

In late 1917 the Royal Flying Corps launched a strategic air offensive against German industrial targets, employing what was then called the Independent Force. It was commanded by Hugh Trenchard, future chief of the Royal Air Force and a foremost proponent of the bombing strategy. Many Canadians served in this force; one of them, Col. R.H. Mulock, was given command of 27 Group, a formation equipped with the period's equivalent of the Lancaster, the Handley-Page V1500 bomber. This four-engined aircraft, with great range, was capable of carrying over three tons of bombs. The RAF staff had great plans for it. A staff paper of September 1918 called for attack upon population concentrations using a bomb load of mixed incendiaries and high explosive. It was estimated that the V1500 could carry 16,000 incendiaries and could lay down a belt of fire 2500 yards long. "If the target is large the operation may be described as simply a plastering of the locality with a predetermined density of fire nuclei," the staff appreciation pointed out. Incendiaries were best used in combination with high explosive; "the effect of depositing high explosives closely followed by Baby Incendiary Bombs could hardly be improved upon. The results might safely be described as terrific, and no ordinary populace could contemplate with equanimity the possibility of further similar attacks." Area bombing doctrine was central to the RAF from its origins.

In the interwar period, Trenchard and his successors defended the independence of the RAF as a service on the grounds of its independent strategic role as a war-winning force, capable of striking at an enemy's economy and at his will to fight through attacks on the civilian population. When, in the 1930s, the rise of Nazi Germany prompted the British government to launch a rearmament program, it was the RAF bomber force which was given priority over the buildup of fighter aircraft. The air service entered the Second World War dedicated to the bombing strategy. RCAF officers who, in the interwar years, took courses at the RAF Staff College, Cranwell, inevitably came in contact with bombing doctrine. In sum, the RAF commitment to the bombing of urban centres was of long standing and there was little that was secret about it. Strategic decisions, whether of 1942 or of any other period, are routinely classified as secret, but there was nothing mysterious or clandestine about the RAF commitment to a strategic bombing offensive against German cities.

The twentieth century has been the century of total war. One of the most prominent features of total war, as distinguished from the more limited wars of the immediate past, has been the obliteration of the line drawn between armed forces and civil populations. Direct action against civilians has taken many forms, but the air weapon has led the way. The British used it against colonial and other populations in the interwar years; the Italians did so in Ethiopia, the Japanese in China, and Germany and Italy in Spain.

In the Second World War, German aerial attacks upon cities were an integral part of *Blitzkrieg*, whether in Poland, Holland, or in the "Blitz" against England. And, of course, German assaults on the civilian populations of Eastern Europe by other than aerial means reached staggering proportions, not only against the Jews but against civilians generally. The dreadful record of this century must form part of the context within which the British – and, later, the American – strategic bombing campaign is to be examined. Making that point, and the further one that Canadians have been involved (if only as followers) from the South African War onwards in the obliteration of limits upon war, would have been a legitimate message to convey.

Quite apart from the historical roots of the strategic bombing offensive, the more immediate springs for it lay in the circumstances in which Britain found itself in 1940. France had been defeated, the United States was neutral, most of Western Europe was under the control of the Axis powers, and there seemed no limit to what Hitler's war machine might accomplish. Shortly after the fall of France, Churchill wrote to Beaverbrook:

When I look round to see how we can win the war I see that there is only one sure path. We have no continental army which can defeat the German military power. The blockade is broken and Hitler has Asia and probably

Africa to draw from. Should he not try invasion, he will recoil eastward and we have nothing to stop him. But there is one thing that will bring him back and bring him down, and that is an absolutely devastating, exterminating attack by very heavy bombers from this country upon the Nazi homeland. We must be able to overwhelm them by this means.

In October 1940, with Cabinet approval, Portal (Chief of the Air Staff) set out the prime objectives of the air offensive as oil and morale; "if bombing is to have its full moral effect it must on occasions produce heavy material destruction."

Thus, in the first year of the war, the objectives of the strategic bombing offensive were fixed at the highest level; they were pursued, with variations in target selection, for the remainder of the war, though German secret weapons, submarine bases, the runup to Overlord, and heavy bombing in support of ground forces were substantial additional uses of the heavy bomber force.

For a good part of the war, bombing was the only means of striking against Germany for both Britain and the United States. It was the only response possible, until 1944, to the powerful Russian pressure for a second front; at the same time, it was an important factor in maintaining Allied morale and an Allied sense that the war was being carried into the German heartland. And, of course, members of the "bomber school," like Portal and Harris and the British prime minister, as well as American counterparts like General Eaker, believed absolutely in the war-winning potential of strategic bombing.

This context is all but ignored in "Death by Moonlight," where the writers' stand is made plain by the actor chosen to play Harris. Harris, by all accounts, was a relentless, single-minded, and quite unpleasant person, but his depiction in the broadcast is grotesque, as is that of his Canadian counterpart, Wing Commander Marvin Fleming, who emerges as a kind of demonic acolyte. Speaking through the actor playing Freeman Dyson, the writers gradually shift emphasis until it is the German night-fighter pilots who emerge as the heroes, not the bumbling and naïve Canadians. As the Dyson character says, "They ended the war morally undefeated ... We had given them ... the one thing they lacked at the beginning, a clean cause to fight for" (Transcript, p. 40).

What is missing from all this is not only the general context I have already sketched, but also the reason why area bombing emerged as the chief *raison d'être* of Bomber Command. Despite the optimism of bombing advocates, the logistic and technological limits on strategic bombing were many. The RAF gave up daylight bombing very early, because of heavy losses to the German defences. Night bombing posed severe navigational problems and made bombing accuracy impossible. Analysis of after-bombing photographs in 1942 demonstrated (as the writers point out) that most crews were not getting within five miles of their designated targets. Far from their bombs dropping on city streets, as the authors suggest, they were cratering German countryside. Area bombing was (as it had always been) the British answer: cities, not factories, were the targets. Improvement in navigational aids, over-target tactics, Pathfinder Group, and target-marking meant more severe attacks on builtup areas and civilian populations as the war went on, but precision bombing at night was a technique mastered only by the most highly skilled of crews.

Bombing cities is a horrible business and its impact is well brought out in the stressful encounter of the two Canadian pilots with Hamburg survivors. It was horrible for the aircrews, given the nature of bombing operations and the exceedingly heavy casualty rate; nearly 10,000 Canadian aircrew were killed. It was horrible for German civilians (as for British civilians); over 400,000 were killed by the joint British-American offensive. It did not succeed in breaking the morale of the German people, just as it had not in the Luftwaffe, V-1 and V-2 offensives against Britain.

But was it a pointless exercise, successful only in killing massive numbers of people, both combatant and non-combatant? Here it is important to remember the nature of the enemy and the objectives of the Allied assault upon Nazi Germany. The Second World War was not only total, but ideological as well; those who fought against Nazi Germany made few distinctions between German forces and the mass of the German people who had supported Hitler's rise to power. The Second World War was war to the knife, as atrocious – arguably more atrocious – than the hecatomb of the First World War. If the bombing offensive against German cities contributed to ultimate victory, then in the minds of the Allies it would have been worth the effort.

There is no analysis in this broadcast of the effect of bombing upon the Nazi state's capacity to wage war. Had there been, the audience at least would have been introduced to the continuing debate over this issue and would have perceived an element to balance against the horrors of bombing. Although this subject, like the broadcast itself, is a tendentious one, the weight of scholarship on the issue is that bombing crippled the German war machine. One has only to read Albert Speer's memoirs to grasp its devastating effect. While it is true that German industrial production continued to rise until late in the war, it rose neither as far nor as fast as it would have had there been no bombing offensive. The dispersion of German industry, the separation of integrated manufacturing processes, the impossibility of deploying skilled labour effectively when large units of production were being broken down into small concealed work-shops: all these effects and more were brought about by the bombing offensive. One of the reasons the Germans failed to develop atomic weapons is because the group of physicists, with Werner Heisenberg as its most prominent member, had to be broken up and dispersed to bunker-laboratories.

It was legitimate for the producers of this program to bring out, vividly, the extremely hazardous nature of bombing operations and the qualities of courage, skill, and endurance called for from aircrew. It was legitimate as well to demonstrate that bombing was not an antiseptic kind of warfare, but a horrific one for millions of people, and that Canadians were deeply involved in it. But the absence of historical context and explanation, the prominence given to a devil figure – Harris – and the lack, either in this presentation or in the previous broadcast on Normandy, of any profile of the nature of the Nazi state and its leaders means that Canadian aircrew are cast, first in the role of sacrificial victims to the aspirations of a manic higher command, and then, by contrast with German night-fighter pilots, as unwitting tools of an evil enterprise.

AFTERWORD

History is a selective process. Out of the immense accumulation of fact and opinion and the endless succession of events, the historian endeavours to select those facts, those opinions, and those events which, according to his or her professional judgment, most fairly describe any given historical development. Historians may plead cases – but first the case must be made, and that can only be done by careful weighing of conflicting evidence and interpretation.

The writers of this series wish it to be viewed as history. They lay emphasis upon the documentation underlying the words of the actors employed in the series; they insist that everything presented is "true," and that much of it has never before been revealed to the world.

My comments in this report should make it clear that I do not regard this series as history, in any commonly accepted sense. The series might be defined as a species of journalism, years after the fact, or as a set of tracts on the horrors of war and the blessings of peace. Had there been, anywhere in these productions, some straightforward declaration of purpose, one might accept the broadcasts as a set of editorials.

But editorials about what? As already suggested, there is a thematic line which runs through all these broadcasts, which goes something like this. Canadian forces, whether serving at Hong Kong, in Normandy, or over Europe, were unwitting, guileless dupes, exploited by their political and military leaders and savaged by the superior forces of the enemy, whether German or Japanese. The operations in which they engaged were fruitless, or worse than fruitless; their blood was spilled to no avail; their sacrifices, existentially, count for nothing. By the time I had finished viewing the series, I was repelled by the pious – and hypocritical – dedication of it to the 44,000 Canadians who had died so unavailingly, and repelled, too, by the requiem-like choral music so tediously employed throughout. Like the admirable Canadian veterans who appeared in each of the episodes, I felt I had been manipulated in the interest of some higher truth possessed only by the writers.

There has been some public discussion of the possibility of placing these films in Canadian schools. In our collective memory of the war, there should be a major place for productions which bring out the terrible destructiveness and futility of war. There should be a place, as well, for productions which address the complexity of human events, have no fear of identifying noble causes, and are not afraid of victory. I can do no better than to commend, to all those interested in the Second World War, the example set by the recent magnificent American series on their Civil War. Using only still photographs, actors' voices reading from letters, diaries, operation orders and other documents, and employing the talents of such balanced historians as the remarkable Shelby Foote, the authors of that series produced a subtle, complex, infinitely moving account of that tragic war, one that met the highest tests both of history and of art. I can only hope that Canadian writer-producers can be found of similar judgment and sensitivity to address the Canadian experience in the Second World War.

DAVID J. BERCUSON

The Valour and the Horror:
A Historical Analysis

GENERAL INTRODUCTION

There is a fundamental difference between a documentary film which attempts to tell the story of a historical event and the event itself.

When a film-maker takes on the role of historian, he/she essentially embarks on an enterprise that is not fundamentally different from the writing of a history. A problem must first be posed, a plan of research is designed, research materials are gathered, and those materials are woven together in an intelligible fashion to tell a story which answers the question posed in the first place.

Professional historians know that history can never be written as it actually happened. For one thing, there is never a complete body of historical evidence. For example, much of history was "made" by men and women whose innermost thoughts can never be fully discerned. Or there may be a paucity of eyewitnesses or of first-person accounts. Historians know that two people may record the same event in very different ways. They also know that they bring their own biases, born of their life experiences, to their work and that these biases will have an impact on what they write even when they do their best to compensate for them.

Thus, the historical documentary film must never be judged solely on its ability to recreate history "as it happened" because, like written history, even of the very best kind, it cannot attain that objective under the best of circumstances.

If the historical documentary film cannot be measured against history "as it happened," against what can it be measured?

It cannot be measured against written history. The act of writing is the act of presenting a large amount of information, factual and/or descriptive, in a relatively economical way which the reader can access at his/her own pace. The act of producing a film is very different. In the production of a good documentary, the film-maker cannot present as much information as a writer on the same subject because the resultant film would be impossibly long. For example, Claude Lanzmann's film *Shoah*, on the Holocaust of the European Jews, was eleven hours long, but the companion book, with the very same text as the documentary script, was only 200 pages. The film-maker also knows that the viewer, for the most part, will not access the film at a pace of the viewer's own choosing even in the age of the VCR, but will view the film at one sitting from start to finish.

The film-maker must, therefore, make his/her point not over many days but in a very few hours, even minutes, and not with a time-consuming narrative but through an artful combination of visual image, sound effects, and the spoken word. It is not so much the imparting of information that is sought after but the triggering of an emotional response in the viewer, one which should produce an effect similar in the mind of the viewer, but much more quickly arrived at, to that which he/she would experience through reading a book about the same subject. Put simply, the art of writing a history book and of producing a historical documentary film are very different.

In our democratic society there is a commonly accepted norm, a norm informing the judicial system, journalism, and the educational system, that all available evidence should be presented and weighed so that independent judgment is rendered. If a documentary history film makes a fair effort *in its own fashion* to present the "available" evidence and to let the viewer make a judgment, then it must be adjudged to be "fair" or "objective" or a good history film. The question at issue here, therefore, is whether the three programs of *The Valour and the Horror* met that commonly accepted standard of "fairness."

SAVAGE CHRISTMAS: HONG KONG 1941

In this segment of the series, the story is told of the two Canadian militia battalions, the Winnipeg Grenadiers and the Royal Rifles of Canada, which were sent to Hong Kong in late October 1941, fought in the brief but savage battle for Hong Kong in December 1941, and were imprisoned by the Japanese after the fall of the garrison on Christmas Day, 1941. The outline of the story is well known and need not be repeated here.

The tone for the film is set early when an actor speaking in the name of infantryman Roger Cyr raises the possibility that "my government would knowingly offer a couple of thousand of its young men as lambs to the slaughter in order to meet some sort of political expedience." That, in fact, is the central theme of this production.

What are the facts as we know them? When the government of Canada agreed to send troops to help Britain garrison Hong Kong in the fall of 1941, it had no way of knowing that war with Japan was imminent even though there was an air of mounting crisis in the western Pacific. After all, Japan had been at war in Asia essentially since 1931. Canada was, therefore, not sending troops to Hong Kong to *fight*; it was sending them to help *garrison* that colony. Col. C.P. Stacey, Canada's official army historian of the Second World War – a man universally admired by both British and American historians for his diligence and objectivity (and widely used by them) – made this observation in his *Six Years of War* (1966): "It must constantly be kept in mind that both British and Canadian authorities believed that the troops were going to Hong Kong for garrison duty, and ... there seemed every reason to anticipate a considerable period during which any training deficiencies could be remedied" (p. 447).

Several observations arise. First, this program suffers from a decided lack of historical context in treating its central theme. No attention is devoted to the general lack of preparedness and small size of the Canadian Army in 1939. No attention is devoted to the actual reasons why Canada agreed to send troops to Hong Kong in 1941. The general lack of preparedness for a Japanese offensive of Americans, British, Dutch, and Australians in the South Pacific and Southeast Asia is barely mentioned. All this ought to have been done to explain both why Canada sent troops to Hong Kong untrained for actual war (as opposed to garrison duty) and why those troops were soon caught up in a war situation. It would also have allowed a comparison between Canada's actions and those of its allies, showing that Canada was not alone in being unprepared for war. It would have demonstrated that sending untrained troops to Hong Kong was clearly a mistake, as Stacey points out (p. 490), but it would have explained how and why that mistake was made instead of charging the government with action bordering on the criminal. Making mistakes is bad but it is not, of itself, evil.

In making Cyr set the tone for the program, the producers are claiming nothing less than that Britain and Canada knew war was fast approaching and that Canada knowingly sent untrained troops to fight in that war. Winston Churchill's oft-quoted musing about the undesirability of reinforcing Hong Kong is quoted to back up that claim, but left unmentioned is the fact that neither Churchill nor anyone else in London or Washington *knew* precisely either that Japan would go to war or where and whom it would strike if it did. Japan

itself did not know; its self-imposed deadline for a peaceful settle-
ment of outstanding difficulties with the United States was 26
November 1941, long after the Canadians were sent to Hong Kong.
It is easy in hindsight to claim that Churchill "knew" war with Japan
was inevitable, but, in fact, he did not "know," he guessed. Many
other Allied leaders, Roosevelt among them, guessed otherwise.

Second, the program fixes blame without acknowledging the
reality that in war, and in the preparations for war, mistakes are
sometimes made by honourable people. There were many errors committed by the Canadian military in the sending of troops to Hong
Kong. One of the most notable was the failure to coordinate the
arrival of the men and their equipment (something *not* mentioned in
the program). But there was no *intention* to deliberately put the lives
of the men in danger. The producers seem not to acknowledge that
human events are rarely predictable and that war is probably the
most unpredictable of human events.

Third, because of the docudrama format, a totally unfounded
charge, one with not a shred of evidence to support it, can be spoken
not by a narrator but by an actor quoting a snippet of a letter or diary
(we are *never* told the original format of these quotes) written by a
man who did not, himself, *know* the facts but who had undergone a
terrible ordeal and was clearly angry about it. Put simply, is Cyr a
credible source regarding the actions and motives of the Canadian
government in sending troops to Hong Kong? Clearly not.

Another error of fact is committed by the narrator when he declares: "The details of what happened to these soldiers were for a
long time suppressed by the Canadian government. The terrible story
is known to very few Canadians." Here a second theme of these programs emerges: secrecy. The producers apparently wish to have their
viewers believe not only that the government deliberately sent Canadians to the slaughter, but that it then tried hard to cover up its
actions.

In fact, a Royal Commission headed by Chief Justice Lyman P.
Duff inquired into the Hong Kong disaster in early 1942. Since the
war was still raging the investigation was conducted *in camera*, but
the final version of the report was *made public* in June 1942. Some
documents examined by Duff were kept secret until mid-1948 but
were then released shortly after the release of the Maltby Report,
prepared by Major-General C.M. Maltby for the British government.
Maltby had commanded the Hong Kong garrison; his report related
events in Hong Kong as *he* saw them. The Duff report exonerated the
Canadian government of wrong-doing; the Maltby report observed
that the Canadian troops were "inadequately trained for modern war

under the conditions existing in Hong Kong," which was undoubtedly true up to a point and which Stacey has admitted. Between Duff and Maltby, therefore, the events of the Hong Kong battle had been well documented by mid-1948. There is, therefore, no basis whatever to the claim that the government "for a long time suppressed" the story. If few Canadians know the story it is because they do not care to read their own history. Three full books have been written on it (Vincent, *No Reason Why*; Ferguson, *Desperate Siege*; Lindsay, *The Lasting Honour*); it was extensively analysed by C.P. Stacey in the official history; and it has been covered in numerous military history texts and general texts on the history of Canada. There was no coverup.

The next problem arising from the program is not an error of fact but an error of omission. The narrator quotes Winston Churchill as saying that Hong Kong could not be held in the event of war (which Churchill did say), but goes on to claim that Britain sought Canadian aid "rather than risk more of their own troops." The implication is clear: Hong Kong is a terrible risk; therefore, send Canadians and not Britons to die there.

The problem with this is that Britain had no troops to send. More than a year after the fall of France, Britain was severely stretched in terms of available manpower. Britain had always been stretched in the Far East and had universally combined British troops with dominion or colonial troops to fill out garrison ranks. A large number of these troops came from India. Not to mention the fact that Britain had no troops of its own to send is a serious error of omission which buttresses the general theme of malfeasance, conspiracy, and secrecy causing the death and agony of unknowing Canadian soldiers.

Shortly after this declaration we are told "incredibly, Canada answered England's call without making an independent assessment of the peril." The producers do not tell their viewers how Canada could have done that (ie, make its own assessment of the situation) when it had no intelligence apparatus to speak of. To see how misleading this assertion is we need to look at the United States; with all the vast intelligence apparatus available to it, including *knowledge of Japan's military and diplomatic secret codes*, the US still did not know when war would begin, or where, and, until late November 1941, it did not even know for certain *if* war would begin.

In the very next sequence the film shows soldiers playing baseball while the narrator says: "The [Winnipeg] Grenadiers had a lot of time to polish their baseball game, but few of them had ever thrown a grenade. Some had never even fired a rifle ... they were officially classified by the Canadian defence department as 'unfit for combat.' "

This assertion, which reflects Maltby, is true on the surface, but it totally ignores the larger context and, in juxtaposing war and baseball, it is also unfair. Here is Stacey on the subject of training: "The two battalions had clearly not reached that advanced state of training which one would wish troops to attain before being sent against an enemy ... but to say baldly that they were 'untrained' is to give quite a wrong impression" (p. 447). He then goes on to make the point, as quoted above, that these troops were not intended for *war*, at least not for some time, but for *garrison* duty. This is a vital point because the general viewing public cannot be expected to know the difference. And yet there is a vital difference. For example, when North Korea attacked South Korea in June 1950, United States troops doing occupation (or garrison) duty in Japan were rushed to Korea to try to stem the advance. They were untrained and unprepared for war and they were crushed. In late 1941 Canada was preparing to send troops of the 4th Canadian Division to Britain – to a war – and those troops were being trained for that task. The troops being sent to Hong Kong were not being sent to a war and it was thought, wrongly as events later proved, that they would have adequate time for further training. That was error, miscalculation, mistake; it was not callousness or worse, as is implied.

By juxtaposing images of soldiers playing baseball with a narration which both overstates the degree of lack of training and ignores the context which explains that lack is to give viewers a definite impression of callousness on the part of the government and the military. Why are these men being prepared for baseball, the producers seem to be asking, when they should be preparing for war?

The theme of government secrecy is further advanced a few moments later when the narrator declares that the troops "had no idea where they were being shipped or what threat they would face." The facts are that (1) soldiers are often not told where they are going in times of increased international tension; (2) soldiers go where they are sent anyway, not where they choose to go (and these were all volunteers); (3) again, *no one knew* what threat they faced.

The lack-of-preparedness theme is reinforced some minutes later when an actress, with tears in her eyes (presumably to add to the pathos and to deepen the impression of innocence in the presence of impending doom) speaks words written (one presumes) by a former nursing sister: "Outside our cabin they're giving them lectures, telling them what this end of the rifle is called, where to put the bullet in. Honestly it's just appalling." Here, again, is Stacey: "The Royal Rifles of Canada and The Winnipeg Grenadiers would doubtless have been more effective units if they had received more advanced training ...

But too much can be made of this. Their casualty lists show that their contribution to the defence was a large one, and ... Japanese accounts ... attest the battalions' solid fighting qualities" (p. 490). Why is this not also quoted in juxtaposition?

Another major theme of the program is that not only were the Canadians untrained for war but their British leaders were incompetent. The British Army was "geared up for First World War–type battles," declares the narrator. What does this mean? There were no "western front" type defences at Hong Kong, there were fortifications. Every nation fighting uses fortifications of some type. Do the producers equate the existence of fortifications with a First World War mentality? Did the United States fight a "First World War–type" battle on Wake Island in December 1941 or on Corregidor in Manila Bay in early 1942? Did the Japanese on Okinawa in 1945? Or the Americans in Khe San in 1968? The statement is both meaningless and pejorative. It is intended to convey the impression of incompetent generals planning to fight the last war to the last drop of the infantryman's blood. It can probably be equally applied to all lost battles!

The sense of pathos which the producers attempt to create is further reinforced some minutes later when the narrator declares: "Overshadowed and often forgotten are the other Japanese attacks in the hours after Pearl Harbor – the Philippines, Malaya, and then Hong Kong." Forgotten by whom? Not by the men or governments involved. Certainly not by two generations of journalists and historians. Hundreds of books have been written and films made about all aspects of the general Japanese offensive which was launched at the start of the war.

The producers' failure to understand the nature of warfare is apparent in their discussion of the reasons for the success of the Japanese attack and the failure of the British defence. It is pointed out that the British expected an attack by sea, but the Japanese came by land. Since sea movement is much easier than land movement, and since sea-power can be projected at any point along a coast, it was an easy assumption for the British to make. In the Second World War, for example, Canada assumed that the port of Halifax would be attacked, if attacked at all, by sea, not by land. Japan's astute planners took advantage of the element of surprise to hit their enemy where he did not expect to be hit. That is war. It is not necessarily malfeasance and was certainly not in this case.

The basic theme of this film is summarized in its last minutes. Once again an actor portraying Roger Cyr comes on to the screen and essentially repeats the statements made in the opening moments of the program, presumably to ensure that any viewer who had not got the point up to then would get it now: "What frightens the daylights out of me ... the thought that my government would have not only willingly, but very actively, placed itself in a situation where it would knowingly offer a couple of thousand of its young men as lambs to the slaughter in order to meet some sort of political expediency." The narrator then proclaims over a shot of soldiers marching in slow motion: "In 1941, these soldiers offered their lives to their country and entrusted their fate to their government. That trust was betrayed."

There is no evidence anywhere yet unearthed by anyone – from archives of Canada or Britain, or in interviews with the principals involved – that these statements are even partially true. Certainly no such evidence is presented here.

Conclusion

Although this film creates a vivid impression of the travails undergone by the Canadians sent to Hong Kong, it fails to present the Hong Kong events in proper historical context, makes assertions about government intentions that are totally without foundation, misreads the evidence regarding the lack of training of these troops and the competence of their leaders, and misleads the viewers by charging that the government attempted to engineer a coverup. The clear impression presented is that Canada, as Britain's lap-dog, either deliberately and knowingly sent its young men, untrained for war, to the slaughter to stay in Britain's good graces, or *should have known* that they were being sent to the slaughter. This is pure fiction. Thus, although much of the film presents a balanced view of the Hong Kong battle and its aftermath, the central theme is developed without regard to *a readily available mountain of evidence* that that theme is a figment of the imagination of the producers. No part of that mountain of evidence which runs counter to this theme is presented to the viewer. Here, the film-makers judged and presented their judgment to the viewer, and they did not present a fair selection of the evidence for the viewer to weigh. Thus, "Savage Christmas" cannot be judged to be either "fair" or "objective" or a responsible piece of history even as a historical film documentary.

DEATH BY MOONLIGHT: BOMBER COMMAND

Introduction: The treatment of the "morality" of "area" bombing as carried out by Bomber Command in the Second World War

This second program of the series focuses on Canadians who flew for Bomber Command during the Second World War. Its central

themes are introduced by the narrator some four minutes into the
film against the backdrop of a Lancaster bomber making a takeoff in
slow motion. The viewers are told that Bomber Command (1) "deliberately hid the truth" about crew survival rates, presumably from
the crews themselves, and (2) "concealed" a "secret plan" adopted in
1942 whereby "Germany would be crushed through deliberate annihilation of its citizens." This, implies the narrator, betrayed the trust
of Canada's airmen who had "joined to save democracy hearing the
words of the Canadian Air Force poet: 'Oh I have slipped the surly
bonds of earth ...' "

Since these themes are repeated throughout the film, they are
worth treating at length here.

This statement links "Death by Moonlight" with the previous program, "Savage Christmas," by once again restating the idea that Canada's fighting men were betrayed by their leaders during the Second
World War. In the previous film betrayal is said to have occurred
when innocent, untrained men were deliberately sent to die in Hong
Kong. In this film, Canada's airmen are said to have been betrayed by
their leaders because those leaders deliberately sent these men to kill
German non-combatants (and did not tell the aircrews they were
doing so) when those men had joined up for nobler purposes.

Three interrelated difficulties arise from this one forty-second
passage. First, there is no evidence that even a single Canadian joined
the RAF or RCAF because he heard the poem *High Flight* by John G.
McGee (an American fighter pilot killed while serving in the RCAF
early in the war). McGee's poem speaks not a word of war, in fact,
but is a celebration of the thrill of flight. To say that aircrew joined
the RAF or RCAF after hearing McGee is to imply that aircrew joined
only for the purest of motives, or, conversely, that only the pure-of-
heart joined. The conclusion can then follow that anything they might
have done in the course of their service that was not quite "pure"
was something thrust upon them by others. This reinforces the main
theme of betrayal.

Second, it is true that Bomber Command did not *publish* ongoing
survival rate statistics during the war. To have done so would have
offered the enemy a powerful propaganda tool and might possibly
have undermined morale among aircrew. The benefits to the war
effort of keeping this and similar news about military plans, operations, and supplies secret are too obvious to require any lengthy
elaboration. It is, therefore, troubling that the producers of this film
raise the subject in the way that they do. The strong implication here
is that RAF/RCAF leaders committed some *wrongdoing* by keeping such
information secret, when they clearly did not. What is the argument
for this? There may be one, but it is not presented here.

Further, although aircrew were not specifically given reports on their own survival rates, they could count. It did not take much figuring to know that if RCAF station Skipton-on-Swale sent up, say, thirty bombers one night and five failed to return, that 35 out of 210 men were either killed, captured, or missing. Aircrew saw the empty beds of missing comrades. Later in the film Ken Brown, one of the featured veteran bomber pilots says: "I don't think I knew it then, the average life of a bomber crew was six weeks." Doug Harvey, the other featured veteran, answers: "We never worried about it. You wouldn't fly if you worried about it." Put another way, these men, like all men in combat, knew that many would die, but to dwell upon the prospect of one's own death was useless once the choice had been made to stay in harm's way.

It should also be pointed out here that crew survival rates changed throughout the war and that crews with more experience had a better chance of survival than "sprog" (ie, untried) crews. No basis for the one-third survival rate as mentioned several times in this film is ever presented. In fact, it is difficult to calculate "survival." Is a gunner who parachutes to safety and is captured and repatriated after the war considered to have "survived" or not? Brereton Greenhous, a historian at the Director General History of the Department of National Defence, has recently written in a book review in *Canadian Defence Quarterly* (winter 1991) that "those who were killed, died as prisoners, and were wounded ... amounted to nearly 42% of the total who flew." According to this, the survival rate was three-fifths, not one-third.

Third, the claim that Allied war leaders, including leaders of the RAF, and especially Sir Arthur Harris, who commanded Bomber Command from late February 1942, deliberately set out to kill German non-combatants is certainly true but is made here, and repeatedly throughout the program, out of context. This failure to provide context leaves the clear impression, whether intended by the producers or not, that the policy was executed *as an end in itself* and not as an integral part of Allied strategy to win what was, after all, a *defensive* war. This is this film's greatest failing.

In October 1942 a memo summarizing RAF bombing policy was circulated within the RAF. It carefully defined what RAF bombers were to do (and not to do) over British, Allied, or neutral territory occupied by the enemy and what they were free to do over Germany. It stated bluntly that when it came to Germany, "the Cabinet have authorized a bombing policy which includes the attack of [sic] enemy morale." Another way of putting this is to say that German morale was to be attacked by bombing designed to induce terror among German civilians and to do so by killing, wounding, and rendering homeless as many of them as possible.

There are a number of important reasons why this policy, duly executed by Harris and Bomber Command, was carried out, but virtually *none* of those reasons is mentioned in this program. Those reasons were:

(1) *The political and military need to respond appropriately to Hitler's "total war."* Put simply, mass area bombing had been pioneered in this war by Germany in attacks against cities including Warsaw, Rotterdam, Coventry, and London. The terrorizing (and mass killing) of civilian populations had been introduced by the Nazis. More than 60,000 British civilians were killed in bombing raids by Germany in this war. Luftwaffe night raids against London were "area" bombing. They were carried out because the Luftwaffe did not have the capability of hitting specific targets at night. The Luftwaffe killed far fewer British civilians than Bomber Command did German civilians only because its twin-engine bombers were not capable of hauling heavy bomb loads. The HE-111, mainstay of the Luftwaffe bomber force, carried 5500 pounds of bombs; the RAF Lancaster carried 18,000 pounds of bombs.

This is, quite possibly, the most important of the contextual factors that is not adequately described here. In fact, the Luftwaffe Blitz against London is treated only twice: in one partial sentence of less than thirty seconds when the narrator declares, "forty thousand British civilians were killed," and in a dramatic segment almost an hour later, when an actor representing an aircrew man tells the viewers that "his" bomb-aimer's mother and sister had been killed by German bombs in Nottingham. That is the extent of the coverage. Max Hastings in his study *Bomber Command* quotes one British Liberal MP as writing in 1942: "I am all for the bombing of working class areas of German cities. I am Cromwellian – I believe in 'slaying in the name of the Lord' because I do not believe you will ever bring home to the civil population of Germany the horrors of war until they have been tested in this way" (p. 147, paperback edition cited throughout). It was simply not conceivable to Allied leaders *at that time* that the German people, having supported their leaders in the launching of this war, should not be made to pay some price for their actions at least as large as the price being paid by the victims of their aggression. This is not to say that revenge or retribution was the prime factor determining the policy – there is simply no evidence to suggest that it was and none is presented in this film – but to point out that possible reluctance to kill German civilians in the pursuit of other goals (for example, undermining morale or destroying industrial capability) was substantially mitigated by the experience of having been on the receiving end of area bombing.

(2) *The knowledge that the* RAF *did not have the capability of making precision strikes against particular strategic targets such as aircraft factories.* For most of the war, the defence was stronger than the offence in the matter of aerial bombardment. Luftwaffe bombing attacks on Britain during daylight in the summer and early fall of 1940 were called off because of heavy losses even though the bombers were escorted to their targets by fighters in most circumstances. It was then that the Luftwaffe switched to night area bombing. RAF bombers were similarly unable to bomb targets during daylight without sustaining very heavy losses, especially since the RAF's most desired targets were in Germany, far out of range of RAF fighters in 1940–42. The Americans attempted to press home with "precision" daylight raids into Germany carried out by unescorted heavy bombers, but suffered such heavy losses by the fall of 1943 that they suspended these attacks until an appropriate long-range fighter was available (the P–51 Mustang). After their early disastrous daylight raids, the RAF switched to night bombing only to find that attacks against "precision" targets were impossible because the bombers could not locate the targets; in some cases they could not even locate the right town or city. Max Hastings summed up this dilemma (pp. 72–3): "Bomber Command was incapable of hitting any pinpoint accurately in the hours of darkness, and was unable to break through the defences in daylight."

The search for a truly effective means of target identification continued through the war, but no foolproof system was devised, not even by the Americans who purported to believe in "strategic" daylight bombing. Hastings believes that one alternative to night area bombing would have been to continue the search for more effective means of hitting precision targets and to do other things (ie, use resources devoted to heavy bomber production in other ways) until that search paid off (p. 146). But he then goes on to observe that in the context of total war – Luftwaffe night area bombing of Britain, etc. – that course was really not an alternative. Thus the real choice available to the RAF if it was to attempt *strategic* bombing in 1942 was either to bomb "areas" of cities or not to bomb at all.

Why, then, bomb areas of cities? In the view of Arthur Harris and others, cities in which the war effort was being served in some fashion or another – factories, port facilities, rail marshalling yards, etc. – were legitimate targets. By destroying whole areas of cities the German war effort would be hindered both by destroying enemy morale (dealt with below) and by rendering German cities uninhabitable, thus destroying their ability to contribute to the war. As Sir

Charles Portal, Commander-in-Chief Bomber Command prior to Harris, wrote in July 1940: "We have the one directly offensive weapon ... by which we can *undermine the morale of a large part of the enemy people*, shake their faith in the Nazi regime, and at the same time and with very few bombs, dislocate the major part of their heavy industry and a good part of their oil production" (Terraine, *The Right of the Line*, p. 261). Harris, for one, was convinced that the war would ultimately be won *only* by the destruction of Germany's cities because that would bring about the "progressive destruction and dislocation of the German military, industrial and economic systems" (Hastings, p. 451). In his view it was nonsense to attempt to bomb precision targets (he called them "panacea" targets) such as ballbearing factories because, quite simply, they could not be hit with precision by day or by night and yet bombers would be lost and crews killed in the attempt (Middlebrook, *The Schweinfurt-Regensburg Mission*, pp. 296–7).

In other words, Portal, Harris, and others thought that bombing *built-up areas* of enemy cities offered the best chance of defeating what they thought of as a wicked and brutal political regime at an acceptable cost in aircraft and aircrews lost. And in the midst of the war which this regime had perpetrated they clearly saw this as a legitimate means of attempting to achieve victory. In one way they were wrong. Hastings observes that it was clear by the spring of 1944 that area bombing would not, by itself, bring victory (p. 421). But it is also true that Germany diverted considerable resources to air defence and these were resources not, therefore, available to counter the Allies in other ways. Albert Speer, the Nazi minister of war production, later observed: "the air war ... opened a second front long before the invasion of Europe." Speer pointed out that 20,000 flak guns were sited for the aerial defence of the Ruhr, for example (Terraine, p. 537). Many of these guns (for example, the much vaunted 88 millimetre) also had use as anti-tank guns; the 88 millimetre is generally acknowledged to have been perhaps the most effective anti-tank gun used by any side in the war. Had *half* of them been available to counter the Allies in Normandy, the fighting there would have been even bloodier than it was. It is entirely fair for the producers to second-guess Harris, Portal, and others on this strategy, but they should have presented the Harris/Portal et al. side of the argument, which they do not. It was a legitimate point of view *at the time*.

(3) *The belief that terror bombing would destroy German morale and bring about victory.* This belief was not unchallenged either within the RAF or among the political leadership of the Allies. There were experts who believed that German morale would not crack and that

the resources being poured into heavy bombers would be better used elsewhere. But the belief itself – termed the Trenchard Doctrine after Sir Hugh Trenchard, first commander of the RAF – was based both on the reaction of Londoners to being bombed by German Zeppelins and bombers during the First World War (there had been considerable panic) and on the writings of several theorists, from science-fiction writer H.G. Wells to air-power strategist Guilio Douhet (Stokesbury, *A Short History of Air Power*, pp. 125ff), all of whom theorized that aerial bombing would invariably create mass panic among civilians. After witnessing the German bombings of London in the First World War, Trenchard came to believe: "The moral effect of bombing stands to the material in a proportion of 20 to 1" (Terraine, p. 9). This was one reason why the RAF developed a doctrine for itself in the interwar years which held that it was not the primary role of the air force to support the army or the navy but to strike "straight at the vitals of an enemy nation, bypassing its armed forces to destroy its war economy" (Carrington, *Soldier at Bomber Command*, p. viii). This was also known as the theory of the "knockout blow."

Here, too, the question to be asked is whether in the midst of this "total" war it was not understandable that Allied political and military leaders would attempt to destroy German morale as a means *to hasten victory*, given the nature of the conflict. They were ultimately proved incorrect in that assumption, but their "side" of the argument warrants telling in some detail to explain their actions.

(4) The inability to make any other significant contribution at that time (and in the foreseeable future) to the effort to defeat Germany. At the time the area bombing offensive began in earnest (the fall of 1942), the USSR was locked in a death-struggle with Germany on the eastern front, but Britain and the United States were a long way away from being able to open a second front in Europe. They had neither the manpower nor the weaponry. They were barely able to succeed in that task in June-August 1944. Aerial bombing was, therefore, one way of maintaining pressure on Germany, as Speer pointed out.

Finally, although "area" bombing became the major preoccupation of Bomber Command for the duration of the war (Hastings observes that 75% of its effort was directed to that end as against "precision" targets), its aircraft did strike both "precision" targets and targets of "strategic" importance. In the first category would be the attack of No. 617 Squadron (the Dambusters) on two German dams in 1943 (covered in this program) and the raid against the German rocket research facilities at Peenemunde in August 1943. The latter is not mentioned in this program at all, which is strange in that the RCAF's No. 6 Group sustained its highest loss rate of the entire war on this one raid and because the raid was an undoubted success, delaying German rocket production for from two to five months. In the second category would be German oil-refining capability. In Terraine's words: "Oil and [German] morale ... [made up] a *pas-de-deux* of alternating targets which was to continue for the remainder of the war" (p. 262).

Virtually none of the above is mentioned *at any point in this film*. The viewers are not told what considerations led Allied military and political leaders to pursue the bombing campaign that they did. Thus the clear impression is conveyed that the killing of German non-combatants was pursued either as revenge or *as an end in itself*, primarily at the whim of Harris.

Specific Comments on the Documentary

1) Approximately seven minutes into the program the narrator says, "Churchill decided that ... devastating attacks against German cities was his only way to win the war." This is untrue. He was, in fact, continuously sceptical about the ultimate value of trying to win the war through aerial bombing, but he gave Harris leeway in the then reasonable hope that it *might*.

2) The narrator says that the RAF's British officers were not pleased by the boisterousness of Canadian aircrews. True, because they believed – correctly – that strict discipline was necessary for survival and that undisciplined behaviour on the ground invariably led to lack of discipline on the approach to, and over, the target.

3) The narrator observes that "The Ruhr was the main target [for Bomber Command] because it was the heartland of German industrial might." The organization of the program leads to the speculation that the producers meant to say specifically that this was true primarily *before* area bombing was initiated in late 1942; that is, it is not until some forty minutes later that we are told by the narrator that "in the second half of the bomber war Harris would turn the killing of thousands of people into a science." If that *is* their intention, they are simply wrong. The Ruhr was a key target throughout the war.

4) Shots of US heavy bombers on daylight raids are used on many occasions, including one with the voice-over, "For the fully loaded [RAF] bombers ..."

5) An actor portraying Freeman Dyson, a scientist working in the Operational Research Section of Bomber Command (we are told only that he worked at Bomber Command "headquarters"), comes on screen to say, "stringent precautions were taken to ensure that any of our command documents on survival rates should not reach the

squadrons." He might have added that much else was also deemed secret from the aircrew and from others.

6) The narrator tells the viewers that "at least one Canadian" committed suicide after being labelled as "lacking moral fibre" (LMF). He ought to have added that tens of thousands of others did not.

7) The narrator says, "In the first four years of the war, Bomber Command seldom tried precision strikes against key industrial targets in Germany." He does not mention any of the mitigating factors mentioned above, such as the RAF's *inability* to bomb with precision at night.

8) In the introduction to the Dambusters segment, the narrator says, "The Royal Air Force had a reputation to uphold ... Bomber Command wanted to focus public attention on something that would create a much better impression than the haphazard bombing of cities." There is no evidence of this in Hastings or Terraine. In fact, an attack on the Ruhr dams had been on the RAF's agenda since 1938 (Terraine, p. 539), which clearly contradicts any claim that the raid was "laid on" as a publicity stunt in 1943. Terraine observes that it was Barnes Wallis* himself who won Harris over to this exploit (p. 539).

The whole treatment of the Dambuster raid in this film is problematic. There is no doubt that the raid was a mistake. The wrong weapon was used on the wrong targets. It was a classic example of error being compounded by error in war. Terraine concludes that the Wallis weapon was used "because it was there," which happens often in war (p. 539). To claim that the raid was mounted because "the public relations benefits ... were undeniable" is a gross distortion *not based on any known fact*. If the producers have such information, they have a responsibility to air it.

Here we see one of the problems with this sort of docudrama. Towards the end of the recounting of the Dambusters story, the actor portraying Freeman Dyson comes on to the screen again to say that the attack "was a public relations triumph." That was true in the *aftermath* of the attack (ie, it was played up then, and later by the RAF), but to have him say this *as he says it* is to give the viewers the clear impression that an important person working at Bomber Headquarters had *knowledge* that the attack was actually *planned* as a public relations stunt, which is totally untrue.

9) After the story of the Dambusters raid is told, the narrator says, "the real lesson that could have been taken from the dams raid is that

---

*   The British scientist who developed the bombs used by the Dambusters.

the precise bombing of industrial targets was possible." To say this after describing the raid as a strategic failure is to be inconsistent. The raid could easily give the exact opposite lesson – that it was *not* possible to affect the war by bombing such targets. There is either something convoluted about the logic here, or the script is simply badly written.

10) The narrator then claims that "the appropriate bomb for the job, the 12,000 pound Tallboy, was eventually developed." In fact the Tallboy was developed as a *tactical* weapon primarily to hit hardened military targets, especially U-boat pens, but including capital warships with thick armour plate on their decks. It was also used against canals, etc. It was a "custom built" bomb, expensive and difficult to make. It was made only in small numbers. Only one bomb could be carried by each specially modified Lancaster flown by a specially trained crew. It was not designed, and was unsuitable, for large-scale raids on sprawling industrial targets such as an oil refinery.

11) The narrator goes on to say that "precision bombing didn't really interest the head of Bomber Command." True, as mentioned above. But *none* of the reasons *why it was true* are mentioned. The viewers are thus left with the impression that Harris believed, or knew, he had a realistic choice between area and precision bombing as two possible routes to the defeat of Germany, but that he chose area bombing with its attendant mass killing. That is not true.

12) The narrator then says that "killing civilians didn't bother Arthur Harris. In fact it was something he joked about" – and the viewers are then treated to the actor portraying Harris responding to a policeman's admonition that his (Harris's) speeding in a car could kill someone by declaring: "Young man, I kill thousands of people every night." This is said with a distinct smile on the actor's face.

Here the producers carry forward the theme that Harris was a dedicated killer, and further embellish it with the notion that he may well have rather enjoyed that killing. In fact, they cannot know at all how much this killing affected Harris because they do not know what went on in his mind. Nor do they know (and if they do they do not reveal) the circumstances under which he uttered those words. He may have said them with great irony. He may have said them in some sense of Shakespeare-like tragedy. He may have said them with great hilarity. The viewers are left to rely upon an actor's (and/or dramatic director's) sense of what happened. Given the potential impact of these words in a film that purports to describe historical reality, this is not appropriate.

13) The viewers are told that at the time that Bomber Command changed its policy to pursue area bombing as a prime strategy (ie, at

the time of the Lancaster's introduction), there was "a sudden desperation to increase the amount of bombs that each plane could carry." This is untrue. The RAF searched for ways of increasing its bombing capacity throughout the war.

14) The narrator then says that Harris had received new orders – "to deliberately target German civilians." Here, and in the segment that shortly follows in which Portal's February 1942 memo on targeting built-up areas is described, absolutely none of the strategic considerations mentioned in the introduction to this segment of the program are mentioned. No explanation is given other than having the actor portraying Harris declare, "We shall destroy Germany's will to fight."

15) The narrator declares shortly after that the Canadian government was not consulted about this policy. He does not mention that Canada's political leaders *sought no role in the making of higher Allied strategy*, a fact well documented by Stacey, Granatstein, and others.

16) Approximately one hour into this program, we are introduced to the first of two segments on the bombing of Hamburg. These two segments together amount to more than twelve minutes out of the one hour and forty-five minutes of the entire program. They are, in one sense, the centrepiece of the program epitomizing the producers' message about the way Bomber Command fought the war.

The Hamburg segments are dominated by reminiscences of the wartime fire-chief and two women who were living in the city at the time. These are buttressed by photographs of the victims of the bombing and of the memorial built to them as well as the mass cemetery in which many are buried. Left unsaid is anything that would have explained the attack or described its outcome.

Hamburg was an important port city with a significant industrial capacity. The RAF bombing which killed more than 50,000 non-combatants and rendered many more homeless was, by all measure, a significant blow to the German war effort. "Nearly a million people fled from the stricken port," Terraine declares. Speer later commented: "Hamburg had put the fear of God in me ... I informed Hitler that armaments production was collapsing and threw in the further warning that a series of attacks of this sort, extended to six more major cities, would bring Germany's armaments production to a total halt" (Terraine, pp. 547–8).

But the RAF did not repeat the performance, and Hamburg's industrial capacity largely recovered. But Hastings observes: "No industry, no urban area could stand repeated punishment on this scale ... But Bomber Command was not to repeat the severity of its attack ... Harris's staff never appeared to grasp the full significance of their success" (Hastings, p. 246). Thus more bombings such as this *might indeed* have shortened the war; more bombings such as this might have saved millions of both non-combatants in Allied countries and Allied soldiers on both fronts. This the producers do not mention.

17) After a sequence showing the Hamburg cemetery where many of the bombing victims are buried, the narrator proclaims that "after Hamburg, the Germans were determined to exact a far higher price from the bomber crews." In fact, they were determined at all times and throughout the war to shoot down as many Allied bombers as they could. Their success depended on their skill and on technical improvements in the methods of finding and tracking enemy bombers.

18) Former German night-fighter pilot Martin Becker says shortly after: "Any inhibitions that any of us had disappeared as soon as we saw our cities burning." This is a self-serving statement. There is no indication given in this film that any German night-fighter pilots had any such inhibitions before Hamburg.

19) The narrator claims that "the Supreme Allied Command ordered Harris to redirect his attacks to precise military targets in preparation for 'Overlord' but Arthur Harris would have none of it." This is totally inaccurate. Harris *resisted* the use of his bombers for this purpose. In the end his aircraft, and those of the USAAF's Eighth Air Force, were placed under the command of General Eisenhower and played a key role in the destruction of the French railway network in the vicinity of Normandy (the Transportation Plan). Further, Bomber Command aircraft mounted attacks on a number of occasions in *direct* support of ground troops (Caen, Walcheren, etc.)

20) The narrator proclaims, in the introduction to the Nuremberg portion, that "Harris liked to pick targets of symbolic importance." The statement is meaningless, but sets the context for what follows in the segment. This is an episode that has been well crafted by the producers to create a sense of the dramatic and to convey the impression that Harris deliberately sacrificed his crews on this night by sending them on a long raid, in full moonlight, to a target that had only "symbolic importance." There are vivid scenes recreating the experiences of one crew interlaced with recollections of the two veteran pilots. There is background music of Beethoven's Moonlight Sonata to accompany film of bombers racing to their targets. It has all the tragedy and pathos of a Hollywood recreation of the Charge of the Light Brigade.

The fact is that the raid of 30 March 1944 was one of eleven Main Force attacks carried out against Nuremberg during the war, with the first raid mounted in August 1942. Some of those raids were carried out in optimal bombing conditions, some not. Losses were very heavy on 30 March 1944, much lighter on other missions. As to the specific reasons why *this* mission was ordered, Martin Middlebrook says: "The reasons why Sir Arthur Harris chose such a target on such a night will never be known." Middlebrook speculates that Harris wanted to hit a "major city with ... strong Nazi connections" to close out his offensive against Berlin and to mark the shift of his forces to the support of Overlord (Middlebrook, *The Berlin Raids*, p. 304). If this is what the producers are referring to in their outright claim to know Harris's motives, they had an obligation to put the matter as Middlebrook did. They did not.

21) After the Nuremberg segment, the actor portraying Freeman Dyson refers to the German night fighters in the context of the bombing of German cities and says, "We had given them, at the end of the war, the one thing they lacked at the beginning, a clean cause to fight for." This, in fact, is the theme of this entire segment, one which conveys the impression that dedicated German pilots were engaged in a just cause to protect home and hearth against the wilful, mindless, murderous destruction of their cities and the innocents living in them.

Whatever the reasons for Dyson making the comment he did – there were others then and now who agree with him – the producers surely had some obligation to present that statement in context. That context is clear: the German night-fighters flew to defend a nation that had supported a regime that had initiated a terrible war dedicated to racial annihilation and the subjugation of half the globe. If Hitler had not begun that war, neither the bombers nor the night-fighters would have been there. Whatever Dyson's personal anguish, Auschwitz was not "a clean cause to fight for."

22) Near the end of the program the narrator proclaims that after the war "many airmen were overcome with doubts about the morality of the area bombing they took part in." That is well and true and speaks volumes about the sort of society we are. But how many is "many"? And what sort of doubts did they have? Besides, "many" airmen, including Brown and Harvey, clearly had no doubts about the morality of what they had done.

Conclusion

A great debate took place in Britain, both in secret and in public, during the Second World War about area bombing. The producers are right to present one side of that debate. But they present almost nothing at all, and certainly nothing substantial, about the other side.

Virtually none of the overall political or strategic context is presented. Virtually none of the debate about the *effectiveness* of area bombing as opposed to other possible methods of bombing is presented. "Death by Moonlight" is a morality play. Harris is the villain, the non-combatant Germans are the victims, the young Canadian airmen are the unwitting tools of Harris, the German night-fighter pilots are the defenders of home and family. "Death by Moonlight" is not fair, not objective, and not good film history.

IN DESPERATE BATTLE: NORMANDY 1944

Introduction: Canada's Normandy Battle in Context

The third segment of *The Valour and the Horror* covers the Canadian Army in Normandy from D-Day on 6 June 1944 to the closing of the Falaise Gap on 21 August 1944.

It is, today, generally acknowledged by military historians, Canadian and otherwise, that the Canadian Army as a whole did not acquit itself well in the Normandy fighting. Although individual men and units fought bravely and well, tactics, training, weaponry, and leadership were too often not up to the occasion. This story is told here and, to some degree, the telling is done accurately.

And yet, significant difficulties with fairness or even-handedness arise early and persist throughout. For example, when the first portion of the story of the Verrières Ridge assault (25 July 1944) is told right at the beginning of the film, the narrator proclaims: "The tragedy that unfolded on this field is only one of the cataclysms that befell the Canadian Army in Normandy ... The true story of those battles has never really been told."

The first part of that sentence is true, but the second is false. The story of Verrières Ridge was first told in detail by the government itself shortly after the war when it issued a public document entitled "The Black Watch (Royal Highland Regiment) of Canada in Operation 'Spring,' 25 July 1944." Cast as an explanation directed to "friends of the regiment," it is a full and complete examination based on war diaries, after-action reports, and interviews conducted by army historical officers. It pulls no punches, freely admits mistakes that led to the disaster of Verrières Ridge, and even admits the damage caused to the attack by friendly shellfire landing among Canadian troops. No coverup was ever intended or carried out.[*]

***

[*] Editors note: This is incorrect. Such a document *was* prepared but not released at the time due to Simonds's objections. The document

In addition to that report, Stacey's *The Victory Campaign*, the official army history of the Second World War published in 1960, contains a full and complete account. So too does Copp and Vogel's book, *Maple Leaf Route: Falaise* (1983), R.H. Roy's *1944: The Canadians in Normandy* (1984), and J.A. English's *The Canadian Army and the Normandy Campaign* (1991). In fact, a good case could be made that the Verrières Ridge battle in particular and the Canadian Army in Normandy in general (also covered in some detail by non-Canadian historians Hastings, Keegan, D'Este, etc.) may be the single *most* studied and written about campaign ever fought by a Canadian military force.

This theme that the tragic story, previously unknown, will now be revealed to the viewers is repeated when the narrator says: "In a sense the [war] artists ... were the only ones allowed to record the truth." But there rests in the National Archives literally tens of thousands of pages of war diaries, after-action reports, and reports of army historical officers which are available to researchers today and have been available for decades. All of these documents "record the truth," or as close to "truth" as anyone is ever likely to get.

A second major problem with this program is its failure to put the events in Normandy into a broader context. Lack of context is the single greatest weakness of the entire series. Although the producers do attempt, in a few brief passages, to explain to their viewers that a small prewar Canadian army expanded rapidly, and that problems arose as a result, they claim that Canadian soldiers' "training was mostly casual or haphazard."

In fact, Canadian soldiers' training was sustained, regular, serious, and aimed fully at preparing Canadian soldiers for modern war (and not gearing them "to refighting the First World War" as the narrator claims in this segment). Although it was not the Canadian Army which pioneered "Battle Drill" (a form of small-unit infantry training and something the producers seem to know nothing about), it *was* the Canadians who adopted it with a vengeance and made it a central part of Canadian Army training doctrine in early 1942.

There is debate as to whether Battle Drill truly prepared infantry for actual combat (English, pp. 107–23), and there is much room to argue that the training Canadian soldiers received was not good enough to sustain them in war, or not the equal to that received by German soldiers. It is, however, false and misleading to say both that

---

became public at the same time that other Second World War material was released. Nevertheless, initial details of Operation Spring were contained in C.P. Stacey's *The Canadian Army: 1939–1945* (1948), and the document's findings were reflected in Stacey's 1960 account.

their training was "mostly casual and haphazard" and that it was "at first geared to refighting the First World War."

A further contextual problem arises here. Granted the Canadian Army was not, on the whole, prepared for the Normandy battle in June 1944 and that it did not, on many occasions, measure up to the German enemy in Normandy. But then neither did many British and American field units up to the corps level. The battle experience of German officers and some of their armour and infantry units, the small-unit training which they received, the technical superiority of some of their armour and most of their anti-tank weapons, and the nature of the terrain – stone-walled villages, numerous streams and low ridges, the almost impenetrable hedgerows – caused untold grief for all the mostly untried Allied formations in Normandy. This factor is virtually ignored but for one sentence mentioning that "on one flank a single German armoured division held back a huge American army," which is untrue. It is ironic, and ignored by the film, that one major Allied formation in Normandy that had had extensive battle experience – the British 7th Armoured Division (the Desert Rats) – also acquitted itself very poorly in the early stages of the battle. Its commander and his corps commander were fired in early August by General Miles Dempsey, General Officer Commanding in Chief Second British Army. That, perhaps, is a measure of just how tough (and effective) the German defence was, and how unready *all* the Allies were. Nor is it mentioned anywhere in this film that at the time the Canadians joined battle in Normandy, one, and then a second, Canadian division had been fighting effectively in Sicily and Italy for almost a year. Those units had been trained in Britain alongside the units bound for France.

To summarize: the overall theme of this program is correct. The Canadian Army was not adequately prepared for the fighting in Normandy in June 1944. But this was not because it did not take war seriously. Further, no other ally was well prepared for the Normandy battle either, and many British and American units performed poorly as did the Canadians.

Specific Comments on the Documentary

1) The narrator states about six minutes into the program that the interwar army "had been assigned mostly to local police actions, aid to the civil power." That had happened in 1923 and 1925 in Cape Breton and in 1933 in Stratford, Ontario. In two of these cases, the militia formed a large part of the force used, not the regular army. Does this constitute "mostly?"

2) The narrator says that Simonds "earned his spurs in civil actions before the war. His troops were used as strike breakers in Nova Scotia." This is thoroughly misleading in view of the extremely limited "action" he would have seen in Nova Scotia. It ignores his schooling at the Royal Military College, his prewar staff work, and his prewar publication of theoretical articles on tactics.

3) The narrator says that Crerar became army commander "despite helping organize both Hong Kong and Dieppe." This places undue blame on Crerar for both. The film might have mentioned that Lord Louis Mountbatten, who was ultimately responsible for Dieppe, went on to become a theatre commander!

4) The narrator tells us what Montgomery thought of Crerar. It should have mentioned that at least one high-ranking British Army veteran, Sir Brian Horrocks, who commanded XXX Corps and knew both men well, thought Crerar was "much underrated, largely because he was the exact opposite to Montgomery" (*Corps Commander*, p. 157, paperback edition). One high-ranking British Army intelligence officer thought Montgomery's attitude towards the Canadians "strange ... [and] far too grand in his attitude to their commanders" (Richard Lamb, *Montgomery in Europe, 1933–1945*, p. 253). This might have provided some context for Montgomery's judgment of Crerar.

5) An actor representing infantryman J. LeBoutelier tells viewers: "I got the order from my officer to come last man off the boat. He says, 'If anyone refuse you, you shoot him.'" This after the narrator relates the story of "battle police" shooting soldiers in the First World War who refused to go over the top. There is not a single recorded instance of any such shooting taking place in the Second World War. Why, therefore, is this mentioned here?

6) The narrator claims that "half the [Queen's Own Rifles] lay wounded or dead" following the initial D-Day landing. Stacey reports the Queen's Own to have sustained 143 dead, wounded, or captured on D-Day. Heavy casualties, admittedly, but not nearly half the regiment of more than 700 men.

7) The narrator claims that "the Sherman ... was just no match for the German panzers." "Panzer" is the generic German word for a hard-skinned or armoured fighting vehicle. Many German "panzers" in Normandy were Pzkv Mark IVs, to which the Sherman was equal. It was the Tiger and Panther which were superior to the Sherman. The "Firefly," an upgunned Sherman with a 17-pounder anti-tank gun as main armament, was capable of knocking out Panthers and, under some conditions, Tigers as well.

8) The story of the Battle of Authie/Buron is told in some detail with dramatizations and interviews with Gen. Radley Walters. This was the action where the 12th SS Panzer was stopped in its drive to the beach on 7 June by the North Nova Scotia Regiment and the Sherbrooke Fusiliers. No mention is made that the SS *was* stopped and thrown back, a victory for the Canadians, however costly.

9) The episode of the SS execution of Canadian prisoners is told in a rather curious manner. The narrator tells the viewers that the Germans explained their actions by claiming "they were often retaliating." What is the evidence for this? The actor representing SS General Kurt Meyer tells viewers that he (ie, Meyer) possessed a notebook from a dead Canadian officer with the notation that "no prisoners were to be taken" and that Canadian prisoners had confirmed this. Surely the producers recognize this for the self-serving statement it is? Are they not aware of the record of brutality, well recorded, of Waffen SS units on both fronts throughout the war? Does this not form a context for the shootings which took place at the Abbaye Ardenne?

10) The second bit of evidence given that the Germans were only retaliating in kind when shooting captured Canadians is that of a British sailor whose description of events is presented without any context.

11) The narrator says, "Some Canadian generals did give orders to take no prisoners." No such order, written or oral, has ever been documented. If the producers had some new evidence to present here, they ought to have done so.

12) The narrator then goes on to say several minutes later that war crimes "are prosecuted only on the side that loses the war." Does this mean that the producers believe the Nuremberg trials were a travesty of justice? They ought to say so outright if they believe it to be so.

This whole episode is problematic. There is more than enough evidence from non-official sources (Foster, *Meeting of Generals*, Mowat, *And No Birds Sang*, etc.) that Canadians sometimes shot prisoners. So did other Allies. There is no evidence to indicate that this was official, decided policy, ever. This stands in sharp contrast to the wholesale shootings of captured soldiers carried out by Waffen SS units on both fronts, shootings that were part of official policy. There is no moral equivalent between random killings by Canadians and the decided policy of the Waffen SS, and it is unfair for the producers to claim there was.

13) The viewers are told after the POW-shooting episode that one German armoured division was holding back "a huge American

army." In fact, the Germans had two armoured divisions and some seventy regiments facing the Americans.

14) The claim is made that Montgomery wanted to capture Caen as a "public relations victory." This claim can only be made by someone totally ignorant both of German strategy to hold Caen at all costs (well documented in at least a dozen serious histories of the campaign) and of the importance of Caen as a transportation centre, river crossing, and the key to the drive to the Seine. Caen dominated the region west and south of the Orne. As long as the Germans held Caen, their position in eastern Normandy was secure. To call the drive to take Caen a "public relations" exercise is simply fatuous.

15) The narrator tells us that Caen was bombed (the words "levelling the place" are used) even though German defences were "centred outside the old Norman city." This is not true. They were centred in the city's northern suburbs, the area heavily bombed. We are then told "the levelling of Caen did not bring any military advantage to the Canadians." In fact the evidence is mixed. Stacey says: "There was no doubt at all of the bombing's results among our own troops ... The effect on the enemy is more doubtful" because "the available contemporary German records ... throw little light on the matter" (p. 158). Stacey goes on to say, "The moral effect upon the German troops ... was probably very considerable." If the producers have evidence which has enabled them to come to a conclusion more definite, or different, from that of Stacey, it ought to be presented.

16) About midway through the program the narrator claims that "in the Canadian Army malingering was more an offense punishable by five years of hard labour in prison. Other armies recognized shell shock for what it was, acute psychiatric collapse." This greatly distorts the truth. There *was* a prison sentence on the books for malingering; this does *not* mean that Canadian Army shell-shock victims (actually, it was called "battle fatigue") received it, although that is the distinct impression created here. In fact the Canadian army was at least as advanced in recognizing and treating battle fatigue as were the other Allied armies. Battle fatigue in the Canadian Army was universally treated as an illness, not a crime. This has been documented by Copp and McAndrew, *Battle Exhaustion* (1990).

17) Again, about one hour into the documentary, the claim is made that Canadian Army training was "casual and haphazard," which is not true.

18) In describing what is known as the reinforcement crisis (ie, when the narrator declares, "The shortage of good reinforcements

was blamed on a conscription crisis at home"), the film fails to mention that it was only later – in the Scheldt fighting of the fall – that the crisis became really acute. Nor is it mentioned that although the reinforcement crisis was undoubtedly caused by faulty casualty predictions for infantry (predictions gained from the British), the unwillingness of the government to send any of the trained infantry conscripts in Canada to Europe made the problem acute.

19) The entire Verrières Ridge episode is marred by the assertion that Operation Spring was fought because Simonds was under "heavy political pressure for that quick victory." The "pressure" was strictly military – to attract German units and hold them to the British/Canadian front while the Americans broke through the German lines to the west. The American attack (Operation Cobra) was launched 25 July, the same day as Operation Spring.

In the same segment the actor portraying Simonds relates that visiting Russian officers had told him they "wouldn't attack unless they outnumbered the Germans by at least five or six to one." Simonds never had any chance to deploy forces so large. They were not available and there would have been no room for them in an already overcrowded Allied bridgehead if they were.

20) When the viewers are told about the fatigue of the 3rd Canadian Infantry Division, they might also have been told that the division had been in the line since 6 June and eventually suffered the heaviest casualties of the three Canadian divisions in Normandy.

21) The viewers are told that Verrières ridge was honeycombed with mineshafts and a film clip is shown of Germans racing through well-lit concrete tunnels. Most of the shafts were *ventilation* shafts and the well-lit, concrete-lined tunnels in the film did not exist there.

22) The entire story of the Verrières Ridge attack is truncated, leaving out key details. The flanks of the Royal Highland Regiment (RHC) should have been protected by the Calgary Highlanders, but the Highlanders could not fight their way into May-sur-Orne. There had been several communications failures in the night battles that proceeded the RHC advance. The meeting between Brigadier Megill and Griffin was to discuss changing the previously prepared fire plan, etc. These details are readily available.

23) After the story of Verrières Ridge, we are told that "the full extent of the calamity was covered up." This statement has no factual foundation whatever.

24) We are told that Simonds stopped Operation Spring when "facing rebellion." This never happened.

25) We are told that the army did not honour Griffin with a medal.

This is true. Had he lived, and had the action been a success, he would most likely have been awarded the DCM.* But the DCM is not awarded posthumously, and the action was most decidedly not a success.

26) Towards the end of the program the viewers are told that the coming of the Typhoon fighter-bomber and the establishment of air superiority were decisive in the eventual victory. In fact, the Typhoon was available throughout the campaign, and the Allies always had air superiority in the battle.

27) The narrator says that the Canadians used "heavy bombing and relentless assaults to push Kurt Meyer's Hitler Youth Division off Verrières Ridge." But they neither used heavy bombing to accomplish this nor did they push the 12th SS off the ridge because the division was not there.

28) After telling the viewers that "there is a lot of controversy" about Canadian generalship – true enough – the narrator says, "General Simonds never answered his critics." This is a gratuitous and pejorative statement. It gives the impression that a specific critic or set of critics levelled charges of poor generalship at Simonds but that he failed, or refused, to answer them. This simply did not happen during the war or during Simonds's lifetime.

Conclusion

There can be little argument concerning the main thesis of this program – that the Canadian Army was unprepared to fight the Normandy battle. But no context is provided in which that theme can be fairly explored, and grossly inaccurate statements are made concerning the training the soldiers received, an alleged government effort to cover up disasters such as Verrières Ridge, and other matters. This and simple errors of fact and omission almost totally undermine the historical value of this documentary. While it does not demonstrate the almost complete failure to present alternative interpretations which mark the first two programs in this series, it clearly reflects the producers' own views to a far greater extent than it does any kind of historical reality.

---

*   Editor's note: This is also incorrect. The medal that Griffin would most likely have been awarded was the Distinguished Service Order (DSO).

PART TWO

The Ombudsman Controversy

Report of the CBC Ombudsman

Gérard Veilleux   6 November 1992
President
Canadian Broadcasting Corporation
Ottawa

Dear Mr. President:

I initially wrote to you on September 26, 1992, in response to your request that, in light of all the material we had discussed, I should prepare a final written summary of the full review I have conducted for you on the program series *The Valour and the Horror*. Since then we have received further representations and material from the producers and program makers of the series. I have reviewed what has been made available and, where appropriate, have made adjustments. Virtually all of what follows is already known to you, of course, and you have seen the material from the producers. So this letter now represents the final summary report which you requested.

BACKGROUND

On January 12, 19, and 26, 1992, THE VALOUR AND THE HORROR, a three-part series, was broadcast on the CBC English Television Network.

There was a strong reaction to the broadcasts, with a substantial volume of calls, letters and other more detailed communications coming in to the CBC, many of them expressing anger or complaining about perceived errors or distortions in the programs as broadcast. Other letters and calls expressed satisfaction with the programs and praise for the producers.

A second airing of the series had been planned to take place on CBC NEWSWORLD beginning Saturday, 28 March 1992, and, in an effort to respond to complaints and concerns which had been expressed, in particular, about the second episode of the series, "Death by Moonlight: Bomber Command," CBC program managers arranged for the second airing of that episode to be followed immediately by a discussion program involving the writer-director of the series and Bomber Command veterans who had expressed objections to that episode after it was first shown.

Controversy about the series continued, however, and the President of the CBC, as is his right under the mandate of CBC's Ombudsman, asked the Ombudsman to conduct a full review of the series for him and suggested that the process include consultation with qualified historians.

PROCEDURES

In carrying out this review the Ombudsman took the following steps:

- Tapes of all three programs, as originally broadcast, were screened a number of times.
- The latest available transcripts of the programs were obtained from the producers and reviewed in detail.
- All correspondence received by CBC on the program series was sought and was read with care and interest. (This correspondence included a number of substantial briefs whose contents have been, in various ways, thought-provoking and helpful.)
- Initially, three historians who were approached agreed to provide detailed commentary on programs in the series. David Bercuson, Professor of History and Dean of Graduate Studies at the University of Calgary, and Sydney Wise, until recently Dean of Graduate Studies and Research at Carleton University, agreed, as requested, to comment on all three programs. Denis Richards, a British author and historian who had written a short history of the RAF in World War II and had met and interviewed Sir Arthur Harris, Commander-in-Chief of Bomber Command from 1942 to 1945, was asked and agreed to comment on the Bomber Command episode only.

Subsequently, two further Canadian historians, whose names were provided by the writer-narrator of the series as historians he and his colleagues would choose to have the Ombudsman speak with, were consulted. They were Steven Harris, an historian with the Directorate of History at the Department of National Defence and co-author of the directly relevant volume of the history of the

RCAF, who stressed that he was speaking strictly as an individual, and Carl Vincent, Government Archivist and author of *No Reason Why – The Canadian Hong Kong Tragedy – An Examination*.

Also considered carefully were the comments of other historians, including those who had written more or less supportive letters at the request of the program makers or the producers of the series.

- Because the time and space constraints of television tend to militate against inclusion of all evidentiary material, the production company was presented by the Ombudsman with a number of written questions and requests for the documentation to support and justify various portrayals, assertions and statements of fact in the programs.
- Upon receipt of responses which the production company had been able to supply, and taking fully into account the comments of all the historians consulted, the Ombudsman proceeded with the final detailed examination upon which the findings in this summary report are based.

ROLES AND RELATIONSHIPS

The auspices under which this series was contracted for and produced are complicated. Principals of Galafilm Inc., the independent production company involved, have stressed, quite correctly, that the series was co-produced with them by CBC and NFB and with the participation of Telefilm Canada.

This review of the series does not, however, concern itself with those or any other administrative or contractual arrangements among co-producers. It concentrates, as the work of CBC's Ombudsman normally does, on the content of the programs as broadcast.

It should also be noted from the outset that the role of The National Film Board is not considered or dealt with at all in this report.

The CBC's Ombudsman is mandated to deal with CBC programming. The NFB is a separate entity with its own structures and standards and, unlike the CBC, does not hold broadcasting licences.

This review has been conducted entirely within the framework of CBC's own particular policies, standards and traditions. What follows should be read in that light only and not as a reflection of any kind on The National Film Board of Canada.

Nor is freedom of expression an issue in this review. The key creative people involved in the series are familiar with CBC journalism policies and aware that anyone producing a program for the Corporation, whether independently or as a member of staff, accepts the constraint of abiding by those policies.

As to the CBC's own responsibilities and traditions, the very first thing that must be said is that the CBC has not merely a right, but an actual responsibility to broadcast programs in the category to which this series generally belongs. Whatever faults may be observed in this particular piece of work, they should in no way be seen as a justification, or even an argument, for an organization like the CBC to draw back, either through fear of causing upset or of political consequences, from the production and presentation of programs which raise difficult and uncomfortable questions, or which force us to look again, for legitimate reasons, at issues on which our views may be settled.

In this particular case, the veterans, despite the unrepayable debt of gratitude that most citizens feel they are owed, do not own an exclusive right to analysis of the events in which they personally participated. Indeed, almost all of those veterans, conscious that they fought, and that many of their friends and comrades died, in defence of our democratic way of life and our personal freedoms, including freedom of expression, would themselves instinctively reject any such idea.

Still, with freedom goes a certain responsibility. Those who make such programs have a duty to ensure that, in questioning conventional views and interpretations, they do not let themselves slip into using their own privileged access to the airwaves to become advocates.

No matter how appealing any new or unfamiliar theory or interpretation may be, or how persuasive the exponents themselves may find it, their presentation should still give reasonable attention to all significant evidence which does not support their theory and should allow us to hear any theory tested against other relevant views, including strongly divergent ones.

This does not mean that there is a policy requirement for delicacy. Sensitivity towards the feelings of people directly concerned in a program's subject matter is largely a matter of courtesy, and perhaps of maturity. It is not a requirement of responsible journalism.

Accuracy, however, is such a requirement, and not always an easy one to fulfil. Accuracy is not achieved simply by making sure that the facts actually chosen for presentation are right. To be accurate means ensuring that all of the relevant facts are present. Accuracy involves a determination to get at the truth and to share it with the audience, even when the result may not perfectly accord with the writer's or producer's pre-conceived notion. If truly controversial issues are involved, a range of relevant opinion as well as facts should be offered. Even those engaged in analysis and interpretation must try to be fair.

Broadcast journalism – or broadcast history – is a particularly difficult and vulnerable enterprise. In the academic world, the historian who presents or publishes work has often done all of the key research personally or has delegated it to graduate students whom he or she has personally trained. In broadcasting, a whole team of researchers from different backgrounds and disciplines may be involved, and they most often do not themselves write the final version of the script. Indeed, by the time that final version is completed several other hands and influences may have been involved. The task of accurately capturing and encapsulating the results of detailed research, often with the researcher not personally present for consultation, under the inevitable pressure for brevity which broadcasting exerts, trying to match a handful of words precisely to the visuals in a few seconds of stock footage, is an extremely demanding and difficult one. Even capable, experienced people doing their honest best to get it right can make slips and errors and the program managers who accept the finished product, doing so on trust, just as a producer does from a writer, or a writer from a researcher and that researcher's contacts, are in a similarly vulnerable position.

CBC POLICIES AND STANDARDS

In order to help program makers and managers to avoid the dangers inherent in these processes, CBC has developed official written policies, approved by the Corporation's Board of Directors, and has made them available in book form to those who work in and with the CBC on journalism or related programs. It may be worthwhile to set down here, from the Corporation's book of journalism policies, the principles upon which those policies are based and some key paragraphs from those policy statements which appear most relevant to this review.

The Corporation's information programming is expected to reflect certain essential principles of journalism:

Accuracy: the information conforms with reality and is not in any way misleading or false. This demands not only careful and thorough research but a disciplined use of language and production techniques, including visuals.

Integrity: the information is truthful, not distorted to justify a conclusion. Broadcasters do not take advantage of their position of control in any way to present a personal bias.

Fairness: the information reports or reflects equitably the relevant facts and significant points of view; it deals fairly and ethically with persons, institutions, issues and events.

Under the terms of CBC's journalism policy, especially when the subject matter is rarely visited and the views or interpretations to be presented are evidently controversial, real and substantial efforts to ensure fairness and balance are required.

Programs dealing with an issue of substantial controversy on a one-time basis should give adequate recognition to the range of opinion on the subject. Fairness must be the guiding principle in presentation, so that the audience is enabled to make a judgement on the matter in question based on the facts.

Another area where particular care is required, especially in light of the highly complex assembly of elements that is involved in a series such as this one, is in the proper editing and juxtaposition of these elements.

The editing process must result in a true reflection of what was originally seen and heard and any terms agreed upon during the preparation of the program.

Editing, the abbreviation of recorded visual, sound or written material, is an essential technique and one of the most demanding in journalism because of the time limitations imposed by radio and television production and the need to be concise and clear. It would be impractical to expect the whole of reality in an edited program. *What in fact results from selection and editing is a compression of reality, a slice of reality – which must nonetheless reflect the essential truth without distortion.* [Emphasis in original]

Under the heading "MIXTURE OF ACTUALITY AND DRAMATIZATION," the policy states:

Journalistic programs must not as a general principle mix actuality (visual and audio of actual events and of real people) with a dramatized portrayal of people or events.

The audience must be able to judge the nature of the information received. The mixture of forms renders such a judgement difficult because it may lend the appearance of reality to hypothesis.

Should a situation arise in which such a mixture of forms is the only adequate method to convey the necessary information, the dramatized portion must be well identified.

GENERAL REMARKS AND FINDINGS

While I do find serious fault with the programs in this series, I want to stress, as I tried to do earlier, that programming which raises legitimate questions about our history, just as about events and circumstances in contemporary society, is an important part of CBC's mandate to inform.

I believe those who made these programs understood this and were trying to carry out their responsibilities to the best of their ability and I find no reason to conclude that they deliberately set out to distort the facts or to mislead their audience.

Nor do I consider, as some people appear to do, that the programs in the series are entirely without merit. One cannot help but admire the courage and humanity of the many Canadians whom members of the audience were able to encounter through these programs, people who clearly saw an unmistakable evil and were ready to risk everything to defeat it and to preserve freedoms we today take for granted.

Even some of those who were not there in person left letters and diaries from which much can be learned. Just a couple of sentences of Martin Favreau, for example, remind us of a proud tradition of voluntary military service among the oldest and most cultivated French Canadian families.

The most powerful and touching parts of the programs – and often the most sound journalistically – are those involving the three pairs of veterans who personally appeared in the films, recalling their own experiences. Their dignity and evident decency were enough to make any Canadian proud to be their compatriot and one might readily apply to any of the six a comment which one of the historians consulted made about the two who appeared in the first episode of the series:

I must record my heartfelt admiration for the two veterans of Hong Kong who appeared in this episode. They were quintessentially Canadian, wholly believable, and some of the sequences in which they appeared were inexpressibly moving.

No program which enable us to meet people like these and to understand something of what they went through can possibly be all bad.

Regrettably, it must also be said that, in some respects, these programs are flawed. Each of the programs seems designed to fit its subject matter within a framework, of which the program makers themselves were apparently convinced, of incompetent, brutal or obsessive and villainous leadership, protected by secrecy or a conspiracy of silence now broken at last by those who made the programs and who are letting the audience hear the "full" or the "real" story for the first time.

The problem is that the case against the leadership is for the most part not proven. The secrecy was either understandable in the context of the time or not evident to others than the program makers. And much of what the narrator claims to be revealing has been known for some time.

In the Bomber Command program and in the Normandy program, attempts to persuade the audience of the villainy of one particular commanding officer, who had been singled out by the program makers, went beyond the available supporting evidence in criticism of the officer in question.

Arthur Harris remains a controversial figure. But even the historian among those consulted who has the least favourable opinion of Harris says that it is wrong to present him as being uncaring about the aircrew in his command.

Similarly, one of the historians consulted observed that the Normandy program seemed to be "stacking the deck" against Lt.-Gen. Guy Simonds. Even Col. Carlo D'Este, an American historian who wrote, at the producers' request, to comment on the Normandy episode, disagreed with the portrayal of Simonds, saying that he was exceptional among senior Canadian commanders.

In these ways, as in others, apparently through efforts to fit the material into a rather arbitrary framework, combined with the pressures of such substantial and complex production activity, the programs fail to meet policy requirements, including, in some cases, the essential test of accuracy.

Reputable, professional historians have pointed out a number of instances where, because important context is not provided to the audience, the information actually presented, or its implication, becomes seriously misleading.

Thus, RAF/RCAF area bombing of targets in Germany, the central issue of the program in which it is discussed, is presented as if precision bombing without calamitous losses of aircraft and men was available as a viable alternative in 1942 and 1943 and as if area attacks were simply preferred by the Commander-in-Chief of Bomber Command because he was obsessed with destroying German cities and killing German civilians. Without exception, however, the historians consulted on this program agree that precision bombing of German targets by Bomber Command was still only becoming increasingly feasible in the Fall of 1944.

Similarly, there are instances in the selection and editing of material from the writings or non-broadcast interviews of people who are represented in the programs by actors where important context and balance were lost.

So, though the actor portraying Roger Cyr is heard in the Hong Kong program talking about the possibility that their government knowingly sent the two Canadian battalions as lambs to the slaughter, we do not hear that, elsewhere in the non-broadcast interview with him, Mr. Cyr says the government decision was based on "the availability of the intelligence and the information of the day."

Similarly, when the same program presents, through an actor, the words of Nursing Sister Kay Christie recalling her concern at hearing rifle instruction sessions on the ship transporting the Canadians to Hong Kong, the audience does not hear the next words from her non-broadcast interview:

But they weren't sent over to fight, they were going over for garrison duty, just to strengthen the British.

Historians may not all agree on the "garrison" argument. It is, however, seen by a number of them as important context, but omitted here.

The audience can also be misled, however inadvertently, by a shift of context, as in the Normandy program where, several times, words from a book by Donald Pearce of the North Nova Scotia Regiment, delivered by an actor, are inserted into discussion of events taking place in Normandy during the summer of 1944, although Donald Pearce did not even arrive in Normandy until later in the year.

There are also errors or confusions of fact, of which a few examples may be illustrative. Kurt Meyer's 12th SS Division are described as eventually being pushed off Verrières Ridge, while all indications, including those from the program makers, are that they were on Bourguébus Ridge and that the producers were trying to simplify to avoid confusing the audience.

General Simonds is described as having "never answered his critics," though he in fact wrote a detailed analysis of Operation Spring. The audience is told that "half of the regiment (The Queen's Own Rifles) lay wounded or dead" on the beach on D-Day, while historians report the Queen's Own to have sustained 143 dead, wounded or captured on D-Day. Tragic, but not half of the regiment. In the Bomber Command program the narrator states that the 545 aircrew killed in the Nuremberg Raid of March 30, 1944, was greater than the number who died during the entire Battle of Britain. The actual figure for the Battle of Britain was 1,485 aircrew killed. In the same program we are told that Arthur Harris, though ordered to have Bomber Command assist with "Overlord," the Allied invasion of Europe, "would have none of it." This is simply not true. While

Bomber Command continued to target Germany it did participate actively in support of "Overlord" and Harris was thanked for that support by General Eisenhower.

The programs contain various interpretations and assertions which the producers were unable adequately to support with documentary evidence and which were questioned or challenged by the historians consulted, including those recommended by the program makers themselves.

Even the Hong Kong film, though the veterans are so impressive and the story of the fall of Hong Kong and its aftermath is generally told well, is marred by several significant unsubstantiated assertions or implications. The notion that the Canadian Government *knowingly* sent 2,000 of its young men to the slaughter is featured prominently, both near the beginning and the end of the program. Elsewhere, the narration suggests that the decision to send the two battalions was made as a result of the Canadian Government's "accepting the Mother Country's assurance that the men would not be in harm's way." Later in the program it seems clearly implied that Canadians were sent to die there because the British did not want to risk any more of their own. The program also suggests that what happened to the two battalions sent to Hong Kong was for a long time suppressed by the Canadian government.

However, the historians who commented on this program challenged these assertions. Even Carl Vincent, who wrote the book on the Canadian Hong Kong tragedy, and who was recommended for consultation by the writer-narrator of the series, while he finds the program reasonably accurate in content and very accurate in theme, had reservations about use of the word "knowingly" and is clearly not convinced that the evidence supports the assertions that the British were willing to sacrifice Canadians rather than risk their own, or that the British provided assurances that the Canadians would not be in harm's way. On the final point, that of suppression, Carl Vincent, while he clearly feels that the Duff Commission report was a "whitewash," says there is no evidence even of deliberate isolation of documents concerning Hong Kong and that treatment by the Canadian government of information on this particular matter was no different from the normal handling of documents in wartime and subsequently by Canada or its allies. Vincent also reports that when he was researching and writing *No Reason Why*, none of the material which he needed was particularly difficult to obtain. In fact, he says, with justifiable pride, that he did not have to resort to oral history because "it was all there in the documents."

Similar assertions or implications in other episodes, including depiction of the Dams Raid in the Bomber Command program as if it was planned from the beginning partly as a publicity stunt needed by Bomber Command to improve its image, and in the Normandy program, where Montgomery's decision to attack Caen was presented as being for public relations purposes, are disputed by the historians who were consulted on those programs.

The last and, in many respects, the most significant area of difficulty with these programs lies in the use of drama techniques. CBC's journalism policy makes it clear that use of drama in journalism programming is discouraged as a general principle because the mixture of forms may make it difficult for the audience to judge the nature of the information presented and because dramatic techniques may "lend the appearance of reality to hypothesis."

Even if one takes the position that, because a number of the people the producers considered it necessary for the audience to hear from are dead, the use of drama segments to present their words may be justified, one cannot avoid the fact that the use of drama in these programs had the effect of helping to create other serious problems and distortions.

If a decision is made to use drama in an information program, the drama segments should be properly identified. That was not done.

Nor, though statements at the beginning of each program seemed to provide an assurance of exact quotation from writings and interviews, were the words put in the mouths of the various people who were represented by actors in every case their own actual words or even a precise reflection, with appropriate context, of what they had actually written or had said on tape with interviewed.

So, at least one quotation delivered by the actor representing Arthur Harris consists of words we have no record that he ever said or wrote. Another quotation, appearing to offer Harris's view of "colonials," seriously distorts the burden of what he actually wrote and the view of him which the audience might draw from it. And, through an important omission, and a shift of context, Harris is shown seeming to say, immediately after pictures of the devastation at Hamburg, that bombing was a comparatively humane method, that there is no proof that women and children died at Hamburg in disproportionate numbers and even seeming to lie about this latter point. Examination of the text of his book shows that important context for his statement about bombing was omitted and that the actual casualty figures he was discussing were for all of Germany, not Hamburg.

Harris is no longer around to speak for himself. Chosen to represent him was an actor who apparently neither looked nor sounded like Harris did, an actor who, in recent years, until his untimely death, had specialized in playing villains, indeed may well have been associated in the minds of members of the audience with any of the many villainous characters he had portrayed, an actor who delivered a number of his lines with a look of cruel menace and, occasionally, even with a curled lip. The dangers in the use of drama in information programs are particularly evident here.

From these examples, and from all of the other material I have discussed with you, I believe it is clear why I find that the series as it stands is flawed and fails to measure up to CBC's demanding policies and standards.

Yours truly,

William Morgan
Ombudsman

BRIAN AND TERENCE MCKENNA

Response to the CBC Ombudsman Report, November 10, 1992, Galafilm Inc.

The purpose of this document is to answer the points raised by the CBC Ombudsman in his November 10 report.

We believe that the CBC Ombudsman's process has been a miscarriage of justice. This purported Ombudsman did not follow most of the generally accepted procedures of an Ombudsman review. He did not advise us of the rules and parameters of his inquiry, in spite of repeated requests. He never questioned us about many of the allegations levelled against us. He did not allow us a proper opportunity to respond in writing to complaints he made against the films.

The Ombudsman has advised us that he did not have to follow the generally accepted steps of an Ombudsman procedure, because this was not technically an Ombudsman procedure. This was a "Special Review" ordered by the CBC President. There were no rules. We believe this was manifestly unfair.

We believe that fair-minded people who review the Ombudsman's process and his report will see that his entire approach has been prejudicial to the filmmakers. We believe in fair and open accountability procedures. This process was neither fair nor open.

In his report, we are struck by the suggestion that we have not been able to provide answers to many of the points he has raised. He has done his best to not even acknowledge the existence of the voluminous documentation we have sent him. After the Ombudsman's review was announced in the spring, we sent him hundreds of pages of documents supporting the film series, in which many of the questions and allegations raised about the film were answered. The Ombudsman doesn't even mention those documents in his report. In his report he makes no mention of the many answers already provided by the filmmakers to the points he has raised.

In the report, extensive reference is made to the Journalistic Policy

Guidelines of the CBC, in a manner which suggests that the filmmakers have broken every cited dictum. While no case is made, the impression is left that the filmmakers have committed infractions in each of these areas. This is unfair.

HISTORIANS

We have repeatedly complained that the choice of the three historians retained and paid by the Ombudsman was inappropriate and prejudicial towards the filmmakers. The Ombudsman was presented with documentary evidence implicating the only Canadian military historian retained by him, and yet the report does not acknowledge this evidence or the Defence Department cover-up of which this historian had knowledge. We review here the supposedly independent and unbiased historians hired by the Ombudsman on behalf of the CBC.

1 Sydney Wise, who is identified by the Ombudsman as former dean of graduate studies at Carleton University. The Ombudsman does not mention that Wise is a former Bomber Command pilot who after the war would become chief of the Department of National Defence Directorate of History. The Directorate of History is responsible for all official versions of Canada at war. The filmmakers have presented the Ombudsman with documentary evidence which suggests that Sydney Wise and the Directorate of History were involved in cover-up [of] the tragic events concerning the Canadian Army in Normandy described in our film series.
2 David Bercuson is a labour historian who has never written a book about the Second World War. Bercuson had already committed himself in print against the series with an attack in the *Calgary Herald* (May 11, 1992) at the time he was hired by the Ombudsman as a supposedly impartial historical advisor.
3 Denis Richards is an official British historian who served with the British Air Ministry Historical Branch. Richards apparently knew Sir Arthur Harris well, and was apparently chosen by the Harris family to write an introduction to a new version of Harris's memoirs. This historian was asked to review *The Valour and the Horror*'s Bomber Command film which severely attacked Harris for sacrificing the lives of thousands of Canadian pilots to pursue a policy of immolating German cities and the civilian population inhabiting them.

Clearly the choice of historical advisors was prejudicial to the filmmakers. None of the Canadian historians who have supported the films were consulted, including Michael Bliss of the University of Toronto, Graeme Decarie of Concordia University and Brian Villa of the University of Ottawa. He also refused to consult the leading international historians who have supported the films, including John Keegan of Britain, one of the world's leading military historians, Max Hastings, the leading expert on Bomber Command, and Colonel Carlo D'Este of the United States, the world's leading expert on the Battle of Normandy.

The Ombudsman pretends that he has consulted historians on our side and they are in fact against us. This is not true. He has contacted Steven Harris, who is writing the Official History of the Royal Canadian Air Force, whom he does not quote in his report, and Carl Vincent, who wrote the definitive Canadian book about the Battle for Hong Kong. In his report, the Ombudsman has paraphrased his conversation with Carl Vincent in a manner that suggests that Mr. Vincent does not support our documentary's treatment of all major issues with respect to Canadian involvement in Hong Kong. This is false.

Carl Vincent is in fact very surprised by Mr. Morgan's characterization of their conversation. Vincent says that he told Mr. Morgan it was a good film, and that Morgan seemed to agree with him. Vincent says that he has only expressed a few nit-picking reservations about small details in the film, but not about the film's general content and theme. Carl Vincent sent us a letter to this effect. The report clearly distorts Vincent's remarks. Its portrayal of Vincent's assessment is totally at odds with Vincent's written appraisal, which we reproduce here:

The salient features of the Canadian Hong Kong involvement are abundantly documented and are as follows:

1 The British War Office considered Hong Kong indefensible both before and after the request for Canadian troops. Only when reinforcements from a "hitherto unconsidered source" (Canada) were thought to be available, were they sent, mainly as part of an attempt to show the United States and China that Britain was standing firm in the Far East.
2 The Canadian government accepted the request unthinkingly and without examination.
3 The Canadian troops were woefully untrained and unprepared, even by the standards of the time.
4 Despite the above, the Canadians put up a brave and astonishingly effective fight, playing the major part in the defence of Hong Kong island.
5 The Japanese were guilty of hideous atrocities when Hong Kong fell.

6 Conditions in the prison camps and during slave labour in Japan were
   appalling and deaths due to neglect, disease, malnutrition and brutality
   were high.
7 After the war the Canadian survivors, many of whom would always be
   affected in mind and body by their ordeal, would have to plead for
   decades before their situation was fully recognized.

The Valour and the Horror while certainly a dramatic portrayal, in no way
alters or exaggerates [the] main facts.

Carl Vincent letter to producers, June 19, 1992

The report chooses to ignore this positive critique offered by Canada's
top scholar on the subject. It fails to even acknowledge its existence.

USE OF DRAMATIC TECHNIQUE

In the following detailed response to the CBC Ombudsman's report,
we will deal first with what Mr. Morgan calls "the most significant
area of difficulty with these programs," namely the use of drama
techniques.

In his written questions to us he never raised the use of drama as
an issue. Now he characterizes it as the most significant issue.

He frames his charge, quoting CBC policy, admonishing filmmakers
against mixing drama and documentary unless the two are well identified.

The Ombudsman condemns the use of dramatic techniques employed in *The Valour and the Horror*. This is astonishing in light of the
fact that the Ombudsman, in his previous incarnation, was Head of
CBC Television News and Current affairs, and was one of the CBC
executives who in 1988 gave the green light to produce *The Killing
Ground*. *The Killing Ground* employed exactly the same techniques of
documentary and drama as *The Valour and the Horror*. This film on the
First World War was the template for the three films on the Second
World War. Strangely, although the dramatizations in *The Valour and
the Horror* are treated in the same way, Mr. Morgan now finds them
unacceptable.

The Ombudsman writes: "If a decision is made to use drama in an
information program, the drama segments should be properly
identified. That was not done."

We would answer that it was done, and that there was obviously
no confusion in the minds of our audience. We saw not a single letter
from any viewer who was confused about what was drama and what
was documentary in the series. Some viewers and critics disliked the

performances of some of the actors representing the soldiers and airmen, but no one for a second thought that these young actors were in fact 70 year old soldiers and airmen. A clear distinction was made to the audience by the highly stylized manner in which the actors in costume addressed the camera, standing in limbo in front of a black curtain. The audience was clearly advised by the narrator on camera before the beginning of each film that actors were employed in the production. It seems that Mr. Morgan is the only person who has made this complaint.

On September 14, 1992, the eminent British historian John Keegan said one of the most distinctive features about the Bomber Command film were the dramatic sequences. "They worked very well," he said. Keegan said he was particularly enthralled by the stories of Martin Favreau and Mary "Bubbles" Moore. Keegan said that in a film such as "Death by Moonlight" it is crucial for the audience to understand where the drama ends and the documentary begins. "The film was very successful at separating the drama from the documentary. The drama was signaled in all kinds of ways, not the least of which was the age of the actors. Clearly that was not the seventy year old Martin Favreau."

Mr. Morgan claims that his review has been "conducted entirely within the framework of the CBC's own particular policies, standards and traditions." How then does Mr. Morgan ignore the fact that the CBC has broadcast many programs mixing drama and documentary. In fact there were other such programs broadcast under Mr. Morgan's direction: "Canada's Sweetheart" (The Hal Banks Story), and the "Mackenzie King Chronicles." This technique has also been used on many occasions in documentaries featured on "The Journal."

In Mr. Morgan's entire treatment of the drama issue, he is clearly not writing as an Ombudsman but as a would-be critic. He perceives the actor playing Arthur Harris displaying "a look of cruel menace and, occasionally, even a curled lip." This is his personal opinion, not an objective fact. It should have no place in his report. He complains that filmmakers chose to play Harris "an actor that neither looked nor sounded" like him. No casting expert would ever accept Mr. Morgan's dictum as a rule of casting.

The Ombudsman complains that, in casting the Arthur Harris role, the filmmakers chose an actor who specialized in playing villains. He is mistaken. Graeme Campbell has played every sort of role, his last being the comic innkeeper in "Les Miserables," a role which de-lighted audiences and brought down the house with laughter and applause every night. We would respectfully submit that Mr. Morgan is not competent as a critic. He should leave that role to those who are paid to be television critics in Canada. Incidently, those critics were almost unanimous in their praise for *The Valour and the Horror*.

PURPORTED DISTORTIONS

Another serious issue is the Ombudsman's insinuation that we made up words and put them into the mouths of actors portraying real people. He focuses on one particular passage read by the actor playing Sir Arthur Harris.

We shall destroy Germany's will to fight. Now that we have the planes and crews, in 1943 and 1944 we shall drop one and a quarter million tons of bombs, render 25 million Germans homeless, kill 900,000 and seriously injure one million.

Firstly, the Ombudsman chose to ignore the manner in which this quotation was framed in the transcript of the documentary. The film makes clear that Harris was reciting orders. Says the narrator, "Bomber Command Chief Arthur Harris received new orders: from now on he was free to deliberately target German civilians." Following this quotation the script makes clear that the orders originated from Sir Charles Portal, Chief of the Air Staff.

Second, in documents supplied to the Ombudsman, it was established that Harris was the co-author of the declaration, a memo prepared with Sir Charles Portal, entitled: "Note by the Chief of the Air Staff: An Estimate of the Effects of an Anglo-American Bomber Offensive Against Germany." Harris's official biographer, historian Dudley Saward, confirms in *Bomber Harris* (p. 176) that the document was prepared "with the assistance of Harris."

The report accuses us of "seriously distorting" Arthur Harris's view of "colonials." This is not true. The Ombudsman has complained that in addition to the Harris quote used, we should have used other Harris comments on this issue that appear later in the text of Harris's autobiography, especially his view that colonial troops "are no better and no worse than the British themselves."

Ironically, had the Ombudsman continued even further down the same page in the Harris autobiography, where Harris applies his musings specifically to the men serving in Bomber Command, he'd have read: "The fact is that an ordinary mixed British crew from all parts of the British Isles is as brave as any crew from any part of the world, and is much better disciplined, and certainly better educated than the average colonial and dominion crew." (Harris: *Bomber Offensive*, p. 64). This statement is one more example of perceived British superiority over the colonial boys. An examination of the other quotes taken from Harris's autobiography show that the other Ombudsman complaints are similarly groundless.

ACCURACY

We now come to the Ombudsman's complaints with respect to accuracy. The Ombudsman has a curious definition of accuracy that we are being measured against. "Accuracy is not achieved simply by making sure that the facts chosen for presentation are right. To be accurate means ensuring that all the relevant facts are present." Says who? Now it is clear that, according to this Ombudsman, the measure of accuracy is not an objective exercise. It is a subjective judgment. Who decides which are the relevant facts required under his definition of accuracy? It is unlikely that every observer will share the same judgment on this matter. Were we required to include all facts that might be considered relevant by any observer when dealing with the thousands of points we raised in our six hours of television? This is the Ombudsman's point of departure, and we consider his approach severely flawed.

It is important to keep the Ombudsman's definition of accuracy in mind when examining the list of supposed "errors or confusions of fact" that he claims to have found in the documentaries.

His first item in this category is a point that has been answered many times, and the Ombudsman is well aware of it. He writes about how Kurt Meyer's 12th ss Division was described as eventually being pushed off Verrières Ridge. He suggests they were never on it.

The point at issue is that there are different names applied to the same ridge. Sometimes it is called the Verrières Ridge. Sometimes it is called the Bourguébus Ridge. Sometimes it is called both. The 12th ss were positioned closer to the village of Bourguébus than to the village of Verrières. We chose, for simplicity, to refer to the ridge only as Verrières Ridge. The Ombudsman is well aware of this explanation.

The second allegation of error is that "General Simonds is described as having never answered his critics, though in fact he wrote a detailed analysis of Operation Spring." No one who has read General Simonds's analysis of Operation Spring would characterize it as an answer to his critics. This is another subjective and minor point that surely cannot be characterized as an "error."

The third allegation of error is a matter of semantics. It concerns the words "half the regiment lay wounded or dead" used to describe the fate of the Queen's Own Rifles on the beach on D-Day. This is military short hand. For example, after the cataclysm on Verrières Ridge a Black Watch officer told us: "We lost the battalion that day."

His reference is to the ridge attack that cost the Black Watch 300 of the 325 men attacking, while the Black Watch battalion actually had a strength of some 900 soldiers. So the battalion "lost" was the section of the battalion that attacked. Similarly with the Queen's Own Rifles on the D-Day beach. At D-Day, the assaulting battalions attacked with an average of 300 men from each regiment. The Queen's Own Rifles's casualties were 61 killed and another 82 wounded, a total of 143 casualties. Thus, in the accepted parlance of the battlefield, half the regiment lay wounded or dead. This answer too has been provided to the Ombudsman, and once again he omits it to create the impression that we have no response.

The fourth allegation of error concerns the observation that the 545 men killed during the Nuremberg Raid was a greater number than those lost in the Battle of Britain. We are of course referring to the widely accepted figure of 537 fighter pilots lost during the skirmishes in the skies over Britain and the English Channel. To make it appear as if we are in error, Mr. Morgan includes in the British figure other aircrew losses in Coastal Command and Bomber Command during the same time period. This is going to ridiculous lengths to make it appear as if we were sloppy in our research. Both Martin Middlebrook in his definitive *The Nuremberg Raid* and Anthony Cave Brown in *Bodyguard of Lies* used exactly the same phrase to characterize the losses over Nuremberg.

The fifth allegation of error concerns the characterization of Arthur Harris's stated reluctance to divert Bomber Command resources to preparations for Overlord. That the words "he would have none of it" are a fair characterization is amply proven by the Harris quote from the film which follows that statement:

It is clear that the best and indeed the only support we can give to Overlord is an intensification of attacks in Germany. If we attempt to substitute attacks on gun emplacements, beach defenses, communications or supply dumps, this would be an irremedial error and lead directly to disaster.

There is a great deal of documentation available on the reluctance of Bomber Harris to divert resources away from his Area Bombing policy to support strategic operations such as Overlord. This characterization cannot be construed as an error.

Clearly Mr. Morgan has been unable to find a single serious error in the entire six hours of television, and is bending over backwards to try and portray these minor nitpicking details as being of much greater significance than any reasonable observer would attach to them.

INTERPRETATION

Mr. Morgan spends much of his report arguing with the interpretation of events reflected in the films. To his eye, they are apparently not the "right" interpretation of the events. Once again he has deliberately distorted the opinion of historians who agree with our interpretations, to make it appear as if they in fact disagree. We have provided the CBC and the Ombudsman with letters from Carl Vincent of Canada, Max Hastings of Britain, Carlo D'Este of the United States and other leading historians who overwhelmingly support our films while quibbling with a few details. In the hands of Mr. Morgan, these documents become more evidence that we got the story wrong and that there is no serious historical opinion supporting the films.

The Ombudsman's approach in this area mirrors his curious definition of accuracy, which we have already dealt with. He claims that "Reputable, professional historians have pointed out a number of instances where, because important context is not provided to the audience, the information actually presented, or its implication, becomes seriously misleading." Once again, our work is to be severely judged, not because of what we actually said, but because of the many other things Mr. Morgan and others wanted to hear that we did not say.

Throughout his document, the Ombudsman is constantly trying to suggest that the filmmakers said things that they never said. Regarding the film about Hong Kong, the Ombudsman observes that "The notion that the Canadian Government knowingly sent 2,000 of its young men to the slaughter is featured prominently, both near the beginning and the end of the program. Elsewhere, the narration suggests ..." Of course, it was not the narrator that suggested this, but an actor playing Roger Cyr, one of the Canadian soldiers sent to Hong Kong. Mr. Morgan cites this as one of our "unsubstantiated assertions." Cyr is quoted in the program saying,

As a soldier, I have no problem with being sent to war. Doesn't bother me. What frightens the daylights out of me ... the thought that my government would have not only willingly but very actively, placed itself in a situation where it would knowingly offer a couple of thousand of its young men as lambs to the slaughter in order to meet some sort of political expediency.

It is the Ombudsman's curious position that documentary filmmakers must prove every line of every statement made by every person being interviewed in every film. The CBC journalistic policy handbook makes clear that it is necessary for the journalist to believe that the interviewee is expressing a reasonably held opinion. Roger Cyr spent four years living in atrocious conditions in prison camps in Hong Kong and Japan. He is entitled to his anger against the Canadian government, which was in his view to blame, and we were certainly justified in including his expression of anger in our film.

In fact Cyr's assertion is a strongly worded illustration of the theme running through Carl Vincent's book, *No Reason Why*. Cyr's statement represents the anger and anguish of a soldier who was sent unprepared into battle, treated as a prisoner of war in a criminal manner, and on returning home was humiliated by army medical officers who dismissed his physical and psychological trauma.

Writes Vincent in *No Reason Why*:

No Canadian soldiers before or since got such a dirty deal or deserved it less. They were, quite literally, dropped into it. Casually sent to a death trap long before they could be considered ready for battle, they nevertheless put up a courageous and astonishingly effective fight against overwhelming odds, endured almost four years of squalid and brutal captivity, and then emerged, often physically and mentally marked by their ordeal, to be rewarded by the sneers of their allies and the neglect of their government.

In his report, Mr. Morgan makes it appear as if Carl Vincent agrees with him that there is no substantial evidence to support the idea that Canadians were sent as lambs to the slaughter. To the filmmakers, Mr. Vincent has said that Roger Cyr was right. "The end result is that they were sent as lambs to the slaughter. They should not have been sent. If the Canadian Government had the brains of a louse, they would not have been sent. 'Lambs to the Slaughter' is essentially what it was." Once again, the Ombudsman is seriously distorting what Carl Vincent says.

It should be noted that Roger Cyr was interviewed by the film's researchers twice for a total of four hours. As the transcripts show, he made it very clear to the interviewer that, having read all of the post-war evidence, he is disgusted with the haphazard way in which he and his fellow members of C-Force were dispatched to Hong Kong and thrown into a no-win situation. And that, using Cyr's actual words, is precisely what the actor representing him expresses in the film.

In selecting lines from the interviews with Hong Kong veterans, the producers always made sure that their words expressed the general sentiment and context of what those particular veterans felt. (A yardstick conscientiously used in all three films in the series.) Nevertheless, anyone wishing to disassemble the general thrust of an interviewee's statement could easily (if unfairly) select one seemingly contradictory sentence. It should also be noted that the interviewed persons portrayed by actors in the film signed releases allowing the portrayal. Many were again consulted in the preparation of the final script read by the actors portraying them.

FRAMEWORK

In another charge, the Ombudsman proclaims these programs "flawed" because the filmmakers were trying to make the subject matter fit a "framework, of which the program makers themselves were apparently convinced, of incompetent, brutal or obsessive and villainous leadership, protected by secrecy or a conspiracy of silence now broken at last by those who made the programs and who are letting the audience hear the 'full' or 'real' story for the first time."

This is a subjective and wholly unsupported characterization of the supposed "framework" of the films. Were the films so damning in their portrayal of the leadership qualities of officers such as Radley Walters, who became commandant of the Canadian Armoured Corps, or Jacques Dextraze, who went on to become Canada's Chief of Defence Staff? Surely not. What about the portrayal of Brigadier Dan Cunningham, or the stories of medical officer Captain Reid, or Lieutenant Scott who saved Bob Clayton's life in Hong Kong, or any of the other officers whose heroic courage was brought to the attention of Canadians by this series? The Ombudsman's allegation is unfounded. Then, having set up the straw man, he turns around and knocks it down with his proclamation, "The problem is that the case against the leadership is for the most part not proven." We submitted detailed documentation supporting what we did say in the film.

In Normandy, for example, we wrote: "To experienced military men, however, it was quickly apparent that the Canadian Army was badly trained and poorly led." That assertion was supported in the film by a statement from Field Marshal Montgomery, the overall commander of the Canadians. It is even supported by C.P. Stacey's official history.

SECRECY AND COVER-UP

Then comes the surprising assertion from the Ombudsman that "the secrecy was either understandable in the context of the time or not evident to others than the program makers. And much of what the narrator claims to be revealing has been known for some time." That the Ombudsman is capable of such a statement, after having been presented with documented evidence of a cover-up by the Canadian Defence Department and its leading military historians, including the only Canadian military historian hired by Mr. Morgan to advise him in this matter, is beyond belief. We will present that evidence here once again.

First, a little background. The film recounts how 26 year old Phil Griffin, under pressure from the High Command, followed orders and led his regiment up Verrières Ridge in a charge that one surviving officer compared to the charge of the Light Brigade. Griffin died on Verrières Ridge and never received any recognition from the army. For many years the Griffin family fought for such recognition.

In 1972, H.H. Griffin, Phil's brother, wrote to C.P. Stacey, the retired official historian of the Canadian Army and Chief of the Directorate of History at the Department of National Defence. Mr. Griffin asked Stacey for help in finding the truth about what happened to his brother in 1944.

Stacey then wrote an astonishing letter to historian Sydney Wise, who took over Stacey's job leading the Department of National Defence's Directorate of History. The Stacey letter appears under the logo of the University of Toronto's Department of History, and is dated the 9th of February, 1972:

Dear Syd,

The attached letter to Mr. H.H. Griffin is largely self-explanatory. See The Victory Campaign, 191–2. It is a sad case. Mr. G. has been discussing it with Murray Hunter.

After the war we made a detailed study of Operation "Spring," of which this grim affair was part (25 July 44). The study led to bitterness between Generals Foulkes and Simonds (in 1944 respectively GOC 2 Cdn Div and GOC 2 Cdn Corps) and they agreed between them that the draft report should be destroyed. All the copies were destroyed, except, by some strange mischance, one. It may still be somewhere in your office. In the event of a visit from Mr. Griffin, it would be well to make sure that he doesn't see this particular piece of paper.

The letter is signed by hand, Charles, and in typeface, C.P. Stacey.

Make no mistake about the impact of what you are reading. This is Charles P. Stacey, the most acclaimed Canadian military historian of his generation, the author of the official account of every major campaign, including the deeply controversial Dieppe, Hong Kong, and the battle for Normandy. At the very least his letter is an admission that he countenanced the destruction of an important report on a battle that was, after Dieppe, the blackest day for the Canadian Army in the Second World War.

The second substantial point contained in the letter is equally disturbing. Stacey counsels Sydney Wise, his successor at the Directorate of History, to conceal the one extant copy of the report on the battle from a military family, the Griffins, who would not let it lie quietly in its archival grave.

At the Directorate of History, we have located what appears to be that document. The cover page describes it as "Report on 'Operation SPRING,' 25 July, 1944," prepared by Captain J. Swettenham. Stacey dispatched his letter to Wise on 9 February, 1972. On the cover page there is a hand written notation by a one Philip Fraplin,* apparently a staff member of the Directorate of History (D Hist), revealing what action Wise took. It reads "not to be released to non-DND researchers without the approval of the director, D Hist." The date is 18 February, 1972.

When we presented this letter to Mr. Morgan, he said it proved nothing. We told him that it certainly proved that his chief historical advisor was being less than candid in suggesting that there were never any cover-ups, that they existed only in the minds of the filmmakers. Clearly there was a cover-up.†

The Ombudsman also attacks the films for suggesting that there was a "cover-up" with respect to the Hong Kong story. Once again, words are put in the narrator's mouth that he did not say. You will not find the words "cover-up" in the Hong Kong documentary. What was said was: "The details of what happened to these soldiers were *for a long time* suppressed by the Canadian Government." Clearly this assertion is supported by the history of the 1942 Duff Commission Report. Once again the Ombudsman portrays Carl Vincent as supportive of his criticism in this area. Vincent has said to the filmmakers: "The Duff Report was a whitewash. It confused the issue and tried to bury it. There's no question about that. The attempt to deceive was definitely there." The Ombudsman consistently misrepresents the views of historians who support the films to make it appear that they are critical.

---

* Philip Chaplin.
† See letter from S.F. Wise to Editor, *Globe and Mail*, 26 Nov. 1992, below, 89.

CONTEXT

The Ombudsman has raised several issues of context, suggesting that we deliberately changed the context of remarks to distort the true meaning. This is nonsense. The Ombudsman referred to a statement by Kay Christie taken from a 1989 interview, where she remembers that she was shocked at the lack of training of the soldiers being shipped over to Hong Kong. On the deck of the ship, the actress portraying Christie describes how the soldiers don't seem to know one end of the gun from the other, and are being told where to put the bullet in. "Honestly," she says, "it is just appalling." The Ombudsman makes much of the fact that in the original interview Christie goes on to say, "But they weren't sent over to fight; they were going over for garrison duty, just to strengthen the British." The Ombudsman then suggests that this statement may have been omitted by the producers "because it ran counter to the case they were presenting." It does nothing of the kind. Christie is ironically commenting upon the complacent attitude and poor planning of the British and Canadian governments that led those 2,000 Canadians to believe they were on their way to a safe posting. If we had included Christie's statement it would simply have reinforced the historical thesis. We did not include it because it was a comment clearly made in hindsight, and would have been inappropriate delivered on the deck of the ship on the way to Hong Kong, especially since the script had just established that the Canadians did not know where they were headed or what their assignment was.

The Ombudsman makes similar unfounded allegations about our treatment of the words of Donald Pearce, which he suggests were taken out of context. He points out that "words from a book by Donald Pearce, of the North Nova Scotia Regiment, delivered by an actor, are inserted into discussion of events taking place in Normandy during the summer of 1944, although Donald Pearce did not arrive in Normandy until later that year." Donald Pearce departed England for Normandy on August 27th, 1944. On his way to the front, as the script accurately notes, he passed the ruins of Caen, and the film quotes his observations on that bombed and desolate city.

Later during the fighting he witnessed an officer dying a horrible death as a result of a shrapnel wound, and his description of that officer's protracted suffering was inserted into the film chapter about the horrors of the battlefield. His third appearance deals with his attitude towards God that is inserted after the reflections on battlefield religion by General Jacques Dextraze. Pearce's last appearance in the film is a long poetic tribute to his fallen comrades in the cemetery sequence at the end of the film. There is absolutely no basis for the allegation that the producers significantly changed the context of Donald Pearce's words to suit their thesis.

CONCLUSION

For every historian attacking *The Valour and the Horror*, there is a serious historian supporting the series. Even the most vociferous critics support many of the film's main points. In the same manner, many of those supporting the films are critical of some sections.

For example, at the Directorate of History, Steven Harris, who is in the last stages of completing the official history of Canada in Bomber Command, was critical of some of the film's controversial elements. But Harris was firm in his support of the film's central thesis – that young Canadians were sacrificed in a campaign to destroy Germany's cities, which resulted in the immolation of at least half a million civilians, mostly women and children. He said "Death by Moonlight" was a pathfinder for his official history – "drawing a lot of flack we anticipated we would get when we published this volume in the coming year."

While it is true that Arthur Harris did not originate the area bombing offensive, it is also true that he supported it longer and more vehemently than anyone else – and in this sense I have no difficulty whatsoever with the prominent place you gave him in the film with respect to the conduct of area bombing.

Similarly one of the world's top historians on the battle of Normandy, Carlo D'Este, while expressing reservations about some aspects of the Normandy episode, saluted the film's major points: "In Normandy, the Canadian soldier was too often let down by a leadership at the higher level that was ill-prepared to suddenly emerge from many years of self-neglect and perform well against the high caliber German army in Normandy." He particularly singled out our chapter on war crimes: "The story was told factually and with compassion. The moral judgements were left to the viewer."

The Valour and the Horror has proven to be six powerful and controversial hours on the Second World War. But in the long history of the CBC and the NFB, they are only six hours among hundreds of hours that have been produced on the Second World War. One of the major documentary series produced by the NFB and run on several occasions by the CBC, was the 13-part Canada at War series. It bore the stamp of the official historian C.P. Stacey. The contrast with *The*

Valour and the Horror led the Defence Department's Steven Harris to muse:

... while challenging your film, no one that I know of has looked at other films, produced in the past, to see if they were at all impressionistic or "guilty" of promoting a particular point of view. (The Canada at War series leaps to mind.) The absolute truth about any event in history is never known – it cannot be. We get closer to it, however, through a process of work, revision, work, revision, and so on – a thoroughly acceptable process. You have played your part; others must have their chance; but for the process to work, no one should be silenced.

In conclusion, we have answered the principal charges levelled by the CBC Ombudsman's report. We believe the procedure followed was manifestly unfair. The choice of the three historians retained was clearly prejudicial to the filmmakers. The Ombudsman's judgments on the films are almost entirely unsubstantiated in fact. This is a clear example of why no one person should sit in judgment and decide whether complex programs are "right" or "wrong." The CBC President has acknowledged this problem in the past. We wish he would have seen fit to allow our programs to be judged by a panel of senior journalists, not by one individual. We are confident that when fair minded observers review the Ombudsman's report and our response, our programs will be vindicated.

Letter to the Globe and Mail and the Montreal Gazette

Sir,   16 November 1992*

The public debate on the television series "The Valour and the Horror" revolves around three issues: the propriety of the Senate sub-committee investigation of these broadcasts; the process followed by the CBC Ombudsman; and the attack on the professional integrity and competence of the historians whose report formed the basis of the Ombudsman's report, published in your newspaper on 12 November.

My opinion on the Senate hearings is not relevant here. With respect to the Ombudsman's Report, I can only say that instead of discussing process, we should be debating substance, and that will not happen until the reports of the historical consultants are released by the CBC. Dr. David Bercuson of the University of Calgary and I have written Mr. Gérard Veilleux, President of the CBC, urging him to release our reports so that some form of rational exchange can take place, instead of the present hullabaloo.

The producer-authors of "The Valour and the Horror" have been as careless of my reputation and integrity as they have of the historical role of the many Canadians whose intelligence and motivation they have chosen to attack for their conduct during the Second World War. They identify me as a "Bomber Command pilot," to indicate my evident bias against one of their films. I had no connection whatever with Bomber Command, serving as a staff pilot in Eastern Air Command during the last two years of the war.

The peg upon which they hang their attempt to destroy my professional reputation is a letter in the files of the Directorate of

---

* Published in the *Globe and Mail*, 26 Nov. 1992, and in the *Montreal Gazette* later that same month.

History, written to me by my predecessor as Director of History, Dr. Charles Stacey. In this letter, Stacey refers to a report concerning Operation "Spring," in which the Canadian Army was involved in some of the bloodiest – and some of the most unsuccessful – engagements in Normandy, towards the end of July 1944.

The crux of the matter is this. Stacey refers to the report as having been destroyed by order of Generals Simonds and Foulkes, who had fallen out over the interpretation of Operation "Spring" in the report. "By some strange mischance," he informed me, "there might be a copy in my office. Should Mr. H.H. Griffin," with whom he and Professor Murray Hunter had had some correspondence, come to my office, "it would be well," Stacey wrote, that he not see the report. This is what is alleged to be a cover up.

The facts are as follows:

1 The sinister-sounding phrase, "by some strange mischance," was Dr. Stacey's way of telling me that he had *saved* a copy of the report ordered destroyed, rather than, as the McKennas have implied, trying to appease the generals. In doing this, he was obeying the most fundamental instinct of any good historian: to preserve, not to destroy, hide or distort. We owe a good deal of our historical heritage to Charles Stacey for his vigour in the preservation of our history, and both his successors have done what they can to emulate him. In sum, then, the report referred to not only still exists, it is in the public record.

2 All the documents connected with Operation "Spring" were classified at the time of Dr. Stacey's letter to me, including the report. There is, may I assure your readers, a considerable difference between normal security classification and "cover ups." No one not a legitimate historical researcher would have been given access to any of them, and the suggestion by the producers of "The Valour and the Horror" that I transferred the report from some accessible classification to one that was not is simply false. The late Mr. Chaplin was simply doing his job; the document was already classified.

3 Why, despite all this, did Dr. Stacey not think it wise for me to waive the rules and permit Mr. Griffin access to the report? Readers should know that the late Mr. Griffin was the brother of Major Griffin of the Royal Highland Regiment of Canada (The Black Watch), who died heroically among the bodies of his comrades on the crest of Verrières Ridge on 25 July 1944. The report, without reflecting in any way upon the undoubted heroism of Major Griffin, contains material which would have been wounding

to the family. Though I might well have denied Mr. Griffin access to classified material in any event, the existence of this material in the report was, I am confident, the reason for Dr. Stacey's advice.

4 Mr. Griffin did not in fact visit me; the document concerned has long since been in the public record. There was no cover up.

I realize that this account of what occurred will be disappointing to many, who have looked for a smoking gun, and probably will be rejected by the McKennas in favour of a more cynical interpretation of the motives of Charles Stacey and myself. I can only rest my case with the hundreds of researchers who, over the years, dealt with both of us, and who know our reputation for openness and our deep interest in historical preservation.

Sincerely,

S.F. Wise
Professor of History
Carleton University

WILLIAM MORGAN

Comments on the November 10 Galafilm Report, 18 November 1992

There was no miscarriage of justice, as claimed by Galafilm. The normal procedure of Provincial Ombudsmen in this country is simply to receive a public complaint, and, in instances where it is deemed appropriate, conduct an investigation privately and then report a finding to the complainant. For a variety of legal reasons, Provincial Ombudsman processes are not public ones.

In this particular case the Ombudsman was asked by the President of CBC to conduct a full review of *The Valour and the Horror* for him. Mr. Veilleux encouraged the Ombudsman to consult qualified military historians and asked that the very first draft of the Ombudsman's findings be shared with the producers of the series.

At the time the review was requested, the producers of the series welcomed the Ombudsman's involvement, sent him copies of material they were preparing for the Senate Sub-Committee and, subsequently, provided written responses to 58 written questions and requests for documentation from him. The program makers' views and advice concerning historians were sought by the Ombudsman and historians whom they felt would not be fair were not considered. When told by the Ombudsman of the historians finally selected for consultation, the only comment from any of the program makers was that two of them "sounded a bit conservative." No question about procedures or the nature of the review was raised by any of the producers or those who made the programs until after they had seen the first discussion draft of the Ombudsman's report, on the Labour Day weekend, whereupon they began, for the first time, to complain about the process and about the choice of historians consulted.

In subsequent months, all further comments, clarifications and representations received from the producers were taken fully into account by the CBC Ombudsman and were reviewed as well by CBC's

General Counsel and the President and Chairman of the Corporation.

In his report, the Ombudsman only indicated that there had been a failure to provide adequate documentation where he had found that to be the case. Where material provided by the producers was found convincing, their view was accepted. Where it was not found convincing, that was reflected in the findings summarized in the Ombudsman's report to the President of CBC.

In quoting from the CBC's journalism policy the Ombudsman was attempting to provide readers of his report with examples from the policy book which seemed most relevant to a review of this kind. The intention was that readers would, as a result, have clearly in mind the kinds of expectations which the Corporation has expressed to the producers and managers responsible for the journalism programming it broadcasts. The programs did, however, offend, at least in part, against each of the policy statements quoted.

Sydney Wise was identified as the former Dean of Graduate Studies and Research at Carleton University because that was the major position he most recently held. A "Who's Who" listing for Wise, as for David Bercuson and Denis Richards, was provided to recipients of the Ombudsman's original discussion draft, including the producers of *The Valour and the Horror*.

Wise was a flying officer in the RCAF but was not, despite the claim made here by Galafilm, in Bomber Command. No attempt was ever made to conceal his background as a pilot or the fact that Wise had once served as Director of History at the Department of National Defence. There are no grounds to justify a suggestion by Galafilm that an experienced and highly regarded historian like Wise cannot be relied upon to conduct himself as a responsible professional simply because of his wartime service.

David Bercuson is not just a labour historian, though he has written books about the Winnipeg General Strike. He is Dean of Graduate Studies at a major university in Western Canada. His book on the life of Brooke Claxton, Minister of National Defence from 1946–1954, is to be published by the University of Toronto Press and he is working on a regimental history of the Calgary Highlanders (sister Regiment to The Black Watch in the 5th Brigade) in World War II and has started work on an operational history of the Canadian army in the Korean War and an analysis on the Canadian military and the making of Canadian defence policy from 1945–1964.

Denis Richards was Narrator and Senior Narrator in the Air Ministry Historical Branch and wrote the short official history of the Royal Air Force in the Second World War. He was chosen by the

publishers to write the introduction for the posthumous reissue of
Harris's book. Richards was consulted by the Ombudsman in the belief that there was merit in hearing from an historian who was alive
at the time and who actually knew a great deal about what was hap-
pening as well as having met and interviewed at some length the
man who was the central figure in the program in question. The producers seem to take the view that a fairer and more accurate picture
of a person and of events can be achieved by taking evidence only
from those who have never met him and were not around at the
time.

The Ombudsman also had available to him letters provided by the
program makers from Michael Bliss, Brian Loring Villa, John Keegan,
Max Hastings, and Carlo D'Este. Professor Bliss, though not a
military historian, or one with military interests, was supportive of
the films. Professor Villa was also generally supportive in his letter,
though he mentioned some criticisms which he did not specify. The
letter which the producers had requested from John Keegan consisted
only of a single short paragraph of general support. Max Hastings,
while making general statements of support for the Bomber Command program and commenting positively on some aspects of the
program, also offered a number of "strictures" about aspects of the
program, including the use of drama techniques. Colonel D'Este,
while offering general support for the Normandy film and its
portrayal of the training of Canadian troops and the performance of
some of their commanders, was also negative about the use of drama,
and disagreed with a central theme of that program, the negative
portrayal of General Simonds.

There was no pretence about the Ombudsman's consultation with
additional historians. Noting their request that he talk to one
specialist historian of the program makers' choosing for each
program, he subsequently did just that with Carl Vincent concerning
Hong Kong and Steven Harris concerning Bomber Command. The
Ombudsman made it clear at the time, when it emerged that the
program makers' recommended historian for the Normandy program
was Carlo D'Este, that he would not pursue Colonel D'Este because
he already had a four or five page document from him, written, as
were the letters from John Keegan, Max Hastings and some others, at
the request of the producers themselves.

Like the other historians already consulted by the Ombudsman,
Vincent and Harris made it clear that there were things about the
programs under discussion with which they agreed and other things
which they considered inaccurate or wrong. In the Ombudsman's

report, having first stressed what he and some of the historians consulted considered meritorious about the Hong Kong program, he then listed a number of assertions and implications contained in the program which Vincent had told him were not adequately supported by the available evidence. Before finalizing his summary report, the Ombudsman read over the telephone to Carl Vincent every word dealing with Vincent's views and comments and Vincent informed the Ombudsman that his views had been reflected accurately.

As for the document from Carl Vincent quoted by the producers in their response, though the Ombudsman has never received it from the producers, the particular points it contains are, in any event, for the most part not in dispute. Some historians might disagree with the statement about training, and it might be argued that the Canadian government did pause momentarily for an assurance that the dispatch of these two battalions would not impair Canada's own ability to defend itself, but neither the Ombudsman nor any of the historians consulted would argue with the rest of these statements. That is why the report contains some praise for the Hong Kong episode and why the Ombudsman found it the most defensible of the three episodes of the series.

What the Ombudsman brought forward in his summary report [were] a number of *other* statements or suggestions in the Hong Kong program which Carl Vincent had indicated to him were not justified by the documentary record.

USE OF DRAMATIC TECHNIQUES

The 58 questions and requests for documentation were intended as a way of seeing the producers' "footnotes," supporting material for their various statements and assertions for which there would be no time or space in a television program but which they should have had on file. The drama issues, by contrast, were self-evident. Though the Ombudsman did intend to discuss them with the producers during the process that was to take place after his initial draft had been shared with them, those detailed discussions never did occur, because the producers refused to participate in them.

The go ahead for THE KILLING GROUND was given by the Vice-President of English television at the time, Denis Harvey, and not by Mr. Morgan.

It is not merely something the Ombudsman has written but the CBC's actual policy which says that, if a mixture of forms is employed, the dramatized portion must be well identified.

Even without information about CBC policy on the matter, more than one of the historians consulted by the Ombudsman expressed concerns and serious reservations about the use of drama in the series. Indeed, two of the historians whom the producers have claimed as supporters expressed similar reservations. Carlo D'Este, in his letter of support solicited by the producers, said he thought "that the use of actors to recreate some of the key characters was misplaced." Max Hastings, writing at the producers' request from England, said: "First, when doing a documentary on an issue of such sensitivity, if it had been produced in this country there would have been a considerable fuss about the use of actors in [the] picture to speak the words of veterans, and about the mixture of documentary and fiction film footage, unless this was clearly labelled in captions at every stage."

As was made clear in the Ombudsman's final summary report, the policy issue of primary concern is the very one that Hastings identified – "the mix of documentary and fiction film footage." That is why the policy book says what it says. The mixture of forms may lend the appearance of reality to hypothesis, making it difficult for the audience to judge the nature of the information received. For this reason, the policy states that, as a general principle, actuality and dramatized portrayal of people or events must not be mixed. If an exception is made on this point, the policy stresses that the dramatized portion must be well identified. That was not done in the case of *The Valour and the Horror*.

The policy is strict on these matters because it is so easy for members of the audience to be misled without even recognizing any confusion. And it is no answer to say, as the producers do, that the actors were young and would not be confused by the audience with 70 year old soldiers and airmen or that the drama was presented in a "highly stylized manner" with the actors "standing in limbo in front of a black curtain." Some of the drama was not presented in this stylized way, but involved dialogue between actors (including dialogue not found in the transcripts on which the producers had claimed that the dramatic representation was based) and took place in dramatic settings such as a battlefield command headquarters. Nor will anyone who saw the program and their portrayals of older men, like Sir Arthur Harris or Major-General Keller, be able to accept that the drama was properly identified just by the youthful appearance of all the actors who appeared in it.

It is difficult to respond to the producers' report of a September 14 telephone conversation with John Keegan. It does appear that the producers sought support from Keegan but so far have only produced a one paragraph letter from him which does not touch at all on the issue of drama.

CANADA'S SWEETHEART – THE HAL BANKS SAGA was originally discussed as a documentary but, because first of the lack of cooperation and then of the death of Hal C. Banks, the program did indeed become one in which drama was interspersed with interview material. However, there was concern about this issue at the time and an honest attempt at differentiation was made. As a result, throughout the main body of the film the dramatized reconstructions of the activities of the late Hal C. Banks, and those who worked for and against him, were shown in black and white film while all of the interview material from living witnesses, including unionists who had opposed Banks, a shipping company owner, and former Minister of Citizenship, Jack Pickersgill, whose government had encouraged and supported Banks, showed them speaking directly to camera and was shot in colour to help underline the fact that these people were speaking contemporaneously and were not part of the black and white drama presentation.

The King program was an experiment in dramatic representation of the King Diaries by the brilliant documentary director Donald Brittain. It was a full-blown drama, including dream sequences, was presented to the audience as drama, with starring credits for leading actors, and did not contain any interviews at all. However, it was still something of a hybrid and perhaps indeed questionable in terms of policy. The use of reconstructions and simulations in THE JOURNAL has been properly identified and within policy.

In writing about the portrayal of Arthur Harris, the Ombudsman intended to illustrate how far drama in an information program can go if great care is not taken. By the choice of actor and the performance obtained from that actor, the producers made up and gave to more than a million people, as if it were an actual reflection of reality, a picture of Arthur Harris which, as far as anyone can tell, no one who knew the man would even have recognized. The producers may disagree, but, even in this awkward area of having actors represent real people, living or dead, it is usual practice to choose an actor who looks and sounds like the person portrayed and for those responsible for the production to try, through makeup, costume and direction of the performance, to make the actor seem as much as possible like the person represented.

What happened in this particular case appears to have been precisely the opposite. As for Thénardier, in "Les Misérables," yes he appears in comic scenes. But he is also the most dishonest, brutal and despicable character in the show and hundreds of thousands of people saw Graeme Campbell play that role, as well as the roles of other villains at the Shakespeare Festival at Stratford, in the years immediately preceding his untimely death.

PURPORTED DISTORTIONS

Regrettably, the producers *did* make up words and put them into the mouths of actors portraying real people. The first speech by the actor representing Nursing Sister Kay Christie in the Hong Kong program includes words which appear in the transcript of the non-broadcast interview with her supplied to the Ombudsman by the producers. But the words "where to put the bullet in," which serves to heighten the impression of the most elementary imaginable training, do not appear in the transcript at all.

In the dramatized encounter between Major-General Keller and Brigadier Cunningham, much of the dialogue delivered by the actor portraying Brigadier Cunningham does not appear in the transcript of the non-broadcast interview with Brigadier Cunningham which the producers provided. And some of that dialogue and the depiction of a fearful Keller run directly counter to what the late Brigadier Cunningham had said in the non-broadcast interview with him.

In each of these cases the producers indicate having obtained the approval respectively of Nursing Sister Christie and the late Brigadier Cunningham for the depiction. However, certain of the words were written by those who made the films and were not, as claimed, words from a documented source.

Then there are the words delivered in the film by the actor representing Sir Arthur Harris:

We shall destroy Germany's will to fight. Now that we have the planes and crews, in 1943 and 1944 we shall drop one and a quarter million tons of bombs, render 25 million Germans homeless, kill 900,000 and seriously injure one million.

The document from which this quote comes was a written "Estimate of the Effects of Anglo-American Bomber Offensive against Germany." It is described officially as "A Note by the Chief of the Air Staff." The Chief of the Air Staff at the time was Sir Charles Portal. The segment from Portal's detailed strategic memorandum is changed slightly and is delivered in the film by the actor portraying the Commander-in-Chief of Bomber Command, Arthur Harris.

The producers say that the film makes clear that Harris was reciting orders.

It is true that the quotation is preceded by narration script which says "Bomber Command Chief Arthur Harris received new orders. From now on he was free to deliberately target German civilians." However, the Portal memorandum was a detailed strategic assessment, not a set of orders. And the actor portraying Harris delivers the words not as if reading orders or even reflecting upon them but as the boast of a man now free "to deliberately target German civilians."

In the alternative, the producers claim that in documents supplied to the Ombudsman it was established that Harris was the co-author of the document. One author has said that the document was prepared "with the assistance of Harris." But this can hardly be accepted as a justification for putting these words from a document signed by someone else into Harris's mouth.

The Ombudsman questioned the statement, delivered by the actor representing Harris, concerning colonial troops because the words used, by themselves, do distort what Harris actually wrote and the impression of him which the audience might form as a result of hearing only those words.

The section of the film in which the "colonial" quote appears has a theme of British disapproval and disdain for "colonials" and, in introducing the Harris quote, the narrator says:

The colonial attitude of British officers came from the top.

The film makes Harris out to be the senior British officer who sets the example for those in his Command to have a low opinion of "colonials." But, though the program makers apparently chose to ignore it in selecting the quote from Harris that they use, in his book, Harris, who was born in India and who grew up in Rhodesia, begins the section in which the quoted words appear by describing himself as "to all intents and purposes a colonial." Elsewhere, in the same passage, and again unquoted by those who made the program, he writes of the "stupidity" of the British Islanders. Yet, in the program he was presented, through the actor, standing beside a British flag and commenting only negatively on the capabilities of "colonial" troops.

In the Hamburg section, the editorial selection by those who made the program, while quoting a few words from Harris in which he speaks of bombing as a "comparatively humane method," leaves out the rest of his statement in which he spoke of it helping to save young men from being cut down in the field and avoiding a blockade of the kind which, in World War I, cost many more civilian lives in Germany and was heaviest in its effect on women and children.

As well, by a shift of context, it is made to seem that Harris is talking about Hamburg only when he is talking about figures for Germany as a whole, and even that he was prepared, untruthfully, to say that there was no proof concerning casualties at Hamburg.

ACCURACY

There is nothing especially unusual about the definition offered here by the Ombudsman. We have all grown up with a legal system in which the oath of witnesses in court is that they will tell, not just the truth, but the *whole* truth and nothing but the truth.

The narration in the Normandy program says: "The Germans often displayed a superior fighting ability, but eventually the Canadians used heavy bombing and relentless assaults to push Kurt Meyer's Hitler Youth Division off Verrières Ridge." The program leaves the impression that Meyer's Division was on Verrières Ridge and stayed there until finally pushed off. That is simply not the case and this was one of a number of inaccuracies in the programs, of which the Ombudsman's report supplied only a few examples.

It is not, in fact, clear that there ever was the kind of focused criticism of General Simonds over Operation Spring the producers implied when they spoke of his never having answered. However, General Simonds did write an analysis of Operation Spring, a document which, perhaps not surprisingly, seems to justify his own actions. If it was an important enough point for the producers to stress in the film, then it is an important enough point to require the relevant context to ensure accuracy.

With regard to the Queen's Own Rifles, on the beach on D-Day, a regiment is usually at least two battalions and a battalion is generally something approaching a thousand men. While recognizing that not every member of the regiment necessarily participated in the D-Day landing, half the regiment means half the regiment. No number was used in the film. The total of 143, incidentally, although it is somehow overlooked here by the producers, included not just dead and wounded but *captured* as well.

With regard to the Nuremberg Raid and the Battle of Britain, if they just meant *fighter* pilots, the producers should have said so. But, it is then hard to see what sense one could make of a comparison only of fighter pilots involved in the Battle of Britain with the whole aircrew of Bomber Command's many aircraft in the Nuremberg Raid.

As far as the views and actions of Harris over Bomber Command's participation in "Overlord" are concerned, the program clearly leaves the impression that Harris was ordered to have Bomber Command participate in "Overlord" but refused to do so and went on with his obsessive efforts to destroy German cities and the civilians who lived in them.

Steven Harris of the Directorate of History, whom the program makers recommended for consultation, commented on this error in the program saying that the truth was that Harris continued to target Germany but that "he did do 'Overlord.' " It is difficult to see how the pointing out of an error as substantial as this can honestly be portrayed as "minor nitpicking."

INTERPRETATION

The Ombudsman has not expressed any view on a "right" interpretation of history. He did, however, try to look with care at the programs and at the comments from the historians, both those whom he had consulted and those who wrote in answer to the producers' requests for support. The people who made these programs have said that they were totally factual, have defended the use of drama by saying there is no fiction in the film and have claimed their research to be "bullet proof."

Yet all three of the historians that the producers mention here – Carl Vincent, Max Hastings and Carlo D'Este – find things about the programs with which they agree and things in the programs that are inaccurate or with which they disagree.

Similarly, a number of the historians, including ones the producers see as supportive, observe and comment on contextual problems in the presentation of information in these films. Dealing with area bombing of targets in Germany in 1942 and 1943 as if precision bombing, without untenable losses of aircraft and crews, was available as a reasonable alternative at the time, but was simply ignored by a commander obsessed with destroying German cities and killing German civilians, is just one example.

Whether one talks, in the terms which historians use, of a lack of context or, in journalism policy terms, of accuracy, fairness and balance, the issue is not that the producers should have told a whole different story because the Ombudsman or anyone else wanted to hear one, but that it is only right and fair to let an audience hear both sides and that the programs too often fail to do so.

This matter of balance and context is dealt with well by Max Hastings in one of a number of admonitions in the letter which he wrote to the producers at their own request for support:

Essentially, what I have always sought to argue, and you could make more of, is the distinction between monstrous, deliberate acts of barbarism, such as the Nazis perpetrated, and errors of war, such as I believe the later stages of the Bomber Offensive became, for reasons I have discussed at length in the closing chapters of my book.

The Roger Cyr statement, presented by an actor, is included in the Hong Kong film in two versions, one near the beginning and one near the end. It is given the pride of place one would normally accord to fact and, on the second occasion it is heard, is followed by a narration statement which seems to accept it as fact and build upon it. The Ombudsman has never suggested that documentary film makers must prove every line of every statement. Mr. Cyr has a right to his opinion, even though no evidence has been brought forward to justify the suggestion that the Canadian government *"knowingly offered its young men as lambs to the slaughter."* But, by the way the producers made use of this statement, they gave it a level of credence and prominence that amounts to endorsement. Having used it in this way in the film, they now say it was just an opinion.

The next section in the producers' response, as with certain elements in the films themselves, involves a confusion on the producers' part about what could be known when and about the special clarity of hindsight.

What Carl Vincent and the Ombudsman agreed, among other things, was that there is no substantial evidence to support the idea that the Canadians were *knowingly* sent as lambs to the slaughter. That is the word which Mr. Cyr used and which the program makers chose to air twice in the film and apparently endorse with narration. The two battalions certainly finished up being lambs to the slaughter, an awful, unnecessary tragedy, but there is no proof that the Canadian government *knowingly* sent them to that fate.

FRAMEWORK

Concerning the framework which the Ombudsman perceives in the structuring of the films, it is quite clear in his summary report that the leaders singled out by the program makers for concentrated negative attention are Arthur Harris and Guy Simonds. In that same summary report the Ombudsman specifically refers in genuinely admiring terms to the veterans who appear in person in the films, including Radley Walters and Jacques Dextraze.

SECRECY AND COVER-UP

Regarding the letter from a former Director of History at the Department of National Defence, C.P. Stacey, to his successor, Sydney

Wise, it is not clear exactly what the producers are accusing either Stacey or Wise of having done, but it seems that the producers have chosen to interpret the letter as proof that Stacey "countenanced the destruction of an important document." Looking at the same information as the producers have seen, Steven Harris has suggested that it is much more likely that, though the Generals may have wished the draft report in question destroyed, it was Stacey who kept a copy so that it would be preserved and that the letter to Wise arose either out of concern and sympathy for Mr. Griffin and a wish not to have him see negative comment about his brother or perhaps to avoid any possibility of the document being used in a legal action.

In any event, if the document which the Galafilm researcher has located in the files is the one mentioned in the letter, then Stacey apparently did not countenance its destruction at all, but, it would seem, intentionally and successfully preserved it for posterity.

The interpretation of these events decided upon and written about here by the producers is at least insulting to the historians in question and probably defamatory.

The Ombudsman's final summary report does not say the film suggested a "cover-up" with respect to Hong Kong. At the suggestion of the producers, it uses the exact words spoken in the film and follows them with an accurate summary of Carl Vincent's comments about the program's suggestion that details of what happened to these soldiers were, for a long time, suppressed by the Canadian government.

CONTEXT

The Ombudsman's report does not say that the further statement by Nursing Sister Kay Christie was omitted by the producers "because it ran counter to the case they were presenting."

What the Ombudsman points out in the case of Nursing Sister Kay Christie is that, though the program presents, through an actor, some words, including ones that are not in the original transcript of her non-broadcast interview, about Ms. Christie's concern at hearing rifle instruction sessions on the ship transporting the Canadians to Hong Kong, her subsequent reference in the non-broadcast interview to the fact that they believed they were not being sent over to fight, but just for garrison duty, was important context but was omitted.

The producers claim that Ms. Christie "is ironically commenting upon the complacent attitude and poor planning of the British and Canadian governments." There is no sense of irony in the printed transcript of the interview with Ms. Christie and the transcript indicates that, after rumours onboard ship from Vancouver, it was confirmed to Ms. Christie and others officially, while still docked in Honolulu, that their destination was the garrison in Hong Kong.

The words of Donald Pearce of the Nova Scotia Regiment were indeed taken out of context as he was shown, portrayed by an actor in combat dress, in circumstances which could easily lead the audience to believe that he was part of the events which began in Normandy in June of 1944, even though he did not sail from England until August 27 of that year. Pearce's observation about Caen was *not* preceded by any scripted notation that he was on his way to the front.

Though the producers do not mention it in this document, in their initial written response to the Ombudsman's question about this point, they replied in part: "The great difficulty in making these documentaries was finding first hand accounts of war experience set down at the time, while the action and experience was still white hot."

CONCLUSION

The producers' statement: "For every historian attacking *The Valour and the Horror*, there is a serious historian supporting the series," considerably exaggerates the apparent support for the series from serious historians.

Steven Harris does indeed say that the Bomber Command program, because of the intensity of the reaction to it, has taken flack which otherwise might have been directed against the book which he and Brereton Greenhous are in the process of completing on the RCAF in World War II. He has made clear, however, that he considers the Bomber Command program wrong on the Dams Raid, wrong to suggest that Arthur Harris was in any way uncaring about the crews in his command, and wrong on "Overlord." The quote from Steven Harris presented in this response appears to be from a document sought from him by the producers, but which contained both pros and cons on the Bomber Command program, and despite requests for it, was never shared with CBC's Ombudsman.

Carlo D'Este, in his lengthy letter, does support a number of points in the Normandy program. However, as earlier indicated, he describes the drama techniques as "misplaced" and, perhaps most importantly, he seems to be in complete disagreement with the producers about General Simonds. The program present Simonds as the villain of the piece in Normandy while D'Este writes that, in his view, Simonds was exceptional among senior Canadian commanders.

Historians see history as an evolutionary process, subject always to new views and new information and this is an entirely reasonable one in terms of the environment in which most historians work and the results of their work are received. But *The Valour and the Horror* was not just one more paper or monograph. It was presented as factual information by a licensed broadcasting organization and each episode was witnessed by considerably more than a million people. It may be many years before television in Canada returns in detail to these subjects and the CBC owes it to the public to ensure that all such programming fully conforms to the Corporation's policies and standards.

PART THREE

Historians' Commentary

JOHN FERRIS

Savage Christmas:
The Canadians at Hong Kong

EDITORS' INTRODUCTION

The central contention of "Savage Christmas," the first of *The Valour and the Horror* programs, was that the two-battalion Canadian force dispatched to Hong Kong in the late fall of 1941 was knowingly sent into a war zone without adequate training. It hangs on the assumption that either Britain or Canada knew, or ought to have known, that Japan was about to launch a full-scale war in the Pacific. That assumption is central to the thesis because if Britain (and Canada) did not know or did not suspect Japan's intentions, it might have been perfectly reasonable at that time to send reinforcements to Hong Kong, trained or not. And if it was a perfectly reasonable thing to have done, no one can be accused of malice in sending those Canadians there.

Although "Savage Christmas" contains much valuable and moving material on the course of the Hong Kong battle and on the later terrible ordeal of the captured Canadians, its essence is contained in the question: "Who, among the British (and the Canadians), knew what about Japan's intentions, and when did they know it?" The question is a reflection of, and not unconnected with, similar questions that have been asked for more than a generation about the lack of preparedness of the US forces in Hawaii when Japan attacked Pearl Harbor on 7 December 1941.

The Japanese offensive in the central and southwest Pacific and in southeast Asia that opened the morning of 7 December 1941 (8 December in Hong Kong) was a genuine strategic surprise to the Americans, the British, and their allies. Strategic surprises do not happen often in wars, or even at the outbreak of wars, but they do sometimes happen. The Israelis, for example, were similarly surprised at the start of the October War in October 1973. When they do happen, they are always the cause of immediate havoc among the victims and long-term controversy among historians. Invariably, when viewed in hindsight, sufficient signs of the impending attack can always be found to prompt such questions as: "Given that this evidence of the attack existed then, and that the intended victims had some reason to be suspicious, and that the victims were reasonably intelligent people with a desire to defend their interests, how was it that they were taken by surprise?" That, in itself, is a perfectly legitimate question. Unfortunately, however, some people who pose that question are never satisfied with an answer that points to the victims' arrogance, or failure to read the signs, or inability to put the larger picture together. They want to believe, instead, that someone must have known, but deliberately and diabolically hid that knowledge to serve some larger conspiratorial purpose.

In the following essay, John Ferris reviews the current historical data regarding British foreknowledge of Japanese intentions and shows how that issue is directly connected to the question of why Canadians who were not trained for war were sent to Hong Kong.

• • •

In September 1941 the British government asked Canada to send reinforcements to Hong Kong. Although Britain knew that the colony was indefensible in case of war with Japan, it also believed that the combined efforts of Britain and the United States could deter Japan from going to war. Indeed, sending reinforcements to Hong Kong was part of that strategy of deterrence.

Canada agreed to the British request and sent some 2000 soldiers of the Winnipeg Grenadiers and the Royal Rifles of Canada to Hong Kong. Those troops were classified by Canada's own military as unfit for combat due to insufficient training. Their presence in southeast Asia did nothing to stop Japan's planned offensive and, in the early hours of 8 December 1941 (Hong Kong time), these Canadian troops were plunged into war along with the rest of the Hong Kong garrison. During the Battle of Hong Kong, 8–25 December 1941, the members of these units fought courageously and creditably, but were finally forced to surrender along with the rest of the garrison. The survivors were badly treated by their Japanese captors and many who survived the fighting died in prisoner-of-war and slave labour camps; 559 of the original contingent failed to return. The Hong Kong calamity ranks with Dieppe as one of Canada's greatest military disasters.

This dark episode in Canadian history is the subject of "Savage Christmas," the first of the programs in *The Valour and the Horror* series produced by Brian and Terence McKenna.[1] This program was the one least criticized by veterans and historians; indeed, except for three minutes of a 104-minute presentation, "Savage Christmas" showed nothing to which any reasonable person could object.[2] However, it is precisely those three minutes that contain two of the most controversial allegations made by the program producers. There, the McKennas present their interpretation of why Canadians were sent to Hong Kong in the first place, criticize the Canadian government for doing what it did, and assert that the dispatch of essentially untrained-for-war soldiers was a monstrous act. In this brief bit of television, the McKennas interpret the events of their documentary, give their views of why the Hong Kong disaster occurred, and name the men they believe guilty of allowing young Canadians to be sacrificed on the altar of Canada's imperial duty to Britain.

The central argument of "Savage Christmas" starts from the claim that "the British ... High Command considered that war in Hong Kong was inevitable, and imminent."[3] The program tells its viewers that British "military authorities" believed that Hong Kong was indefensible and that they refused to send British reinforcements there. Nonetheless, the British chose to make a "symbolic attempt" to defend an indefensible position and selected Canadian rather than British soldiers to pay the price. In order to do so, the British are said to have deliberately misled Canada about the danger of the mission. The Canadian government, in turn, is accused of "knowingly" sending its boys like "lambs to the slaughter" because this "offered an opportunity to wave the flag." The McKennas assert that Ottawa did this without checking the facts, even though it knew, or should have known, that war with Japan was inevitable and imminent. The viewers are thus left to infer the motives behind Canadian and British actions, but they receive a strong hint to look for nasty ones.

In presenting their view of the background to the Hong Kong debacle, the McKennas treat the actions and attitudes of several people over a two-year period as though they were those of one person at a single time. In so doing, any differences that emerge among the views of individual British decision-makers are taken to prove that "the British" were guilty of a kind of collective hypocrisy. Two crucial terms are left undefined – viewers seem to be expected to understand "symbolic" as meaning only "the maintenance of British prestige," while "knowingly" could mean anything from "deliberately placed men in a situation known to have potential dangers" to "deliberately sent men to a hopeless position despite knowing that war would occur." Such slack usage of language makes analysis difficult: one definition of "knowingly" points to a mistake, the other to a crime.

The arguments presented in "Savage Christmas" about how and why Canadian forces arrived in Hong Kong stem entirely from Carl Vincent's book, *No Reason Why*.[4] The McKennas rely completely on his evidence and they interpret his argument carelessly. Not only that, they also utterly distort his views. Vincent states that the British government "had plenty of information at their disposal in September 1941 to show that war in the Far East was virtually inevitable sooner or later," and his vague argument can be read as indicating that throughout 1940–41 Britain did believe that war with Japan was inevitable and imminent.[5] Such an interpretation, however, is accepted by no reputable authority. The McKennas either ignore this fact or are ignorant of it. They do not seem to have read more than one of the hundreds of other accounts of the outbreak of the Pacific war. Against this, they ignore the arguments and lengthy quotations on this matter by C.P. Stacey, the official historian of the Canadian Army in the Second World War. Stacey's analysis represents the verdict of virtually every serious student of the outbreak of the Pacific war, excluding only Pearl Harbor conspiracy theorists.[6]

The McKennas use Vincent as an authority where he is not. Despite his knowledge of Canada's role in the Hong Kong affair, Vincent is no expert on British policy towards Japan. His sum total of primary research in Britain consists of fourteen files from one archival series which bear solely on the narrow question of Hong Kong itself. If his notes are any indication, Vincent did no research in the main body of material about British relations with Japan – hundreds of files in dozens of other Admiralty, Air Ministry, Foreign Office, and War Office series, in the central archival sources for British strategic decisions, the PREM files and the Chiefs of Staff Papers (CAB 79 and 80), and in collections of private manuscripts. His bibliography cites only one of the hundreds of articles and monographs that discuss British and American policy towards Japan. The McKennas' bibliography also ignores this literature.[7]

In order to explain why Canadian forces were sent to Hong Kong, one must distinguish between the knowledge and the intentions of several layers of Canadian and British decision-makers and to place these events in context. Above all, one must remember two points. Authorities in London believed that Hong Kong would be indefensible in case of war, but they also believed that there would be no war. This belief was bolstered by a bad reading of good intelligence. The British and American governments were both reading Japanese diplomatic codes and they both entirely misconstrued what Japan would do. In particular, when the decisions to send Canadian troops to Hong Kong were taken, both these governments doubted that Japan would attack the British Empire. Neither government believed that war was imminent or inevitable. Even the Japanese did not know they would start such a war until 1 November 1941, three days after the Canadians sailed from Vancouver. The British and Americans did not discover this fact – to their shock and dismay – until after the Canadians had disembarked in Hong Kong.[8]

Perhaps British authorities should not have made these errors, but they did. This makes them fools, possibly, but not villains. They did not consciously risk Canadian instead of British lives for the sake of prestige. They did not deliberately sacrifice Canadian troops. Nor was there a single set of motivations for British decision-makers – their motives varied with the time and the man. Until the fall of France in June 1940, British authorities generally believed that Japan would not attack the British Empire and that the European war would end with both speed and success. During the six months following the French capitulation, British authorities were concerned primarily with European affairs. They recognized that Japan was a greater potential threat and more likely to enter the war than had been believed a few months before, but, even so, Churchill and the British Chiefs of Staff concluded that war with Japan was neither imminent nor inevitable. By October 1940, with the Battle of Britain under their belt, they thought that the chances of war and the scale of any Japanese threat had declined markedly.

By December 1940 a string of smashing victories over Italy increased British confidence still further. Consider the views of Air Vice-Marshall Brooke-Popham, who, as commander-in-chief far east, loosely controlled all British forces in southeast Asia. He argued that these North African successes had so dramatically increased Britain's bargaining position against Japan that Tokyo should be given two blunt choices: "to follow footsteps of Mussolini as Jackal of Hitler" or else back down: "At the present moment we have more military and political trumps in our hand than at any time during the last 5 years. It would probably be worth using them boldly while the hand still remains to be played."[9]

Over the next twelve months, perceptions in London swung from fear of war in the Pacific to a smug assumption that such a war could never happen. In February 1941 some intelligence information seemed to indicate that Japan was increasingly hostile to Britain. For a few months thereafter most British authorities were no longer entirely sure that Japan would stay out of the war. In February and May 1941 the intelligence analysts for the Chiefs of Staff – the Joint Intelligence Committee – refused to predict what Japan would do, but conceded that it might attack Britain, or might not. Some British authorities drifted towards the belief, as the Foreign Office phrased it, "that the only safe course for us is to proceed on the assumption that a Japanese attack is imminent and that only strong reaction by the United States will frustrate it." Churchill, however, rejected the idea of danger. He told Franklin Roosevelt that "the odds are definitely against" a Japanese attack on Britain and the United States, although he admitted that "no one can tell." An irritated Alexander Cadogan, professional chief of the Foreign Office, wrote that Churchill "is now determined that nothing will make [the Japanese] come in."[10]

In any case, two events led virtually all British decision-makers to accept Churchill's views. For five months after the German attack on Russia in June 1941, Whitehall believed that Japan was more likely to strike north than south – that it was unlikely to attack Britain and absolutely unlikely to start a war with the United States.[11] Simultaneously, Roosevelt promised to stand by Britain against Japanese aggression. From this point on, the British and American governments linked their policies in the Pacific. British authorities, especially Churchill, denied that the Japanese would risk war against so powerful a coalition. While they knew that Japan might go to war against them, they were convinced that it was far more likely that Japan would back down. Churchill told the foreign secretary and the Chiefs of Staff on 16 July 1941:

I must repeat my conviction that Japan will not declare war upon us at the present juncture, nor if the United States enters the war on our side. I agree with the views of the Chiefs of Staff that we are in no position to declare war upon Japan without the United States being in on our side. Therefore I do not consider that a war between Britain and Japan is likely at the present time. If contrary to the above views Japan should attack us, I am of the opinion that the United States would enter the war as the weight upon us would clearly be too great. Nevertheless, since the threatened Japanese moves in Indo-China are of serious concern to us, further precautions in the Far East should be taken so far as they are possible without condemning us to misfortune in other theaters.

In a memorandum of 29 August 1941 that has been in the public domain for more than forty years, Churchill repeated this view almost word for word. Indeed, on 2 December 1941 he still hoped that Japan would not attack Britain and the United States.[12]

These perceptions of Japan's intentions and the unlikelihood of an Anglo-Japanese war determined the role of Hong Kong in British planning. Between 1931 and 1939 British military resources were stretched thin, and authorities in London refused to strengthen Hong

Kong to any notable degree. They had trouble enough building up
the vital Singapore base. These attitudes became even more pro-
nounced between August 1939 and August 1941. During that period,
however, British commanders in Asia began to adopt an entirely
different policy – especially Brooke-Popham. In January 1941 he
argued that the garrison of Hong Kong was too small for effective
defence but that the addition of just two more battalions would make
a prolonged defence possible. This, in turn, would also prove Britain's
"determination to defend Hong Kong [and] encourage [the] Chinese
in their resistance to Japan and would be [an] important feature in
our policy of firmness toward Japan which is calculated to reduce
likelihood of aggression by her." Brooke-Popham also believed that
Britain could use Hong Kong as a forward base in a war against
Japan: "To us out here, it seems no longer a question of reducing our
losses in Hong Kong but of ensuring the security of places that will
be of great value in taking offensive action at a later stage of the
war."

Brooke-Popham's proposals were rejected by the Chiefs of Staff
and by Churchill, who argued that, in case of war with Japan, Hong
Kong would be indefensible and Britain did not have the resources
to reinforce it. Above all, Churchill rejected Brooke-Popham's
arguments about deterrence: "Japan will think long before declaring
war on the British Empire, and whether there are two or six battalions at Hong Kong will make no difference to her choice."[13]

The view from the Far East was different, however. In the last
days before the Pacific war, the senior Canadian officer at the colony,
Brigadier J.K. Lawson, wanted yet more of his countrymen sent there,
and the garrison commander, Major-General C. Maltby, argued, "Is
not value of Hongkong as bridgehead increasing every day and
Hongkong becoming potential centre of ABCD [American-British-
Chinese-Dutch] front?"[14] Moreover, Brooke-Popham and both generals who commanded the Hong Kong garrison in 1941 had an entirely
different policy from their superiors. They wanted reinforcements for
Hong Kong from any source, and not just for symbolic purposes.
They truly believed that just a few battalions more would make Hong
Kong impregnable and deter Japan from war. Canada's involvement
in Hong Kong stemmed from this level of British command and its
connections with the "old boy" army network that connected British
with Canadian army officers.

In August 1941 General Edward Grasett retired as commander of
the Hong Kong garrison. Grasett, a Canadian serving in the British
Army, then returned to London via Ottawa. On the way, he visited
his old classmate from the Royal Military College, H.D.G. "Harry"

Crerar, chief of the Canadian General Staff. Exactly what passed between them remains a mystery. Vincent has concluded that Crerar actively led Grasett to believe that Canada would welcome a request to provide reinforcements for Hong Kong.[15] Vincent's inference is certainly plausible but rests entirely on circumstantial evidence and cannot be proven. It also contradicts Crerar's testimony of 1942 to the judicial inquiry into the Hong Kong affair (the Duff Royal Commission). In any case, when Grasett reached London he repeated the well-worn argument to the Chiefs of Staff that reinforcement of Hong Kong was necessary from several points of view, but added a new twist: If Canada was officially asked, it might send those additional men. He may even have stated that Crerar would welcome a request to do so.

The Chiefs of Staff did not have to pursue Grasett's proposal; they would clearly not have done so in January 1941, but they did pursue it in September because this appeared to be an offer that Britain could no longer refuse. British (and American) authorities believed that war with Japan would not break out if Japan could be deterred. In order to show Japan that such a war would be suicide, a solid diplomatic front needed to be maintained with the United States and Nationalist China, and whatever small reinforcements were available must be sent to Asia. To London, the issue of war or peace with Japan seemed to rest on tough negotiations with Japan and on Britain's ability to keep China and the United States on its side. So long as the United States was committed, British authorities believed that Japan was unlikely to risk war. This encouraged the British to take firm action; they believed that without this stand the United States might cease to cooperate with Britain. It was, in essence, a vicious circle of reasoning. Thus, by the time Grasett arrived in London, British decision-makers had changed their minds about Japan and about reinforcing Hong Kong. These reasons emerge clearly in the Chiefs of Staff recommendation that Grasett's proposal be adopted:

3. ... Our defences in Malaya have been improved and Japan has latterly shown a certain weakness in her attitude toward Great Britain and the United States.
4. A small reinforcement [of Hong Kong] of one or two battalions would increase the strength of the garrison out of all proportion to the actual numbers involved, and it would provide a strong stimulus to the garrison and the Colony. Further it would have a very great moral [sic] effect in the whole of the Far East and it would show Chiang Kai Shek that we really intend to fight it out at Hong Kong.
5. The United States have recently despatched a small reinforcement to the

Philippines and a similar move by Canada would be in line with the present United States policy of greater interest in the Far East.[16]

The key issue was no longer indefensibility in war but the deterrence of war. These arguments caused Churchill to change his mind about Hong Kong, and on 19 September the British government asked Canada to provide reinforcements for that colony.

Until Canadian troops had actually landed in Hong Kong, British authorities concurred that Japan would back down rather than risk war. The Chiefs of Staff, for example, told Brooke-Popham that while Hong Kong was still regarded as indefensible, reinforcements there were part of a broader policy of deterrence:

It has now become possible for U.S.A. and ourselves to take a more forward line in the Far East. U.S.A. have on their part recently displayed greater interest in this theatre and have despatched reinforcements to garrison of Phillipines [sic]. Our reinforcement of Hong Kong will show China that in spite of other commitments we intend to fight it out at Hong Kong and it will also have salutary effect on Japanese ... Canada, by providing these troops, will be accepting wider commitment in imperial defence similar to that assumed by Australia in Malaya.

Only in late November did Britain – for the first time – realize that war with Japan was inevitable and imminent.[17]

Britain did not intend that 2000 Canadians die or surrender at Hong Kong. It wanted them, at a small risk of disaster, to increase what they thought were the already favourable chances of preventing war. Of course, this scenario turned out to be wrong. In effect, British incompetence did create a Canadian disaster. Britain did risk Canadian lives and it did know that risk was involved. But it also put its own troops at risk. Exactly as the decisions about Hong Kong were made, the British and the Americans deployed other reinforcements to east Asia, including two British capital ships and 3000 sailors, 100 American B-17 Flying Fortresses, and thousands of American soldiers. Not just Canadians, but all these reinforcements were killed or captured within a few short months.

Nor did Britain use false evidence to manipulate Canada into providing reinforcements. The British request to Canada repeated virtually word for word the Chiefs of Staff assessment to Churchill, which did reflect British expectations.[18] This message did not state that Britain intended to hold or relieve Hong Kong in case of war, nor did it deny that risk was involved. It simply implied that the risk was low and manageable, because that was what Whitehall believed. The problem lay not with the honesty of the statement, but with its accuracy. Both before this date and after, Britain gave Canada a large and representative sample of its reports and assessments on Japan, including, in the autumn of 1940, a lengthy memorandum explaining why Hong Kong was indefensible.[19] Only two significant pieces of information were not given to Canada. For security reasons, Britain did not provide copies of the decrypted solutions of Japanese diplomatic messages. Nor did it provide Churchill's opinion of January 1941 that he considered Hong Kong to be indefensible – that had been his private opinion expressed to his chief advisers. Such private opinions were, for good or ill, rarely circulated to his own cabinet, let alone the dominions. Moreover, by September 1941 it was an obsolete opinion because he had changed his mind on the issue.

If Britain did not mislead Canada, however, Canadian authorities helped mislead themselves. In 1941 Canada had no independent means to assess any strategic situation. They received enough material to appraise the issue on their own from Britain, but they did not attempt to do so. Canadian authorities do not appear to have read carefully any of the material sent by Britain. Even if they had, however, there is no reason to think they would have bettered the dismal British and American performance at evaluating Japanese intentions. Their performance at strategic analysis left much to be desired, as every single commentator has argued.[20] They relied on their own intuition and their allies' assessments rather than on any independent analysis of the evidence, but this was also true of most other Canadian decisions in the war.

The claims of "Savage Christmas" about why 2000 Canadians were sent to Hong Kong are false. They are a Canadian version of the conspiracy theories that have surrounded American (and, to a lesser degree, British) decisions ever since 7 December 1941 – that Roosevelt or Churchill knew about the attack on Pearl Harbor and let it happen for their own fell purposes.[21] The McKennas' view does not even have the charm of novelty. The Canadian politician George Drew formulated and publicized virtually identical views in the 1940s, views that received wide currency in the press.[22]

The traumatic events of December 1941 stemmed from one of the greatest strategic and intelligence miscalculations in history. In hindsight, it is hard to believe that anyone could ever have made such errors. Hence, it is easy to believe that the decisions that led to the disasters could not have been errors at all and that they happened because someone wanted them to. Such views are comprehensible but they are not correct. Stupidity, not conspiracy, dispatched 2000

Canadians to Hong Kong and the American Pacific Fleet to the bottom of the sea.

This error of judgment by Ottawa led to a host of other errors. Most notorious were the limitations in training of the Winnipeg Grenadiers and the Royal Rifles of Canada. Specialists differ on the question of just how trained those men were. There is no right answer; any conclusion about the level of training these men should have had before leaving Canada must depend on a judgment about the potential danger they faced. This question of training was the second major reason why "Savage Christmas" was criticized.

Here the McKennas stand in an orthodox and defensible position. Correctly, "Savage Christmas" reports that many of the Canadian soldiers sent to Hong Kong had not properly trained with their weapons: "Few of them had ever thrown a grenade. Some had never even fired a rifle ... they were officially classified by the Canadian defence department as 'unfit for combat.'" All this is true, and it is not the worst of the facts. About 20 per cent of the Royal Rifles soldiers had not passed the most elementary tests with their rifles. Neither unit was capable of using mortars and machine-guns effectively – their main source of organic firepower. Neither was adequately trained in tactics. In 1948 the chief of the Canadian General Staff, Charles Foulkes, was scathing about these issues:

The most regrettable feature arising out of the inadequate training and equipping [of the Hong Kong reinforcements] was the effect on the morale and fighting efficiency of the Canadian troops, which unfortunately was interpreted by their British superiors as a lack of courage, willingness to fight and even in some cases cowardice. On the other hand this had caused in the minds of Canadian troops bitterness, lack of confidence and resentment in their British superiors.[23]

Still, certain points should be noted for the record. These two battalions were no worse trained than many other Canadian units of that period. They were not expected to fight in Hong Kong, but to serve as a garrison during which time further training could be conducted.[24] Above all, as Stacey emphasized:

The two battalions had clearly not reached that advanced state of training which one would wish troops to attain before being sent against an enemy ... but to say baldly that they were "untrained" is to give quite a wrong impression ... The Royal Rifles of Canada and The Winnipeg Grenadiers would doubtless have been more effective if they had received more advanced training ... But too much can be made of this. Their casualty lists show that their contribution to the defence was a large one, and ... Japanese accounts ... attest the battalions' solid fighting qualities.[25]

However shameful to the country which sent them there, these units' lack of training was ultimately of little significance. Had two experienced Canadian battalions, trained to a standard that would have been expected of Canadian infantrymen in 1945, been present instead, Hong Kong would have fallen almost as quickly and would have inflicted just a few hundred more Japanese casualties. Foulkes and Bernard Montgomery espoused this view after the war. Robert Clayton, a veteran quoted in "Savage Christmas," correctly says, "It wouldn't have mattered even if we were well trained. Okay, we would have killed a few more of them."[26]

One part of the Canadian Hong Kong force put up a superlative performance that matches anything done by a Western unit during the Pacific war. At the battle of the Wong Nei Chong pass, D Company of the Winnipeg Grenadiers fought alone for four days, almost literally to the last round, often surrounded, holding out against a force twenty times their own strength, each Canadian killing or wounding five Japanese soldiers. Yet the rest of the Canadians were not heroes, they were just brave and increasingly tired men doing their best. They fought well, far better than anyone had any right to expect, but the flaws in their training hold true. Small Canadian forces on the defensive fought better than large ones on the attack. After four days of combat, almost 50 per cent of the soldiers in these units were dead or wounded, and both battalions had been burned out. Nonetheless, their courage, self-sacrifice, and combat value won praise from the most parsimonious and significant of sources – the Japanese officers who opposed them. In a soldiers' battle where command collapsed, amid close-quarter combat where courage counted for as much as technique, the Winnipeg Grenadiers and the Royal Rifles were well prepared. In fact, they rank among the best-trained and most dangerous soldiers the Japanese faced any- where in December 1941. Only one of the other four battalions in Hong Kong (the Middlesex Regiment) was better prepared.[27]

How did the training and preparedness of the Canadians rank against that of other Allied soldiers at the start of the Pacific war? The quality of training for virtually all British and Indian soldiers in Malaya was a scandal; the performance of Dutch, Filipino, and American Army forces in the first months of the Pacific war was little better.[28] Fewer than 10,000 of the 400,000–odd Allied soldiers who fought Japan in December 1941–March 1942 matched the fighting quality of the Winnipeg Grenadiers and the Royal Rifles of Canada. None surpassed it. This says much for their courage but more about the general unpreparedness of the Allied military for what befell them. It was not only Canada that sent untrained and badly prepared men into an area where war was not supposed to break out.

In explaining why Canadians were sent to Hong Kong, "Savage Christmas" adopts Robin Hood history, filled with villains, victims, and heroes. British authorities are cast as King John, Canadians as the Sheriff of Nottingham, and their actions as murder in the first degree. None of this is true. The key agents in these events were Canadians, not Englishmen; the key factor was the linkage between decision-makers in Canada and in Britain. The underlying cause was the colonial status Canada still had in British and Anglo-Canadian military minds. The crime was not premeditated murder but manslaughter – a crime every government is bound to commit in a war against a serious enemy, when errors are inevitable and every one is deadly. While these British actions were marked by an unusual degree of reckless stupidity, the fact of British stupidity destroys any case for British treachery.

None of these events would have happened without Grasett – a Canadian serving as a middle-level British officer who had the opportunity to gain the ear of both the British Chiefs of Staff and of Crerar, a man able to use his position to help erode Whitehall's resistance to a policy increasingly favoured by British military authorities in Asia. These authorities held sincere but erroneous views of Britain's ability to deter or defeat Japan. Without Grasett, authorities in London would never have thought about Canadian reinforcements. They followed his proposal because it suited a sincere but flawed policy of deterrence. As for the authorities in Ottawa, they did not "knowingly" send men to destruction. The case of Charles Gavin "Chubby" Power surely destroys this view. As associate minister for national defence for air, Power was a combat veteran of the First World War with access to all the information available in Ottawa about Hong Kong. Despite his access to that information, he agitated to send the Royal Rifles regiment on that mission, one in which his own son was an officer. The available evidence does not indicate that Canadian authorities "knowingly" thought this mission involved serious risks. Their assessments and actions were tragically misguided, even reckless, but no more.

In any case, to look for guilty men is to overlook the cause that sent Canadians to Hong Kong – and to war. In many crucial ways, the Canada of 1940 and 1941 remained a colonial society. Canadians defined Britain's cause as their cause; they went to war because Britain was in peril. Even today, no one ought to be astonished at this relative simple-mindedness. Canadians may have been wrong to think that Britain embodied only good, but Nazi Germany and Imperial Japan were fair embodiments of evil. Canadians did the right thing when few peoples did, and they did it of their own free will. They voluntarily fought against evil, no doubt in part for the wrong reasons, but without those wrong reasons they would not have done the right thing. In the minds of English Canadians, they and the mother country were fighting a world war in which risks and costs were unavoidable. The Canadian government was striving to reduce the scale of those risks and sacrifices in the face of great popular pressure to increase them. Canadians went to Hong Kong because Canadians and their government wanted to do their part. J.L. Ralston, minister for national defence, told the Canadian Cabinet War Committee: "It was Canada's turn to help ... Australia had been doing a great deal in Libya and elsewhere; the New Zealanders had been in Crete; and the South Africans in Abyssinia." Similarly, after the fall of Hong Kong, Richard Hanson, leader of the Opposition, said in the House of Commons:

I offer no criticism at all of the government for having sent these two battalions to Hong Kong. If we are to be in a total war effort, and to undertake a total war effort ... we must expect to share, in common with the other gallant soldiers of the British empire, and of our democratic allies, the fortunes of war ... Hong Kong? – before this war is over perhaps there will be more Hong Kongs. We have got to make up our minds, the Canadian people have to make up their minds, and the people of the democracies who to-day are faced with a situation more serious than that which has ever confronted the peoples of the world have got to make up their minds that there may be more Hong Kongs.[29]

If one must find villains behind the Hong Kong debacle, one need merely look in the mirror. The guilty men were a Canadian society and government that starved its military forces for years on end and then one day sent them off against well-equipped enemies, in pursuit not of national interests defined by Canadian politicians but of international interests defined by external authorities. Hong Kong was not the first example of this phenomenon or the last. It happened in the First and Second World Wars, in the Korean War, and in the Gulf conflict. The risk was taken in NATO and everywhere Canadians have served as UN peacekeepers. It is the Canadian way of war.

NOTES

I am indebted to Christopher Bell for allowing me to examine his notes about the role of Hong Kong in British defence planning between 1919 and 1941, and to David Taras for loaning me his files on the controversy about *The Valour and the Horror*. I am particularly grateful to Elizabeth Herbert for comments on earlier drafts of this paper, and to Patrick Brennan for illuminating the Canadian militia myth. All citations from CAB, PREM, and WO files are taken from material held by the Public Records Office, London, and appear by permission of the controller of Her Majesty's Stationary Office.

1 "Savage Christmas: Hong Kong, 1941."
2 For the views of two leaders of major veterans' groups – Bob Ford, dominion chairman of the Royal Canadian Legion, and Cliff Chadderton, chief executive officer of the War Amputations Society of Canada and chairman of the National Council of Veterans' Associations – see Fourth Session, 34th Parliament, 1991–92, *Proceedings of the Standing Senate Committee on Veterans' Affairs*, Issue 6, column 6:83 (hereafter *Proceedings*); *Saturday Night*, May 1993, 49. The final report of the *Standing Committee* in effect ignored "Savage Christmas." For a representative sample of historians' attitudes, see Terry Copp's analysis in *Proceedings*, Issue 3, 25 June 1992, columns 3A:3–3A:7.
3 Throughout this article, unattributed quotations are from the program.
4 Carl Vincent, *No Reason Why: The Canadian Hong Kong Tragedy – An Examination* (Stittsville: Canada's Wings 1981).
5 Ibid., 25–34.
6 C.P. Stacey, *Official History of the Canadian Army in the Second World War*, vol. 1: *Six Years of War: The Army in Canada, Britain and the Pacific* (Ottawa: Queen's Printer 1955), 437–91.
7 The McKennas' bibliography is found in M. Weisbord and M. Simonds Mohr, *The Valour and the Horror: The Untold Story of Canadians in the Second World War* (Toronto: HarperCollins 1991), the companion volume to the television series. See also Vincent, *No Reason Why*, 14–23, 41; *Proceedings*, Issue 9, 6 Nov. 1992, column 9A:10. The McKennas also claim that an encyclopedia article by an official historian at the Department of National Defence, Brereton Greenhous, supports their "central thesis," whatever that may have been. Greenhous, however, says nothing about the intentions and knowledge of the Canadian and British governments in 1941.

The best account of British strategy and diplomacy in the Pacific during 1940–41 is Ian Cowman, "Anglo-American Naval Relations in the Pacific, 1937–1941" (PhD thesis, University of London 1989). More general work on the topic include Bradford Lee, *Britain and the Sino-Japanese War, 1937–1939* (Stanford: Stanford University Press 1973), Paul Haggie, *Britan-*

nia at Bay: The Defence of the British Empire against Japan, 1931–1941 (Oxford: Oxford University Press 1981), James Neidpath, The Singapore Naval Base and the Defence of Britain's Eastern Empire, 1919–1941 (Oxford: Oxford University Press 1981), S.W. Kirby, Singapore: Chain of Disaster (New York: Macmillan 1971), and Peter Lowe, Great Britain and the Origins of the Pacific War (Oxford: Oxford University Press 1977). Hong Kong is generally relegated to the background of British policy in the Pacific. Christopher Bell, "The Problem of Hong Kong and Britain's Strategy towards the Far East, 1921–1941" (MA thesis, King's College, London 1992), is the only specialist study of the topic, and a good one. These works differ on various points, but all concur with the points made in the text and none support the McKennas' case.

The same is true of the literature about the outbreak of the Pacific war and relations between Britain, Japan, and the United States in 1940–41. That literature is too vast to be fully cited here; those interested in more detail can find it in John S. Sbrega, The War against Japan, 1941–1945: An Annotated Bibliography (New York: Garland 1989), 69–147, although this account omits the memoirs and biographies of major British and American decision-makers. The works that most clearly explain American and British perceptions of Japanese intentions are Gordon W. Prange, Donald M. Goldstein, and Katherine V. Dillon, At Dawn We Slept: The Untold Story of Pearl Harbor (Toronto: McGraw-Hill 1981), and Pearl Harbor: The Verdict of History (New York: McGraw-Hill 1986), Roberta Wohlstetter, Pearl Harbor: Warning and Decision (Stanford: Stanford University Press 1962) (amended by reference to David Kahn, "United States Views of Germany and Japan," in Ernest May, ed., Knowing One's Enemies: Intelligence Assessments before the Two World Wars [Princeton: Princeton University Press 1984], 500). The best introduction to the diplomatic background is Akira Iriye, The Origins of the Second World War in Asia and the Pacific (London: Longmans 1987).

8 Nobutake Ike, Japan's Decision for War: Records of the 1941 Policy Conferences (Stanford: Stanford University Press 1967), 210–40; compare Prange et al., At Dawn We Slept, 327–8.

9 For a characteristic example of the Foreign Office's views before the fall of France, see Dening to Stirling, 2 May 1940, CAB 21/1010. For views between June and December 1940, see memorandum by the chiefs of staff (COS), COS (40), 592, 15 Aug. 1940, CAB 80/15; memorandum by COS, COS (40), 843, 18 Oct. 1940, CAB 80/20; memorandum by John Godfrey, director of naval intelligence, "NID 1986," "Attitude of Japan," 21 June 1940, WO 208/1217A; Commander-in-Chief Far East to COS, 18 Dec. 1940, WO 106/5402B; compare FO 371/24737, F5742, and FO 371/27887, F1185.

10 Memoranda by Joint Intelligence Committee, (JIC) (41) 55 and JIC (41) 61, 7 Feb. 1941, FO 371/27886; memorandum by JIC (41) 175 revise, 1 May 1941, CAB 122/72; memorandum by Foreign Office, 15 April 1941, FO 371/27957;

Francis L. Loewenheim, Harold D. Langley, and Manfred Jones, eds., *Roosevelt and Churchill: Their Secret Wartime Correspondence* (New York: E.P. Dutton 1975), 130; David Dilks, ed., *The Diaries of Sir Alexander Cadogan, 1938–1945* (New York: Putnam 1971), 375.

11 For a representative sample of government opinion, see minute by Dening, 23 June 1941, FO 371/27880; compare note 42.

12 Memorandum by Churchill, COS (41), 139 (0), 16 July 1941, CAB 80/58; Winston S. Churchill, *The Second World War*, vol. 1: *The Grand Alliance* (London: Cassell 1950), 774; minute by Churchill, 2 Dec. 1941, FO 371/27913.

13 Brooke-Popham to COS, 18 Jan. 1941, COS (41), 51, Annex 11, WO 106/2418.

14 Bell, "Hong Kong," 33–5, offers the clearest account of this issue.

15 Vincent, *No Reason Why*, 25–34; compare Stacey, *Six Years of War*, 439–40.

16 Hollis to Churchill, 10 Sept. 1941, and minute by Churchill, 15 Sept. 1941, PREM 3/157/1.

17 Commander-in-Chief Far East to War Office, 1 Oct. 1941, and memorandum by MI 2(c), 2 Oct. 1941, WO 208/876 – the file is filled throughout the autumn of 1941 with material on British assessments of the likelihood of war; War Office to Brooke-Popham, 6 Nov. 1941, WO 106/2409; compare FO 371/27883, F9164, F10117, WO 172/15, and CAB 122/73. For other useful accounts of these issues, see John Ferris, "From Broadway House to Bletchley Park: The Diary of Captain Malcolm Kennedy, 1934–1946," *Intelligence and National Security* 4, 3 (July 1989): 439–40, and J.W.M. Chapman, "Pearl Harbor: The Anglo-Australian Dimension," in the same issue, 451–61. See also Richard J. Aldrich, "Conspiracy or Confusion? Churchill, Roosevelt and Pearl Harbor," *Intelligence and National Security* 7, 3 (1992): 335–46.

18 Compare Hollis to Churchill, 10 Sept. 1941, PREM 3/157/1, with Stacey, *Six Years of War*, 439–40.

19 Carl Vincent, *No Reason Why*, 18–23; Patricia Roy, J.L. Granatstein, Masako Iino, and Hiroko Takamura, *Mutual Hostages: Canadians and Japanese during the Second World War* (Toronto: University of Toronto Press 1990), 62.

20 Vincent, *No Reason Why*, 262–3; Stacey, *Six Years of War*, 440–2, 450–2.

21 For good examples of the American variant of this view, see Robert Theobald, *The Final Secret of Pearl Harbor* (New York: Devin-Adair 1954), Harry Elmer Barnes, *Pearl Harbor after a Quarter of a Century* (New York: Arno Press 1972), and John Toland, *Infamy: Pearl Harbor and Its Aftermath* (Garden City: Doubleday 1982). For refutations, see Prange et al., *At Dawn We Slept* and *Pearl Harbor*.

   For the British variant, see James Rusbridger and Eric Nave, *Betrayal at Pearl Harbor: How Churchill Lured Roosevelt into War* (New York: Summit Books 1991); for refutations, see the articles by Aldrich, Chapman, and Ferris cited in note 17.

22 Canada, House of Commons, *Debates*, 1948, vol. 2, 1549–54, 1631–40, 1771–4; 1948, vol. 4, 3429–30; and 1949, vol. 2, 1055–6.

23 "Savage Christmas: Hong Kong, 1941"; Vincent, *No Reason Why*, 56–66, 262–9.

24 Stacey, *Six Years of War*, 447; *Proceedings*, Issue 3, meeting 25 June 1992, appendix VA-1, 3A-5-6.

25 Stacey, *Six Years of War*, 490.

26 Vincent, *No Reason Why*, 262; "Savage Christmas: Hong Kong, 1941."

27 Oliver Lindsay, *The Lasting Honour: The Fall of Hong Kong, 1941* (London: Hamish Hamilton 1978), 17–20; Kenneth Taylor, "The Challenge of the Eighties: World War Two from a New Perspective, The Hong Kong case," in Christon Archer and Tim Travers, eds., *Men at War: Politics, Technology, and Innovation in the Twentieth Century* (Chicago: Precedent 1982), 203–4; Stacey, *Six Years of War*, 457. The literature about the battle of Hong Kong is weakest where it most follows the apologias of senior surviving British officers. In particular, Maltby's dispatch, both in its original and censored form, is unusually unreliable even for the genre. For these reasons, Tim Carew's two works, *The Fall of Hong Kong* (London: Anthony Blond 1960) and *Hostages to Fortune* (London: Anthony Blond 1971), are worthless, while Lindsay, *Lasting Honour*, is misleading, unless used with care. The account in the British official history – S.W. Kirby, C.T. Addis, J.F. Meiklejohn, G.T. Wards, and N.L. Desoer, *The War against Japan*, vol. 1: *The Loss of Singapore* (London: Her Majesty's Stationary Office 1957), 110–29, is judicious, although brief. The regimental and/or official histories of units involved are also useful: B.K.D. Bhargava and K.N.V. Sastri, *Campaigns in South-East Asia, 1941–1942: Official History of the Indian Armed Forces in the Second World War, 1939–45* (Kanpur: Orient Longmans 1960); Augustus Muir (pseudonym), *The First of Foot: The History of the Royal Scots* (the Royal Regiment) (Aldershot: Gale & Polden 1961), 109–11, et passim. The works by Canadian authors – Stacey, *Six Years of War*, 461–90, Vincent, *No Reason Why*, 127–209, and Ted Ferguson, *Desperate Siege: The Battle of Hong Kong* (Toronto: Doubleday 1980), 45–215 – offer the best accounts of the Canadian role. They are reasonably accurate about the performance of other units and they also offer lengthy translated excerpts from the surviving reports from Japanese commanders. A translation of another Japanese account, though of limited value, can be found in "Japanese Monograph No. 71, Army Operations in China, December 1941–December 1943," in Donald S. Detwiler and Charles B. Burdick eds., *War in Asia and the Pacific, 1937–1949*, vol. 8: *China, Manchuria and Korea* (Part One) (New York: Garland 1980), 21–49. Roy et al., *Mutual Hostages*, offers a good, succinct account of the battle of Hong Kong, including the most accurate statement of the damage inflicted by D Company, and, along with Daniel Dancocks,

In Enemy Hands (Edmonton: Hurtig 1982), offers an excellent account of the experiences of Canadians as prisoners of war.

28 John Ferris, "Worthy of Some Better Enemy? The British Estimate of the Imperial Japanese Army, 1919–1941, and the Fall of Singapore," *Canadian Journal of History* 28, 2 (Aug. 1993): 248–55.

29 House of Commons, *Debates*, 1941–42, vol. 4, 4473–4; Vincent, *No Reason Why*, 32–4; the standard account of the political background is J.L. Granatstein, *Canada's War: The Politics of the Mackenzie King Government, 1939–1945* (Toronto: University of Toronto Press 1975), chaps 4–6. Roy et al., *Mutual Hostages*, 62–5, also offers a precise account of the Canadian background to the Hong Kong affair.

BILL McANDREW

The Canadians on Verrières Ridge: A Historiographical Survey

EDITORS' INTRODUCTION

Dr Bill McAndrew, author of the following article, has chosen not to confront directly the historical issues raised by *The Valour and the Horror* in its treatment of the role of the Canadian Army in the Battle of Normandy. Instead, he has decided to concentrate on Operation Spring, the failed Canadian attempt to dislodge German forces from their positions on Verrières Ridge, the centrepiece of the episode entitled "In Desperate Battle." His essay brings out the immense complexity of this operation and provides a sharp contrast with the simplicities of *The Valour and the Horror*. McAndrew discusses the ambivalent nature of Field Marshal Montgomery's strategy, the difficulty in interpreting the intentions of corps commander General Simonds, the conflicting testimony of other officers involved in the operation, and the variety of interpretations subsequently put forward by historians who have written about it.

McAndrew's analysis, informed by his grasp of the literature and his expert knowledge of the ground (he regularly conducts many battlefield tours, not only in Normandy but in Germany and Italy), is a historian's response to the assertion made by the authors of *The Valour and the Horror* to have discovered "the truth" about the Canadian army in Normandy. Was the Canadian Army badly trained, badly armed, badly led? Did it face an enemy superior to it in every respect? Was Canadian treatment of prisoners of war on the same moral level as that exhibited by their Waffen SS opponents? Was the Canadian Army's attitude towards soldiers who suffered from battle fatigue ("shell shock") as primitive and arbitrary as *The Valour and the Horror* suggested?

McAndrew's responses to these questions are those of a professional historian deeply aware of the nature of battle. They will acquaint the reader with the complexities inherent in the study of war and with the rich bibliography awaiting those who wish to inform themselves more fully. A former infantryman, McAndrew is the co-author, with Terry Copp, of *Battle Exhaustion: Soldiers and Psychiatrists in the Canadian Army, 1939–1945,* and, with Donald E. Graves and Michael Whitby, of *Normandy 1944: The Canadian Summer.* He is currently completing a book on the Canadian Army and the Battle of Normandy.

• • •

One of the perpetual optical illusions of historical study [is] the impression that all would have been well if men had only done the other thing ... Where so much is obscure, it is clear as day that there was no easy solution to the problem of the attacker. The critic of the solutions that were in fact adopted must first arm himself with better ones; he must then be sure that they were available amidst the confusion, the misinformation, the fluctuating hopes and the sheer worry and exhaustion of the battlefield.[1]

Operation Spring, the attack by 2nd Canadian Corps on 25 July 1944 against Verrières Ridge south of Caen in the Normandy bridgehead, was an almost unmitigated disaster of Canadian arms. Six infantry battalions and three tank squadrons attacked separately along an eight-kilometre front against entrenched German positions well sited on commanding high ground. One battalion, the Royal Hamilton Light Infantry, reached its objective and held it against repeated German attempts to drive them off. The others were unsuccessful. When they attempted to take the village of Tilly-la-Campagne, the North Nova Scotia Highlanders were severely mauled by a reinforced half-battalion of 1st SS Division panzer grenadiers. The Cameron Highlanders of Canada, the Calgary Highlanders, and Le Régiment de Maisonneuve were as severely treated when they tried to secure the connected villages in the Orne River valley at the other end of the ridge. Following them, the Canadian Black Watch suffered worst of all, taking more than 300 casualties – virtually the battalion's entire rifle strength. It was a Second World War tragedy akin to that experienced by the Royal Newfoundland Regiment, which lost 90 per cent of its men in an hour at the Somme on 1 July 1916. Except for 19 August 1942 at Dieppe, this was the Canadian Army's costliest single operation of the Second World War, causing about 1500 casualties, almost a third of them killed. Canadian units had suffered another 1600 casualties in the few days preceding Spring.[2]

Because of its appalling costs, Spring understandably looms large to Canadians, and several explanations have been advanced over the years to describe what went wrong – some of them self-serving, some critical, some exculpatory, yet others conspiratorial. Curiously, however, within the broader course of the Normandy bloodbath, Spring seems a trifle, barely rating mention. Other armies had their own comparable disasters to analyse and, in general histories of Normandy, Spring is just one more battle among many that the Allied armies fought to break out of their Normandy bridgehead. In the month of June, for example, Allied forces had more than 60,000 casualties, 8500 of them killed, and between 6 June and 29 August, around 210,000.[3]

The Canadian debacle of 25 July can only be understood by fixing it within this larger framework of Allied operations in Normandy and tracing its sources deep in the seven weeks of continuous fighting after D-Day. However well known, the course of those events provokes continuing interest and still causes acrimonious debate among participants, observers, historians, and journalists. As Eric Larrabee has written in *Commander in Chief*, his gracious essays on President Franklin Roosevelt's military commanders:

Forty years afterward, the Normandy campaign is still being argued over. Was it well or badly done on our side? ... Could the Germans ... have conducted an even more resourceful defense than they did? Was it a "failure" on Montgomery's part not to capture Caen promptly, as he asserted he would do? Did the eventual American breakout to the west proceed according to Montgomery's prior design, or had he seriously meant his own attack east of Caen to be the major effort? ... Ultimate success has not prevented these points from remaining in dispute.[4]

Following the reasonable premise that the fastest pen wins the interpretive war, Field Marshal Bernard Montgomery, the Allied ground forces commander in Normandy, was first to offer what became a quasi-official British version of events in *Normandy to the Baltic*.[5] The essence of his argument, reinforced in his *Memoirs*, was that he fought his battle in Normandy exactly as he had planned before the invasion.[6] He wrote that following the air and sea assault on 6 June, the bridgehead was linked and secured while reinforcements, resources, and supplies poured ashore at a faster rate than the Germans could concentrate their forces to drive the invaders into the sea.[7] During the dogfight, British and Canadian divisions on the eastern flank deliberately attracted the main German armoured reserves to their front around Caen, to keep them from interfering with the western, American, sector from which General Omar Bradley's troops broke spectacularly out of the bridgehead at the end of July. The decisive victory in Normandy, Montgomery asserted, was the natural culmination of the brilliant operational concept to hold on the left and move on the right that he had foreseen well beforehand. This perspective was codified in the official British history, *Victory in the West*, and argumentatively buttressed by his official biographer, Nigel Hamilton, in *Monty: Master of the Battlefield, 1942–1944*.[8]

Montgomery's viewpoint, which directly or implicitly exaggerated his role at almost everyone else's expense, was not universally accepted as an accurate or even truthful account of events. Critics, mostly but not solely American, challenged Montgomery on several grounds. Although temperate in tone, the memoirs of his peers, General Dwight Eisenhower's *Crusade in Europe* and General Bradley's *A Soldier's Story*, firmly suggested that Montgomery's interpretation was overly simplistic.[9] Rather than following a pre-written script, they argued, Allied commanders were forced by Germans and the Normandy terrain to adapt and modify their operations almost daily in response to continuously changing conditions on the battlefield. In their view, Montgomery had to share the glory as well as the pain of Normandy operations with other commanders. A number of scholarly accounts elaborated their arguments with informed critical analysis – for example, Forrest C. Pogue's *The Supreme Command* and Russell Weigley's *Eisenhower's Lieutenants*.[10]

Several works published around the time of D-Day's fortieth anniversary amplified the debate and raised important related aspects that affected events in Normandy, among them manpower, technology, training, and morale. Richard Lamb, *Montgomery in Europe*, Max Hastings, *Overlord*, and John Keegan, *Six Armies in Normandy*, stand out, but in a class by itself is Carlo D'Este's *Decision in Normandy*.[11] With scrupulous balance, D'Este marshalled a wide array of previously unused sources to produce the best researched and, arguably, the most persuasive discussion of Normandy yet. Among the several myths he effectively demolishes is the one that Montgomery fought the battle exactly as he had planned it. D'Este traces the documentary record meticulously to demonstrate that Montgomery initially intended to seize Caen and the plateau extending south to Falaise, and then to fight aggressively to break through the German defences in that sector. When this proved not to be possible, Montgomery modified his operational plan to one of holding on the left and breaking out on the right. Unfortunately, Montgomery failed to make his intentions clear to General Eisenhower and other senior commanders, who became acutely disturbed over what they perceived to be a large gap between Montgomery's predictions and his achievements. As D'Este demonstrates, it was essentially this miscommunication that lay behind the acrimonious, sometimes bitter differences among senior Allied commanders over the conduct of the campaign. Intriguingly, D'Este concludes that Montgomery was a better general than his tiresome self-portrait allowed. Rather than rigidly following a plan left redundant when its premises changed, Montgomery displayed admirable flexibility in responding to unexpected conditions. D'Este's work remains indispensable to any study of Normandy.[12]

This interpretative difference is much more than an esoteric debate, because it affected the conduct of the Normandy campaign and the lives and deaths of a great many soldiers. The German achievement in confining the Allies to a narrow bridgehead following their extraordinarily successful air and sea assaults on 6 June produced a two-month stalemate that led minds to contemplate, however reluctantly, Gallipoli or the attritional trench ordeal of 1914–18. It was a long march to Berlin, and doubts arose that it would ever begin as Canadians, British, and Americans advanced the front only slowly and incrementally, taking heavy casualties all the while. The Americans cut the base of the Cotentin Peninsula and besieged Cherbourg, but were hemmed in by effective German resistance in difficult bocage country: small fields rimmed by hedges and sunken roads that had to be cleared one by one at great cost.[13] Canadians and Britons had to negotiate several kilometres of wide open terrain before they could reach the main German positions on commanding ground. All the while, German observers directed devastating artillery and mortar fire on any movement below. Not until the middle of July were Canadian and British units able to secure Caen, which had been a prime D-Day objective. The price of getting there was brutal, wearing out scarce troops and raising serious doubts about Montgomery's capacity to break the stalemate.[14]

Failing to secure the vital terrain around Caen, Montgomery then developed his plan to attract and keep German panzers on the British/Canadian front in order to allow the Americans to break through the German defences at the base of the Cotentin and get into Brittany. This is what he later said he intended with Operation Goodwood, the attack by three British armoured divisions east of the Orne on 18 July. Unfortunately his explanations to General Eisenhower at the time implied that he meant Goodwood to achieve a decisive breakthrough. When it stalled, a serious gap widened between Montgomery's words and his deeds, raising doubts about his competence and leaving a corrosive legacy of unfulfilled expectations.

Montgomery's neck came under a sharp axe. The American secretary of war, Henry L. Stimson, visited Normandy in July and became as irritated as his chief of staff, General George C. Marshall, at the lack of progress. Marshall urged Eisenhower to stop deferring to Montgomery and to take more active control of operations. They were feeling pressure from the American press, which was comparing casualties and asserting a disparity of sacrifice: alleging that Americans were dying while Britons and Canadians loafed. Prime Minister Churchill berated his chief of the Imperial General Staff, General Brooke, about Montgomery's apparent cautiousness and became more upset when Montgomery tried to prevent him from visiting Normandy. Air Marshal Sir Arthur Tedder, Eisenhower's deputy, who was especially bitter because Montgomery had failed to deliver the airfield space on the Caen-Falaise plateau that the air force needed to project its air power, urged Eisenhower to sack him. Churchill apparently considered doing so but was dissuaded by Brooke.

The result was enormous pressure on Montgomery, both to keep German tanks in the east and to deflect American criticism. Eisenhower flew to Normandy on 20 July and strongly urged Montgomery then and in a confirmatory letter the next day to keep attacking in the eastern sector in order to keep the German armoured divisions on their front. This doomed the Canadians and British to an endless series of seemingly fruitless holding operations, the least desirable of military options. It was from this murky source that Operation Spring bubbled.

As pressure on him increased, Montgomery naturally passed it down the chain of command and eventually to fighting soldiers, including Canadians. The Canadians in the bridgehead in early July, when this high-level drama was being played out behind and beyond them, were a mixed lot. D-Day assault units, the 3rd Canadian Infantry Division and the 2nd Armoured Brigade, were still in the line, both having been bloodied further in battles for Carpiquet airport and Caen in early July. They had learned much in the operational training school of Normandy, but, inevitably, had paid a price. Major General Rod Keller, commander of 3rd Division, was showing overt signs of stress, and increasing rates of battle exhaustion suggested that some soldiers were approaching a stage of burn out. The old-timers were then joined in the bridgehead by General Charles Foulkes's inexperienced 2nd Division and II Canadian Corps, commanded by Lieutenant General Guy Simonds. A combination of operationally worn-out and operationally inexperienced soldiers, a situation not unique in Normandy to Canadians, produced conditions that were hardly ideal for introducing a new corps to battle.

II Corps' first action on 18 July, to pinch out the city of Caen, marked the end of one protracted phase of fighting and the beginning of another still tougher one: to advance the thirty-five kilometres to Falaise. First they had to climb Verrières Ridge. The ridge itself is not of great height, but it is tactically significant because it controls all the bare approaches to it. On its eastern end the ridge is cut by Route Nationale 158 running from Caen to Falaise. On the western side is the valley of the Orne River, with the interconnected villages of St-André, St-Martin, and May-sur-Orne. West of the river the ground rises once more; local legend holds that "he who holds Hill 112 holds Normandy,"[15] a point British and German units had been demonstrating in the severest fighting for several weeks. Running along the forward crest of the ridgeline is a lateral east-west road connecting St-Martin–Beauvoir and Troteval Farms–Bourguébus–Tilly-la-Campagne. On the reverse slope behind the crest of the ridge are the towns of Fontenay-le-Marmion, Verrières, and Rocquancourt, which the Germans turned into fortified strongpoints.

The Germans considered the sector the key to their Normandy defences, the open plateau behind it being the best terrain on which they could concentrate their tanks for a counter-offensive to eliminate the bridgehead. Conversely, an Allied breakthrough there would force the Germans to withdraw to the Seine. While the Germans had been able to stop the British armoured divisions that attacked in Goodwood at the base of the ridge, the threat of massed tanks there caused them to reinforce their defences facing the Canadians with five armoured divisions and elements of two others. As was their practice, the Germans deployed in several defensive lines in depth. They strung their outposts along Verrières Ridge, giving them the task of delaying and blunting attacks that a second, stronger line in the fortified towns beyond would absorb. Further behind were mobile armoured reserves ready to counter-attack any threat immediately. The benefits the Germans had from favourable terrain and from time to entrench themselves were enhanced by other factors. Weapons technology gave a distinct advantage to defence over offence, especially in Normandy where German panzers and anti-tank guns outranged all but a few Allied tanks and enabled them to sit under cover on commanding high ground and pick off Shermans advancing through open wheat fields. Attackers, any attackers, were at serious risk.

This was the unenviable task facing the 2nd Canadian Corps in July 1944. Any assault on Verrières Ridge, however arranged by whomever, presented a most perplexing tactical challenge. Was an attack necessary? In Montgomery's maturing concept of operations, the bulk of German armoured forces had to be kept around Verrières Ridge while General Bradley prepared his breakout. General Eisenhower ordered continuous pressure, Montgomery agreed, and the unrelenting insistence to break the Normandy stalemate moved inexorably down the chain of command through Generals Simonds,

Keller, and Foulkes, to brigade and battalion commanders, and to the lieutenants, corporals, and riflemen who had to implement their tidy map plans. On 25 July Operation Spring tried to flow uphill against the strongest German armoured force in the west. That same day, the Americans began their epic breakthrough against light German tank forces.

It is impossible to describe any battle precisely and completely: too many physical and psychological realities intervene and each participant's war is an intensely personal experience.[16] Because it was so controversial, however, Spring's course has been traced more fully than most. The first attempts to document what happened were those of the historical officers attached to both 2nd and 3rd Divisions and II Corps Headquarters. They were part of a unique system of recording the Canadian Army's Second World War experience instituted by Colonel Charles Stacey. With varying degrees of success the historical officers followed closely behind the fighting troops, observing, collecting documents, supervising the compilation of unit war diaries, and interviewing officers and soldiers as soon after the fighting as possible.[17]

In his personal war diary, Captain Jack Martin reported the attempts by the North Nova Scotia Highlanders to take the village of Tilly-la-Campagne. On the way in at night they bypassed camouflaged German heavy weapons that destroyed their supporting tanks while entrenched panzer grenadiers in the village shot the infantrymen. Instead of helping them, artificial moonlight, created by bouncing searchlight beams off low clouds, apparently lit them up.[18] Captain Joe Engler had more to report on 2nd Division's attack. His remarkably accurate initial description, largely confirmed as more evidence materialized, told how the Royal Hamilton Light Infantry fought a skilful and spirited action in taking the village of Verrières, while elsewhere everything went wrong. The Royal Regiment of Canada was unable to get much beyond Verrières; the Cameron Highlanders of Canada, the Calgary Highlanders, and later Le Régiment de Maisonneuve were unable to secure the villages in the Orne valley that were the start line for the Black Watch's attack up the ridge; when the Black Watch's commanding officer was killed, his young successor paused to rearrange his attack and marched the battalion up Verrières Ridge to be annihilated; meanwhile, General Simonds decided not to commit his two reserve armoured divisions that had the task of exploiting any initial success into the Caen-Falaise plateau.[19]

Engler's and Martin's accounts, amplified in the narratives that followed, described the bare bones of what happened, but the scale of the debacle soon prompted questions that have reverberated through the years about how and why events took the course they did. What was Spring's purpose and intention? Was it effective and did it achieve anything? Who was responsible, especially for the Black Watch disaster that has become synonymous with Spring?[20]

Charles Stacey was the first to explore these and related questions at war's end in 1945 when, while preparing a booklet on the Normandy operations, he was made aware of General Simonds's sensitivity on the matter.[21] Shortly after, Stacey accepted an appointment as official army historian and immersed himself in Spring, laying out the documentary record that culminated in his *Victory Campaign*.

The first item to be clarified was Spring's purpose. While Stacey and his staff were still locating survivors to interview, some just released from prisoner-of-war camps, Montreal constituents of defence minister Douglas Abbott began pressing him for an explanation. Stacey prepared a draft paper that Abbott apparently did not release, but it prompted Simonds to write his own account of the operation.[22] According to Simonds, Spring was a holding operation for limited objectives designed to conform with Montgomery's plan of holding German tanks in place while the Americans broke out of their western end of the bridgehead.[23] Unfortunately, he explained, "of all the operations of the war, the 'holding attack' is that least understood by the layman for casualties seem to be out of all proportion to apparent gains."[24] General Foulkes, 2nd Division's commander, disagreed with Simonds, telling Stacey that Spring was meant to achieve more, that it was the first phase of a large-scale operation intended to break out onto the Falaise plain, and, he added later, that he doubted Simonds's intention had been a holding attack: "I doubt this very much. Certainly if he did know he did not disclose this to his subordinates and he was in a violent rage when General Dempsey called off the battle on the evening of 25 July."[25]

These two perspectives have found their way into most later studies, with different authors choosing to emphasize one or the other explanation. For reasons of morale it is unlikely that Simonds would inform Foulkes he was committing soldiers to die for no evident greater purpose, but Simonds's plan strongly suggests he had more in mind than simply holding German tanks in place. A key part of his plan foresaw two British armoured divisions under his command exploiting towards Falaise, and when Stacey interviewed Simonds further in the spring of 1946 his notes record Simonds saying, "The corps plan actually legislated both for success and the lack of it."[26] Because the historical evidence will sustain either argument, any interpretation depends on the observer's predelictions; one view emphasizes the plan's flexibility to exploit opportunity should it arise;

the other deplores the plan's fuzziness and lack of clear intent. Spring, it seems, was to be a breakthrough if possible, but possibly not a breakthrough.

Simonds and Foulkes also disagreed over what went wrong with the operation that caused so many casualties for such little gain. Simonds, as unfortunately he was wont to do, decided that Spring's failure was not the result of any fault in his plan but of units that failed to implement it properly. "That we suffered what were, in my opinion, excessive casualties," he wrote, "was due to a series of mistakes and errors of judgement in minor tactics ... Such heavy losses were not inherent in the plan nor in its intended execution. The action of the Black Watch was most gallant but was tactically unsound in its detailed execution."[27] Foulkes, in contrast, attributed failure to his division's inexperience. "When we bumped into battle-experienced German troops we were no match for them," he reflected; "it took about two months to get that Division so shaken down that we were really a machine that could fight."[28] Putting the best face on it, Simonds claimed partial success, because Spring gave him a foothold on Verrières Ridge that was a springboard for later operations. Foulkes seems to have concluded that the operation had achieved little, if anything at all.

Simonds's and Foulkes's views were doubtless coloured by their personal and professional rivalry. At the end of the war their respective positions as superior and subordinate were reversed when Foulkes was appointed chief of the General Staff, while Simonds's career was left in limbo for a time.[29] If the major actors in the battle were not entirely sure of their purpose, however, or of the reasons for the operation's many reverses, it is little wonder that historians ever since have had ample scope to emphasize different parts selectively.

As official army historian, C.P. Stacey trod a tortuous path through the evidential minefield in preparing The Victory Campaign, especially while the major actors, differing among themselves, remained in authority as Stacey's military superiors. That he produced such a balanced and judicious account, openly weighing for readers the sometimes contradictory evidence on which he based his judgments, was a remarkable achievement, even if one may disagree with some of his conclusions.[30] Stacey persuasively documents the holding-attack argument, accepting that Spring was a necessary part of a grand overall plan, a tactical sacrifice to achieve a greater operational end. Spring achieved its purpose, he concluded, because it diverted the Germans for two vital days from acknowledging the significance of General Bradley's breakout offensive, Operation Cobra. The Canadian operation, he observes:

was merely the last and not the least costly incident of the long "holding attack" which the British and Canadian forces had conducted in accordance with Montgomery's plan to create the opportunity for a decisive blow on the opposite flank of the bridgehead. There had been an urgent strategical need for it; and the urgency was strongly underlined in the Supreme Commander's communications to Montgomery. The opportunity had now been amply created, and the American columns, rolling southward from St. Lo, were grasping it to the full.[31]

Stacey's conclusions, which lasted for a generation, were accepted for the most part in two books published around the fortieth anniversary of D-Day. Reginald Roy's excellent operational narrative, *1944: The Canadians in Normandy*,[32] is a valuable source that follows the course of the fighting from June to August in an honest, thorough manner and doesn't condemn. J.L. Granatstein and Desmond Morton's attractive account, *Bloody Victory*,[33] is upbeat and celebratory. Like Roy, they describe what occurred rather than how and why. In contrast, Terry Copp and Robert Vogel's *Maple Leaf Route: Caen* and *Falaise*, is more judgmental. They reckon that, more than a mere holding attack, Spring was meant to be "a new breakout battle on the eastern flank of the bridgehead," that corps and divisional headquarters quickly lost control of its conduct, and that both headquarters remained "out of touch with reality" throughout.[34]

More recently, four books have re-examined Spring and its context in the Normandy campaign: Terry Copp, *The Brigade: The Fifth Canadian Infantry Brigade, 1939–1945*; Dominick Graham, *The Price of Command: A Biography of General Guy Simonds*; J.L. Granatstein, *The Generals: The Canadian Army's Senior Commanders in the Second World War*; and John A. English, *The Canadian Army and the Normandy Campaign: A Study of Failure in High Command*.[35] These new works examine several areas in depth through additional printed sources and interviews with participants, yet their conclusions regarding Spring's purpose, conduct, and results follow those of their predecessors. Graham and English are entirely approving of Simonds's explanation of events. On Spring's purpose, English deflects the holding-attack–breakout question, remarking enigmatically that "too much has always been made of whether or not 'SPRING' was a holding attack."[36] Graham observes that "a holding operation, which SPRING was without any doubt, is thankless, for there is no compensatory gain in territory. However the pill was sugared by SPRING being represented as a holding operation with a thin chance of [going further]."[37] Copp expands on his earlier view that the matter was not so clear cut. He acknowledges a Montgomery directive ordering that "the Germans must be induced to build up strength east of the Orne so our affairs on the western flank can proceed with greater speed," but quotes a later one indicating that Montgomery changed his plans and told Eisenhower he was not going to "hold back or wait" for the breakout to begin in the west.[38] It is revealing that none of these exhaustive studies has conclusively clarified either Spring's purpose or its results. Graham declares it successful as a holding operation that was stopped when it achieved its aim. English doesn't comment directly. Copp observes that Simonds rationalized Spring as having achieved its primary purpose, and concludes it was a "successful military operation" to the extent that it distracted and inflicted casualties on the Germans, especially when they exposed their panzers to Canadian anti-tank guns during counter-attacks on 26–27 July.[39]

Copp notes that the Germans do not seem to have taken Spring very seriously. After Goodwood they estimated that Montgomery had massed about 1000 tanks around Caen for another massive assault, and consequently packed the sector defences with seven of their nine panzer divisions. Expecting a powerful tank assault, they took "the view that the attack begun this morning ... [that is, Spring] is not the anticipated major attack, as in the first place the enemy air arm has not yet appeared in sizeable dimensions."[40] Ironically, it was the threat of an attack in the Canadian sector, rather than the attack itself, that achieved Montgomery's operational aim of keeping German tanks away from the American front.

The third question is equally complex: Who or what was responsible for Spring's failure? No convenient scapegoat stands out, although a brigade commander and two battalion commanders in Third Division were sacked and General Keller barely retained his job.[41] Simonds apparently said he wanted to replace Foulkes as 2nd Division's commander, but he did not do so.[42] Clearly, senior commanders placed the onus for failure on their subordinates. Writing as a sympathetic biographer, Graham absolves Simonds from almost all responsibility, placing it instead on "the detachment of divisional and brigade commanders from tactical reality." While critical because they "neither demanded, sought for themselves, nor received accurate and timely information on which to conduct their battles,"[43] Graham doesn't comment on the failure of Simonds's headquarters to make available the accurate information his subordinate commanders needed to fight their battles effectively.[44]

Copp is also critical of commanders, observing that, instead of commanding, Foulkes acted simply as a conduit through whom Simonds's detailed orders flowed downward to those who had to implement them. Having interviewed Brigadier William Megill, commander of 5 Brigade, Copp is not as disposed as others to lay most of the blame for the Black Watch debacle on him. Megill, he writes, was "appalled by the plan for 'SPRING' which seemed to have been prepared by someone who could not read a contour map and had never seen the ground," and he describes Megill's difficulties in trying unsuccessfully to persuade Foulkes of its inadequacies. Copp also quotes Megill's description of the impossible ambience in which he was operating, where "the Corps commander was pressing the divisional commander and he was pressing us to get on with an attack which we knew was almost hopeless. Under these circumstances one does not quit. You do as much as you possibly can and hope that someone will see the light and give you some relief." Copp reckons that Simonds's plan, which left his subordinates with "little latitude," was fundamentally flawed and overly rigid. It ignored actual conditions at the front as well as the Germans, and it failed because it was flawed "by poor operational intelligence, communication failures and the kind of mistakes that inexperienced troops were bound to make."[45]

Copp's interview with Megill sheds light on the difficulties inherent in trying to reconstruct the course of any battle in which each participant – tired, hungry, fearful, and stressed out – has a unique perspective on the same events. Major Phillip Griffin, a twenty-four-year-old company commander, assumed command of the Black Watch when Lieutenant Colonel Cantlie was killed around first light as the battalion was moving towards its start line before wheeling to climb the ridge. The unit was dispersed, daylight was removing their night cover, their scheduled artillery program was timed to begin, their start line had not been cleared of Germans, and they were under fire from several directions. Griffin sensibly decided to reorganize his companies and modify the timings of his fire plan. Out of communication with Griffin, Megill went forward to meet him on the verandah of a house in the village of St-Martin. Megill recalled many years later that he thought Griffin's plan was "a dicey proposition" but, because Griffin was calm and confident that it was sound, he declined to intervene.

It is exceedingly doubtful that we will ever know the precise content and tone of that fateful conversation. Megill may have simply accepted Griffin's view; he may have urged or insisted that Griffin go because his superior commanders were pressing him to hurry; or the two inexperienced battle commanders may have agreed they had a chance. Rather than pronounce a fatuous categorical judgment on that human dilemma, we would be better advised to consider its nuances and hope that none of us has to experience what these men faced that early morning.

As the subtitle of his book – *A Study of Failure in High Command* – suggests, English is the harshest critic of this and other Normandy operations, finding serious fault with almost everyone involved in Spring except, curiously, its responsible commander, General Simonds. Like Graham, he concludes that the "major responsibility for the disaster appears to lie at the divisional level of planning and execution." But English's analysis goes far beyond Spring to expose the flawed training system that underlay it and, ultimately, the basic inadequacies in prewar defence practices that deprived the army of a war-fighting capacity. His is the angry complaint of the professional regular officer against the historical reality of Canadian military affairs in any era: how to define an army's purpose, policies, and capacity to prepare for war in the face of public peacetime indifference. English's verdict is bitter: "Looking at Canadian Army performance in Normandy up to the end of July 1944, it would seem fair to say that the lives of many soldiers were unnecessarily cast away." Rejecting explanations of experience or "the myth of German fanaticism" to explain failures, he concludes that the "responsibility must rest with the high command."[46]

Was that failure inherent in the Canadian Army's condition during the Second World War? Granatstein's canvas in *The Generals* is broader than English's. He is less concerned with operational details than with higher political and diplomatic issues that often confine military options, and that professional soldiers prefer to ignore. He observes: "Nations get the politicians they deserve. That truism might also apply to generals." Consequently, he expects that there will be faults in command, and cites Theodore Ropp's quip that no one should be surprised that the tiny prewar army produced no military geniuses because "one might just as well try to sort out the real intellectuals among Canada's barbers or dentists." That observation applies, of course, not just to Canadian commanders but to those in all of the Allied armies in Normandy. Similar critical comments can and have been written about United States and British generals and the combat effectiveness of their armies.[47] All experienced serious command, doctrinal, and technological faults in Normandy and elsewhere during the Second World War.

It seems unlikely that much that is new can be written about the ill-fated Spring, unless startlingly new primary sources – letters, recollections, unearthed documents – unexpectedly materialize. Any review of the literature reveals a surprising reliance on the same fundamental data – albeit filtered through different minds, attitudes, and predilections – that Captains Joe Engler and Jack Martin began collecting on 26 July 1944. The story is virtually all there, in and between the lines of Stacey's measured *Victory Campaign*, as later accounts offer variations of its familiar themes with differing emphases.

How to explain Spring? The two self-evident reasons Spring ran off course were the terrain and the Germans. A small number of Canadians, from one new and one burnt-out division, were sent into an attack, exposed and uphill, against the strongest part of the German defences. As a tactical means to further a greater operational end it may have contributed something, but Verrières Ridge was a bloody classroom in which to teach combat's harsh lessons. Many factors worsened an already tenuous situation: information about the German defences was scanty and overoptimistic; the corps plan was inflexible; divisional commanders sent too few men against too strong objectives[48] and failed to inform themselves sufficiently of the actual conditions units faced on the ground; and infantry, tanks, and artillery actions were inadequately coordinated. Not for the first or last time a tactical operation was allowed to proceed after the premises on which it had been based had changed fundamentally. The results were predictable but not unusual. Disasters plagued all armies in the Second World War: in France, Holland, the Rhineland, and Italy. Canadians in the forgotten Italian campaign fought as part of a gigantic holding operation for much longer, and with equivalent cost. Unfortunately, that was the nature of the Second World War. Because of its inherent drama, and because its appalling costs were so highly concentrated in time and space, Spring will continue to interest coming generations, if for no other reason than it exposes so many fundamental questions about men in battle. Canadians, not just military buffs, should pay it heed, bearing in mind that it is the search for understanding, rather than any proclamation of illusory definitive answers, that truly informs the historical process.

Considering the range of human behaviour among soldiers caught up in combat poses other obstacles to understanding. For the most part, previously cited studies have been top-down, concerned with commanders and their tactics. Considerably less has been written about soldiers, individually or en masse. John Keegan applied his extraordinary historical and imaginative skills to reconstruct Agincourt, Waterloo, and the Somme in his justifiably celebrated *Face of Battle* but unfortunately, he did not extend them to the Second World War. Two estimable works, John Ellis's *Sharp End of War* and Richard Holmes's *Acts of War*, look thematically at the human face of battle, and several memoirs and novels have added valuable if idiosyncratic elements to enlarge our awareness of the singular conditions of the battlefield. But, as Paul Fussell asserts in *Wartime*, only a frontline fighter can ever know truly what combat is like, and it is impossible for him to describe it fully to anyone.[49] One young Canadian infantry officer, haunted by the deaths of his men, would have agreed: "No one has really been in the same places as anyone else; and I refuse to play the game of comparing experiences," he wrote. "The whole war seems to me a quite private experience; I mean for everyone. Each man talks about a quite different war from mine, and ultimately everyone is separated from everyone by layers of privacy and egoism."[50]

While we can extrapolate from these general studies of men in battle over the centuries, we know even less, specifically, about the battlefield behaviour of Canadian soldiers. A few memoirs and novels are indispensable, but, like all anecdotal evidence, they are difficult to generalize. Terry Copp and Bill McAndrew, in *Battle Exhaustion*, attempt to isolate one manifestation of soldiers' reaction to the extreme stress of combat and suggest that psychological dysfunction was just one of many behaviours, some arbitrarily classified as medical, others as disciplinary.[51]

As much as commanders preferred to avoid these complex behavioural questions, the protracted Normandy fighting did not allow it. At Verrières Ridge, unit incidence of battle exhaustion rocketed upwards from about 10 per cent of physical casualties to 30 per cent and more. Two classic patterns were evident: 2nd Division soldiers, new to battle, who lost their self-control from battle fright in the unanticipated chaos of combat, and 3rd Division troops who were burnt-out from overexposure to intolerable stress. Because this incidence challenged strongly held attitudes about proper soldierly behaviour, commanders and doctors alike found it exceedingly difficult to determine if these strung-out soldiers were genuinely ill or were malingering cowards; whether their reaction to combat was normal or aberrant. A soldier could be effective one day and incapable the next. Motivation and morale could fluctuate daily as a result of battle stress or personal distress, and the line distinguishing medical from disciplinary diagnoses wandered maddeningly. Commanders, reluctantly taking advice from psychiatric advisers who were themselves unsure of the etiology or proper treatment for such cases, and faced with a looming shortage of combat infantrymen who took more than 75 per cent of the casualties, felt obliged to apply a disciplinary tourniquet to stem the manpower bleeding. With the death penalty unavailable as a deterrent, sentences of imprisonment for three to five years were awarded instead.[52] At the same time, Canadian commanders acknowledged that some psychological casualties would not be able to return to combat, and they established special units which employed them on constructive labouring tasks behind the front.

The treatment of prisoners of war prompted behaviour even more difficult to comprehend, both for those directly involved and for historians trying to reconstruct events. To be blunt, is mistreatment of prisoners a normal and expected part of war? Reports of murder began circulating within 3rd Canadian Infantry Division, and among Germans, immediately after D-Day, each side accusing the other of having begun a tragic and stupid slide to infamy by taking no prisoners. Canadians soon had a documented case, when several months after the battlefield had moved beyond Normandy to Holland, the French owners of the Abbaye Ardenne, situated on Caen's northern outskirts, discovered the remains of several Canadian soldiers buried in their garden. More bodies were unearthed a few kilometres west around the Château d'Ardrieu. A high-level Court of Inquiry, employing forensic advisers, investigated and concluded that 134 Canadian soldiers had been murdered while in captivity between 7 and 17 June 1944 by soldiers in the 12th SS Panzer Division. Some had died from close-range gunshot wounds, others from multiple bullet wounds, still others from blows to the head.[53] Charges of war crimes were raised against the commanders of the two panzer grenadier regiments whose troops had occupied the murder sites at the time, Colonels Kurt Meyer and Wilhelm Mohnke, and four others. Meyer was apprehended, tried, and sentenced to death for having been responsible for the actions of his soldiers at the Abbaye Ardenne. His sentence was commuted to life imprisonment and he served several years in Dorchester penitentiary before being returned to Germany. The others were not tried. Mohnke was captured in Berlin in 1945 and imprisoned in the Soviet Union for several years before being repatriated to Germany. Periodically the question of his culpability has been raised, but to date no further action against him has been taken.[54]

There is a qualitative distinction between shooting an enemy in the immediate aftermath of fighting and the deliberate execution of one in captivity. Did Canadian soldiers also shoot prisoners? Unlike the meticulously documented cases of gross German misbehaviour, allegations of Canadian misdeeds are entirely anecdotal, and this presents clear problems of evidence for both jurists and historians. In his trial, for instance, Meyer testified about having found the bodies of several German soldiers in circumstances that suggested they had been shot while captives.[55] Several accounts tell stories, based on interviews with veterans, of Allied soldiers shooting prisoners. When he commuted Meyer's death sentence, Major General Chris Vokes claims he told his superiors that he and most other Canadian commanders would be equally culpable if they were held responsible for the misdeeds of their soldiers. Tony Foster, in *Meeting of Generals*, cites his father, Major General Harry Foster, president of the court that sentenced Meyer, as having similar views.[56] One private soldier recalled many years later that the stress of combat affected all types of behaviour:

To borrow from Farley Mowat's nice term, "the worm of fear" ate at all of us at varying speeds. As the worm feasted on one's courage, the booze consumption increased in late summer and beyond. Even properly controlled, I doubt if the booze consumption did more than extend one's time in the front line by more than a few days or a few weeks. Beyond that we became [a battle exhaustion casualty]. Another byproduct was the shooting of German prisoners and wounded Germans that summer.[57]

For historical and judicial purposes, however, it is extremely difficult, if at all possible, to pursue these allegations beyond the anecdotal.[58] Two comments apply. The first, which may be self-evident to Vietnam and Bosnian generations, is that mistreating prisoners – or bombing hospitals, killing civilians, rape and looting – is part of the brutalization of war, any war, and it would be naïve to expect that no Canadian soldiers ever mistreated prisoners. If no one had, this army would have been unique.

The second comment is that anecdotal observations often suggest that behaviour varied widely among units; that the command climate – some tolerating, others prohibiting mistreatment – was possibly the key determining factor. A Normandy veteran recalled that "when we faced the murderous psychopaths of the 12th SS (Hitler Jugend) ... we found out that they had murdered some of our men who had been taken prisoner, [and] we never thereafter took an SS prisoner."[59] In contrast, a unit history recounts a more complex response. Three of its men were taken prisoner and shot in the back while being marched away, but one was just wounded and returned to his lines. "Many stories began to circulate through the regimental area about other reported cases of the shooting of prisoners in the back by the Germans and the troops were fighting mad over these outrages." That Sunday, the regimental padre held his first church service in Normandy.

Sensing the temper of the men his sermon was brief and to the point. With quiet sincerity he stated that although the enemy might shoot prisoners in the back, the Hussars must not seek revenge by doing likewise. Adding that he did not wish to be padre in a unit which did so he gave the sound advice that playing the game would, in the long run, bring fewer casualties. This church service considerably alleviated the tenseness within the Regiment.[60]

Who can say what tangible influence the padre's words had on individual attitudes and behaviour? Anyone probing further would be well advised to bear in mind one historian's thoughtful observation: "If it is the responsibility of the historian to record such unhappy events, it is perhaps better left to men of greater wisdom and deeper understanding of the human heart to interpret them."[61]

NOTES

1 N.C. Phillips, *Official History of New Zealand in the Second World War, 1939–45. Italy, I: The Sangro to Cassino* (Wellington: War History Branch, Department of Internal Affairs 1957), 353.

2 The best starting point in the literature is Colonel C.P. Stacey, *Official History of the Canadian Army in the Second World War, III: The Victory Campaign: The Operations in North-West Europe, 1944–1945* (Ottawa: Queen's Printer 1960).

3 The estimates were American, 127,000; British/Canadian/Polish in 21st Army Group, 83,000. Allied air forces lost another 17,000. Estimates of German losses were 200,000 killed and missing, and a similar number of prisoners of war.

4 Eric Larrabee, *Commander in Chief* (New York: Harper and Row 1987), 463–4.

5 Montgomery presented his views to a meeting of the Royal United Services Institute in October 1945: *Journal of the RUSI* (Nov. 1945). *Normandy to the Baltic* (London: Hutchinson 1947) was apparently prepared from Montgomery's official papers by Major General David Belchem, who headed his operations staff. It became the formal account on which, for several years, the military history entrance examination for the Canadian Army Staff College was based. In this author's experience, no interpretive variations or deviations were accepted. Belchem later wrote two books of his own that echoed the same theme: *All in the Day's March* (London: Collins 1978) and *Victory in Normandy* (London: Chatto and Windus 1981). See also the comprehensive account in Chester Wilmot, *The Struggle for Europe* (London: Collins 1952), which persuasively argues Montgomery's views, as does, but with more balance, Francis de Guingand's *Operation Victory* (London: Hodder and Stoughton 1947).

6 Montgomery, *Memoirs* (London: Collins 1958).

7 The race to determine which side would successfully concentrate sufficient forces to break the other was anything but assured. As one planner wryly

observed, Operation Overlord might easily have become Operation Overboard because "the number of divisions required to capture the number of ports required to maintain those divisions is always greater than the number of divisions those ports can maintain." Quoted in Roland G. Ruppenthal, "Logistic Planning for Overlord in Retrospect," *D-Day: The Normandy Campaign in Retrospect* (Lawrence: University Press of Kansas 1971), 88.

8 L.F. Ellis, *Victory in the West*, vols. I and II (London: HMSO 1962–68); Nigel Hamilton, *Monty: Master of the Battlefield, 1942–1944* (London: Hamish Hamilton 1983). See also the account by Eversley Belfield and H. Essame, *The Battle for Normandy* (London: B.T. Batsford 1965). A dispassionate analysis of Montgomery's generalship is Ronald Lewin, *Montgomery as Military Commander* (London: B.T. Batsford 1968).

9 Dwight D. Eisenhower, *Crusade in Europe* (London: Heinemann 1948); Omar N. Bradley, *A Soldier's Story* (New York: Henry Holt 1951). Bradley published a later memoir, with Clay Blair, as *A General's Story* (New York: Simon and Schuster 1983), which is much more critical of Montgomery than the first.

10 Forrest C. Pogue, *The Supreme Command: United States Army in World War II, The European Theatre of Operations* (Washington: Office of the Chief of Military History 1954); Russell Weigley, *Eisenhower's Lieutenants: The Campaign of France and Germany, 1944–1945* (Bloomington: Indiana University Press 1981). See also the memoir by Eisenhower's deputy commander, Lord Tedder, *With Prejudice* (London: Cassell 1966).

11 Richard Lamb, *Montgomery in Europe: Success or Failure?* (London: Buchan and Enright 1983); Max Hastings, *Overlord: D-Day and the Battle for Normandy* (London: Michael Joseph 1984); John Keegan, *Six Armies in Normandy* (New York: Viking 1982); Carlo D'Este, *Decision in Normandy: The Unwritten Story of Montgomery and the Allied Campaign* (London: Collins 1983).

12 A valuable dissection of the evolution of Montgomery's plans and actions is in Martin Blumenson, "Some Reflections on the Immediate Post-Assault Strategy," in *D-Day*, 201–18. Blumenson concludes that Montgomery had a master plan sufficiently general to allow him to adapt it to changing conditions, but that attracting German tanks to the Caen sector was incidental. He argues that the Germans would have concentrated them there in any case because of its communications network and because the terrain best allowed them to concentrate their armoured divisions for a massive counter-stroke: "The Germans massed their forces in that area, not because Montgomery drew them there but because they were trying to fulfil a purpose of their own. Traditional German military thought and doctrine stressed the attainment of victory by a decisive act rather than by strategy of gradual and cumulative attrition" (215). Explaining why Montgomery preferred to portray himself as rigid and inflexible is perhaps best left to a

psychiatrist, but some of the insights of Norman Dixon in *On the Psychology of Military Incompetence* (London: Jonathan Cape 1976) may apply.

13 See the official United States Army histories: Gordon A. Harrison, *Cross-Channel Attack* (Washington: GPO 1951), and Martin Blumenson, *Breakout and Pursuit* (Washington: GPO 1961).

14 It is generally agreed that the Allies held on primarily because of their overwhelming superiority in air power, naval gunfire support, and *matériel* abundance, as well as because Allied code-breakers effectively read German signals traffic. See, for example, John Ellis, *Brute Force* (London: Andre Deutsch 1990); Ralph Bennett, *Ultra in the West* (New York: Charles Scribner 1979); and F.H. Hinsley, *British Intelligence in the Second World War*, vol. 2 (London: HMSO 1981).

15 Quoted in Belfield and Essame, *The Battle for Normandy*, 82.

16 See W.J. McAndrew, "Recording the War," *Canadian Defence Quarterly* 18 (winter 1988): 43–50.

17 The Canadian recording system differed from that pioneered by S.L.A. Marshall for the United States Army and from the British system. The historical officers' reports and the war diaries were used as raw material for detailed historical narratives and as case studies in the army's training system.

18 On the artificial moonlight silhouetting the attacking infantrymen, see Will Bird, *No Retreating Footsteps: The Story of the North Nova Scotia Highlanders* (Kentville, NS: Kentville Publishing Company, nd). For reasons that remain obscure, General Keller decided to commit just one battalion in his initial attack, and the German positions were much too strong for so few troops.

19 See the reports in the war diary of No. 2 Historical Section, 25 and 26 July 1944. NA, RG 24, vol. 17, 506. Engler was killed in action in October 1944.

20 In his essay on historical inquiry, Clausewitz describes the several stages of research: to find out what happened; to relate cause with effect; and to extrapolate essential constants in military history that can usefully inform later generations of soldiers. He is careful to distinguish between idle criticism and critical analysis. See Karl von Clausewitz, *On War* (New York: Modern Library 1943). The historical narratives compiled during and immediately after the war by Stacey's staff represent the first phase, and his *Victory Campaign* the second. Historians and soldiers are still exploring the implications of the last stage.

21 When Stacey sent a draft of a paper on Canadian operations in Normandy to Simonds for comments, the latter complained "rather strongly about certain passages." See C.P. Stacey, *A Date with History: Memoirs of a Canadian Historian* (Toronto: Deneau 1983), 175.

22 Simonds elaborated in the spring of 1946 in an interview with Stacey. Copies in NA, RG 24, vol. 12, 745.

23 This is the same argument – a tactical sacrifice to achieve a greater opera-

tional end – that is frequently used to explain Dieppe, most recently in Denis and Sheleagh Whittaker, *Dieppe* (Toronto: McGraw-Hill Ryerson 1992).

24 Simonds memorandum, "Operation Spring," in NA, RG 24, vol. 12, 745, has been published in *Canadian Military History* 1 (fall 1992): 65–8.

25 Foulkes made this comment when he reviewed Stacey's draft of *The Victory Campaign*. D Hist 83/269.

26 Stacey, "Memorandum of Interview with Lieut-General G.G. Simonds, C.B., C.B.E., D.S.O., at Canadian Military Headquarters, 19 Mar 46," copy in NA, RG 24, vol. 12, 745.

27 Simonds, "Operation Spring." His inclination to blame units and soldiers for not implementing his faultless plans raises serious questions about command responsibility, suggesting that responsibility lies at the bottom, not the top. Rather than Selection and Maintenance of the Aim as the first principle of war, Simonds's response suggests that he preferred Selection and Maintenance of the Plan. The difference is fundamental and says much about the Canadian way of war.

28 Stacey, *The Victory Campaign*, 276.

29 See the accounts in Dominick Graham, *The Price of Command: A Biography of General Guy Simonds* (Toronto: Stoddart 1993), and J.L. Granatstein, *The Generals: The Canadian Army's Senior Commanders in the Second World War* (Toronto: Stoddart 1993).

30 For example, Stacey found the principal fault of the Canadian Army to be too many idle and ineffective regimental officers who did not take training seriously enough. This is a rare instance where he does not present persuasive evidence, and where he ignores the fact that senior officers bore the responsibility for training and supervising their regimental officers. Nor does his criticism acknowledge faults in the army's training and doctrinal system.

31 Stacey, *The Victory Campaign*, 195–6.

32 Reginald Roy, *1944: The Canadians in Normandy* (Toronto: Macmillan 1984). See also Roy, "Black Day for the Black Watch," *Canadian Defence Quarterly* (winter 1982/83). A useful and informative earlier account is Alexander McKee's *Caen: Anvil of Victory* (London: Souvenir Press 1964).

33 J.L. Granatstein and Desmond Morton, *Bloody Victory: Canadians and the D-Day Campaign 1944* (Toronto: Lester and Orpen Dennys 1984).

34 Terry Copp and Robert Vogel, *Maple Leaf Route: Caen* and *Maple Leaf Route: Falaise* (Alma, Ont.: Maple Leaf Route 1982, 1983).

35 Terry Copp, *The Brigade* (Stoney Creek, Ont.: Fortress Publications 1992); John A. English, *The Canadian Army and the Normandy Campaign: A Study of Failure in High Command* (New York: Praeger 1991).

36 English, *The Canadian Army*, 260.

37 Graham, *The Price of Command*, 146.

38 Copp, *The Brigade*, 66.

39 Ibid., 83–6. See the excellent article, which uses a range of German sources, by Roman Johann Jarymowycz, "Der Gegenangriff vor Verrières: German Counterattacks during Operation Spring: 25–26 July 1944," *Canadian Military History* (spring 1993): 75–89.

40 Quoted from German War Diaries in DHist, AHQ Report No 50, "The Campaign in North-West Europe: Information from German Sources."

41 These were Brigadier Ben Cunningham, commander of 9 Brigade; Lieutenant Colonel Charles Petch, whose North Nova Scotia Highlanders had been unable to take Tilly-la-Campagne; and Lieutenant Colonel G.H. Christiansen, who, with considerable moral courage, refused to commit his Stormont and Glengarry Highlanders in a futile daylight assault against Tilly after the North Novas' disaster. Christiansen lost his job but saved, not only his personal honour, but more important his battalion to fight again in more promising circumstances. Much of this and other information on personal relations among commanders was unavailable until the late 1980s, when previously closed papers of General H.D.G. Crerar were opened at the National Archives.

42 See Graham, *The Price of Command*, 146; and George Kitching, *Mud and Green Fields* (Vancouver: Battleline Books 1983).

43 Graham, *The Price of Command*, 143.

44 While understandable in an approved biography, Graham's double standard of judgment, one for Simonds and a quite different one for everyone else, gets in the way of dispassionate critical analysis.

45 Copp, *The Brigade*, 66–86.

46 English, *The Canadian Army*, 237–62. English does observe that Corps Headquarters might have coordinated their operations more effectively with British troops on their right, across the Orne.

47 See, for example, the illuminating comparative studies in Allan Millett and Williamson Murray, eds., *Military Effectiveness*, vol. 3: *The Second World War* (Boston: Allen and Unwin 1988). See also R.L. Brownlee and W.J. Mullin, *Changing an Army: An Oral History of General William E. DePuy, USA Retired* (Washington: US Center of Military History 1988). D'Este, in *Decision in Normandy*, and Hastings, in *Overlord*, present information that demonstrates similar training and tactical difficulties in the United States and British armies. See also the astute critical observations on combat performance by New Zealand brigadier James Hargest, "Notes on Normandy Landings," CAB 106/1060, copy in DHist.

48 Sending too few men against too strong an objective was a persistent theme cited by scores of officers evacuated to hospitals in Britain as having had an adverse affect on morale. Another was that rigid plans devised at higher command levels unduly restricted their flexibility and initiative. See the after-action questionnaires in NA, RG 24, vol. 10, 552. One German

officer commented that Canadians "were perhaps less calm and more enterprising and tougher than the soldiers from the mother-country. I had the impression that the individual Canadian was a brave child of nature, and that therefore his average combat efficiency was superior to that of the British city dweller. The lower command of the Canadians, also, was good. On the other hand the British leadership of larger units seemed superior to me." Quoted in DHist, AHQ Report No 50, 69.

49 John Keegan, *The Face of Battle: A Study of Agincourt, Waterloo and the Somme* (New York: Vintage Books 1977); John Ellis, *The Sharp End of War: The Fighting Man in World War II* (London: David and Charles 1980); Richard Holmes, *Acts of War: The Behaviour of Men in Battle* (New York: Free Press 1985); Paul Fussell, *Wartime: Understanding and Behavior in the Second World War* (New York: Oxford University Press 1989).

50 Donald Pearce, *Journal of a War: North-West Europe, 1944–1945* (Toronto: Macmillan 1965), 179.

51 The novels and memoirs include Donald Pearce, *Journal of a War* (Toronto: Macmillan 1965); C.M. Johnson, *Action with the Seaforths* (New York: 1954); Fred Cederberg, *The Long Road Home* (Toronto: General Publishing 1984); Colin McDougall, *Execution* (New York: St Martin's Press 1958); Farley Mowat, *And No Birds Sang* (Toronto: McClelland and Stewart 1979); see also Terry Copp and Bill McAndrew, *Battle Exhaustion: Soldiers and Psychiatrists in the Canadian Army, 1939–1945* (Montreal: McGill-Queen's University Press 1990). On memoirs and fiction, Thomas Hobbes is supposed to have observed that "imagination and memory are but one thing for which divers considerations hath divers names."

52 See Bill McAndrew, "The Soldier and the Battle," in David Charters, Marc Milner, and Brent Wilson, eds., *Military History and the Military Profession* (New York: Praeger 1992).

53 As well as a Court of Inquiry, the grisly discovery prompted soldier poetry:

> Destruction and atrocities
> Are kindred things of war,
> That makes us wonder if this world
> Is still worth fighting for.
> A world where murdering monsters
> Can stalk defenseless prey,
> As were our nineteen comrades
> Taken prisoners in the fray
> ... May God, too, judge the killers
> In trial by Bible truth,
> And the guilty will be sentenced –
> Eye for eye and tooth for tooth.

From James Pearson, "The Silent Martyrs," in Jane and Walter Morgan, eds., *Soldier Poetry of the Second World War* (Oakville: Mosaic Press 1990).

54 A member of the Court of Inquiry and later Canadian prosecutor of Meyer, Lieutenant Colonel B.J.S. McDonald wrote his account as *The Trial of Kurt Meyer* (Toronto: Clarke, Irwin 1954). A thorough and well-balanced treatment of the issues is in Craig W.H. Luther, *Blood and Honor: The History of the 12th SS Panzer Division, 'Hitler Youth,' 1943–1945* (San Jose: R. James Bender 1987). The 12th SS Division's operations officer wrote its official history as Hubert Meyer, *Kriegsgeschichte des 12. SS-Panzerdivision 'Hitlerjugend,'* 2 Bd. (Osnabruck: Munin Verlag GmbH 1982). An English translation is pending.

55 The "Record of Proceedings" of Meyer's trial are in DHist 159.95023 (D7).

56 Cornelius Ryan, *The Longest Day* (London: Simon & Schuster 1959); Alexander McKee, *Caen: The Anvil of Victory* (London: Souvenir Press 1964); Max Hastings, *Overlord* (London: Michael Joseph 1984); C. Vokes (with John P. MacLean), *Vokes: My Story* (Ottawa: Gallery Books, nd); Tony Foster, *Meeting of Generals* (Toronto: Methuen 1986).

57 Personal communication.

58 An excellent recent account of a complex and perplexing ethical incident at the end of the war is Chris Madsen, "Victims of Circumstance: The Execution of German Deserters by Surrendered German Troops under Canadian Control in Amsterdam, May 1945," in *Canadian Military History* (spring 1993): 93–113.

59 Personal communication.

60 *A History of the First Hussars Regiment* (np, nd), 76.

61 Luther, *Blood and Honor*, 185.

SCOT ROBERTSON

In the Shadow of Death
by Moonlight

EDITORS' INTRODUCTION

The central contention of the "Death by Moonlight" episode of *The Valour and the Horror* series was that the strategic bombing campaign against Germany during the Second World War was both immoral and ineffectual. Since many thousands of Canadians served as aircrew in Bomber Command of the Royal Air Force, either in RAF squadrons or in 6 (Canadian) Group of the command, it follows that these airmen were complicit in a monstrous crime against humanity and a purposeless one, since the bombing campaign brought mass murder and devastation but not victory. At the same time, some attempt is made by the writer-producers to provide a "cover story" for Canadian aircrew by asserting that they were deceived and betrayed by the politicians and air marshals, who exploited their patriotism and courage. It was small wonder that Canadian survivors of the bombing offensive objected angrily to being portrayed as either accomplices or dupes.

Many issues of historical accuracy arise from an examination of "Death by Moonlight," but at the heart of the question is the adoption of night area bombing by the RAF, its prosecution throughout the war by Air Marshal Sir Arthur Harris, the commander of Bomber Command, and its contribution (and that of the American bombing offensive) to Allied victory. Why did the RAF decide on night area bombing instead of "precision" raids? Why did the British government sanction a mode of warfare that would inevitably bring high civilian casualties, instead of pursuing some alternative strategy? Did the rules of war, as enunciated in the Hague Convention and other conventions of international law, forbid the bombing of enemy cities?

These are some of the questions Scot Robertson investigates in the following article, endeavouring to supply a series of contexts notably

absent from "Death by Moonlight." It is an extraordinary fact that, despite
the massive Canadian participation in the bombing offensive against
Germany and the extremely heavy casualties suffered, there has never
been any public discussion of the issues raised by the bombing campaign.
In this sense, it was of course legitimate for the authors of "Death by
Moonlight" to address these issues, but they were swiftly lost sight of in
the controversy that followed.

   Dr Robertson is a student of the strategic bombing campaign. His
thoughtful article contributes to our understanding of the issues surrounding it and to our knowledge of the considerable literature devoted to it. He
himself is preparing a book on the strategic bombing campaign for Praeger
Publishers of New York.

● ● ●

Nearly half a century after the bombings of German cities by the
combined forces of RAF Bomber Command and the US Army Air
Forces during the Second World War, a controversy rages as intense
as the fires that engulfed those cities. Questions regarding the legal
and moral nature of those attacks generate the debate – a debate that
has recently flared up in a very public fashion. The cause of public
controversy was, in one instance, the decision to erect a memorial to
Sir Arthur Harris, wartime commander-in-chief of Bomber Command,
at St Clement Danes Church in the Strand. On the one hand, mayors
of several German cities expressed dismay that a memorial could or
should be raised to the man whose actions they saw as responsible
for the death of untold thousands of German civilians. On the other
hand, there were numerous veterans of Bomber Command who felt
that this modest memorial was a long-overdue testament to the
bravery and courage of those who carried the war to Nazi Germany
at a time when little else was, or could be, attempted in the West.

   A second instance, this time in Canada, raised similar questions.
The spark on this occasion was the airing of the television documentary *The Valour and the Horror* and, in particular, the episode "Death
by Moonlight" that dealt with part of the air war. For a brief moment,
it appeared that a meaningful discussion would ensue on a question
that is still fraught with many complexities for historians. Unfortunately, discussion on substance was overwhelmed by a fierce and
seemingly unresolved dispute over the nature of the television
presentation. This is not the place to revisit that ongoing, bitter
dispute, except to say that television may not be the best medium for
exploring a subject so complex as the strategic bombing campaign
against Nazi Germany. The documentary, as far as it went, painted

a fairly accurate picture of a series of discrete events; however, it failed to concede that its treatment was partial and incomplete and that there were aspects that could not be given fair consideration within the time allotted to the producers. In any event, much of the subsequent discussion appeared to degenerate into a shrill exchange concerning freedom of the press.[1] To the historian, this is disappointing because there are so many aspects of the strategic bombing campaign that deserve fuller attention and more reflective treatment.

One of the difficulties that has plagued, and will no doubt continue to plague the efforts of historians is the fierce controversy regarding the strategic bombing campaign in Western Europe. David MacIsaac identified four principal themes that have driven this debate:

1 the ineffectiveness and inhumanity of RAF Bomber Command's avowed policy of area bombing directed against German civilian morale;
2 the long-delayed effectiveness of US precision bombing efforts;
3 the drift of the US attacks by early 1945 towards a bombing effort more clublike than swordlike; and
4 given that victory through air power alone proved unattainable in the prevailing circumstances, whether the immense material and human resources devoted to the bombing campaign might have been better employed in other ways.[2]

The "Death by Moonlight" episode of *The Valour and the Horror* series attempted to address the first and fourth of MacIsaac's themes – the matters of effectiveness and the legal/moral aspects of the bomber offensive. In so far as the episode arrived at any meaningful con- clusions, it would appear that the producers held that Bomber Command's offensive was both immoral and of questionable legality, and that there were perhaps better ways to employ the vast material and human resources devoted to the strategic offensive. Neither of these conclusions is startling; each has been made before in the historical literature. In fact, the debate of these two themes has been one of the constants in the historiography of the strategic bombing campaign in general and of Bomber Command in particular. Unfortunately, "Death by Moonlight" failed to concede that the debate is still ongoing, that the available evidence permits other conclusions than those presented, and, perhaps of greatest concern, that the bombing offensive was not carried out in a vacuum. This article will offer an alternative perspective to the themes raised in "Death by Moonlight."

HISTORIOGRAPHY OF THE BOMBING CAMPAIGN

As with most debates on momentous issues, there is enough evidence
to sustain several arguments. What is distressing in this case is how
rarely the debate reached beyond the emotional level and sought to
understand the underlying causes. In the case of the bomber offensive
against Germany, this is more than a little surprising, given the
attention it has received over the past half century. Noble Frankland,
a British historian of the air war, observed that most people have
preferred to feel rather than know about strategic bombing; our own
debate squares with his judgment.[3] Not that the emotional aspects of
the bombing offensive are not powerful in the extreme: the horrific
effects of area bombing on German civilians and the extraordinary
courage and stoicism of Bomber Command aircrews are cases in
point. But why was such devastation visited upon civilians, and why
were crews asked for such sacrifices? In sum, why did Bomber
Command carry out its campaign as it did – a question never really
addressed by The Valour and the Horror.

Robin Higham aptly characterized the story of the Royal Air Force
(and perhaps by extension the RCAF) in the Second World War as "a
multi-faceted diamond of which only perhaps two or three faces have
been polished."[4] Perhaps the brightest face is John Terraine's
magisterial book, A Time for Courage, which will set the standard for
many years to come.[5] Richard Ovary's The Air War, 1939–1945 is
perhaps the best single synthesis of the air war viewed from the
perspective of each of the major combatant nations.[6] The Bomber
Command War Diaries: An Operational Reference Book, 1939–1945 by
Martin Middlebrook and Chris Everitt is an invaluable reference work
for historians.[7] It provides a detailed account of Bomber Command
operations for each and every day of the war. Although it cannot
supplant archival research, it is certainly a welcome addition to the
literature, particularly for those unable to make frequent and regular
use of British archives.

Despite this material, the historiography of air power during the
Second World War remains relatively underdeveloped. It still tends
to be a field dominated by squadron or group histories, personal
reminiscences and diaries, operational accounts of particular battles,
or detailed works on individual aircraft or other technology that
contributed to the air war.[8] In their historiographical essay, Stephen
Harris and Brereton Greenhous wrote: "A long-standing difficulty in
air history is that most air historians also have been air protagonists,
not inclined to tarnish the image various air forces have so carefully
cultivated to strengthen their credibility as independent entities."[9]

While this was indeed the case up to 1984, things have begun to change. Perhaps this is a sign that air power as a field of historical inquiry is coming of age. More and more, historians are subjecting the air war to critical scrutiny and integrating discussions of it into the larger question of the overall war effort. Terraine's book is an example of this emerging trend. So too is MacIsaac's essay, "Voices from the Central Blue: The Air Power Theorists."[10] An extremely valuable addition to the literature is a volume edited by Horst Boog containing the papers given at an international symposium hosted by the Militargeschichtliches Forschungsamt in Freiburg, Germany, in 1988.[11] Interestingly, and perhaps ironically, this renaissance in air history has flourished most in the United States. Michael S. Sherry's *The Rise of American Air Power: The Creation of Armageddon*, Conrad C. Crane's *Bombs, Cities and Civilians*, and Alan J. Levine's *The Strategic Bombing of Germany, 1940–1945* are but a few of the more notable works that have appeared recently.[12]

THE DEVELOPMENT OF AIR POWER AND THE WAR AGAINST GERMANY

The earliest identified example of modern air war can be traced back to the late eighteenth century, when hot air balloons were used to provide observation platforms, mainly for artillery spotting. The mid-nineteenth century bore witness to the first use of the aircraft to deliver ordnance against ground targets when, in 1849, Austrian forces launched unmanned bomb-carrying balloons at Venice. By 1908 Germany developed the means to deliver bombs with some measure of accuracy from dirigibles (rigid air ships) capable of carrying a load of bombs over considerable distance and to manoeuvre over the target area.

During the first year of the Great War, the appearance of German dirigibles over London caused a degree of panic in the streets. Indirectly, this led to the formation of the Royal Air Force in 1918. Even though the British were capable of mounting an effective area defence against the Zeppelin, it could be said that a threshold had been crossed. No longer was fighting limited to the front-line engagement. The Zeppelin attacks had demonstrated that the enemy nation could be put at risk. This new aspect of war was reinforced by the appearance of German fixed-wing bombers over London and Paris and the appearance of Royal Naval Air Service and, later, Royal Air Force bombers over major German cities.

The theory of strategic air power, therefore, had its roots in the First World War. Following the German campaign directed against the British homeland, calls for reprisals were heard from many circles in Britain. The pressure to carry the war well beyond the zone of fighting to the German homeland resulted in the creation of the Independent Air Force and the Royal Air Force. A principal mission of the RAF was to prosecute a strategic air campaign against Germany. This campaign was to include attacks against industrial and transportation targets and the seat of the German government. An underlying objective was to undermine the will of the German nation to continue the war – in other words, to break the morale of the people. It was hoped that, as a consequence, Germany would sue for peace.[13] In the event, the RAF's strategic offensive was relatively puny and fell far short of producing the desired end.[14]

Although limited payload and accuracy meant that the damage inflicted was relatively little compared with the investment, it became obvious that a new form of warfare had been inaugurated. Nowhere was this notion more alarming than in Britain. Unlike continental Europe, where, for centuries, both soldiers and civilians experienced the ravages of war, Britain had remained largely insulated by the English Channel. The advent of air war changed that, and dramatically so, forever altering the basis of British security policy. The notion that Britain was vulnerable, that it was no longer an "island," had a profound impact on the British. Barry Powers has written that "England's defensive security was lost with the development of the airplane and ... England existed thereafter in grave jeopardy. This fundamental shift in England from confidence to insecurity about its defensive position was of major consequence during the interwar years."[15] Such a viewpoint pervaded British society. Malcolm Smith has commented that "the idea of aerial bombardment was almost as haunting an aspect of contemporary culture as nuclear weaponry was to become later."[16] As Uri Bialer has so ably demonstrated, the bomber cast a long shadow – one might even say a pall – over British foreign and defence policy for much of the interwar period.[17]

Strategic air power was one consideration, if not the dominant one affecting the organization and equipping of the British armed services during the interwar period. Under the influence of Air Marshal Sir Hugh Trenchard, chief of the Air Staff from 1919 to 1929, the RAF succeeded in placing strategic air power at the centre of interwar British defence policy. It did so by convincing successive governments that air power would obviate the need to prepare an army for large-scale war on the Continent. This struck a receptive chord among politicians and public alike, both infused with the desire never again to engage in the slaughter brought on by stalemate. Trenchard and his disciples capitalized on this sentiment, arguing that air power could bypass an enemy force in being, strike directly at the sources of enemy power, and quickly break the will of the enemy to continue with a war. It apparently mattered little that Trenchard's and the RAF's claims lacked substance.[18] For politicians and the general public alike, it was sufficient to hold up the theory as one that would deter war, and if deterrence failed, win quickly. Either no one seemed alarmed at the prospect of a bombing match in which civilians would be the target, or it was accepted as a better alternative than a repeat of the trench stalemate of the Great War. Whatever the case, the RAF's theory stood, and its development throughout the interwar period drove it down a path towards the strategic bombing offensive carried out by Bomber Command during the Second World War.

In the last few years of peace, however, the RAF began to worry that it was ill-prepared to carry out its strategy. For a variety of reasons, many internal but some the result of Treasury parsimony, Bomber Command found itself with a force that its commander-in-chief, Air Marshal Sir Edgar Ludlow-Hewitt, deemed unable to take to the skies and prevail. Bomber Command lacked all manner of technical equipment to carry out its strategy in daylight. Moreover, a heavy bomber was still something Bomber Command did not have in its squadrons in sufficient numbers. Given these shortcomings, it is not surprising that on the eve of the Second World War, Britain adopted a "gloves on" approach. The bomber forces that had been built up during the last years of the interwar period were restricted, in the British case, to strikes on German naval targets and propaganda raids involving the dropping of leaflets. Yet even those restricted attacks by Bomber Command resulted in heavy casualties for the attacking force, as Max Hastings has described.[19]

On 4 September 1939, for instance, fourteen Wellingtons of Number 3 Group set out to attack German naval targets. The Wellingtons targeted the ships *Scharnhorst* and *Gneisenau* in the Elbe estuary, failing to score a single hit and losing two aircraft. On that same day, fifteen Blenheims of Number 2 Group targeted the *Admiral Scheer* at Schillig Roads, pressing home their attack at low level. Although four hits were recorded, none of the bombs exploded. The cost was five aircraft. Overall, the scorecard was bleak. Twenty-nine aircraft set out. Of those, seven were shot down, or 24.1 per cent. Such a casualty rate was very high. No military force can suffer casualties on the order of 25 per cent and hope to sustain operations for long.

Be that as it may, Bomber Command persisted. On 12 December 1939 twelve more Wellingtons from 3 Group again took off to attack the Schillig Roads. That time the raid "ended in tragedy, with the loss of half the force."[20] According to Hastings, those raids were "deliberately conceived as a means of testing Germany's defences and Bomber Command's tactics, rather than a serious assault on German sea power. There is no other way to explain the command's lack of concern about the failure of their aircraft to sink or damage a single enemy ship."[21] Despite the failures and the staggeringly high casualty rate, Bomber Command again threw itself into the breach on 18 December 1939. On that occasion, twenty-four Wellingtons took off to attack enemy warships in and around the Schillig Roads and Wilhelmshaven. Twelve survived!

In the case of Bomber Command it is possible to see – at least with the aid of hindsight – the seeds of later developments. If the theory so painstakingly developed by the Air Staff during the interwar years was victory through air power, then victory would have been very far off indeed. At the rate casualties were being sustained, Bomber Command would have been eviscerated in a short time, with little to show for its efforts. The cause of those alarming losses was an effective and largely unanticipated German defence. At low levels, where accuracy would have been better, German flak was murderous. At high levels, the fighter defences were equally devastating. The German defences were exacting a toll well in excess of Bomber Command's ability to replace its losses.

In view of this alarming turn of events, Bomber Command was forced to re-evaluate its approach. The elaborately crafted Western Air Plans, developed before the outbreak of war, were by and large abandoned.[22] Daylight strategic bombing had proven to be far beyond the capability of Bomber Command, forcing the Air Staff to cast about for alternatives. Yet the search for an alternative strategy – a complicated matter at best – was made more so in that it had to be carried out during wartime. While this doctrinal re-evaluation was being conducted, the RAF was still required to contribute to the war, even though it was at that stage a "phoney war." During the Battle of France, the bombers of the Advanced Air Striking Force based in France were used tactically against the advancing German ground forces, to no great effect but with punishing losses. On several days, the loss rate was 50 per cent or more.

At the same time, the strategic forces of Bomber Command again attempted precision daylight attacks on naval targets. As in earlier raids, the results were depressing. In one attack directed against the *Scharnhorst*, five out of fifteen Halifaxes were lost. In another attack on merchant ships tied up in Rotterdam harbour, seven out of seventeen Blenheims failed to return. In Winston Churchill's view, "the losses in our bombers have been very heavy this month, and Bomber Command is not expanding as was hoped. While I greatly admire the bravery of the pilots, I do not want them pressed too hard."[23] As a result of the losses sustained, and the limited result obtained, Bomber Command was, in effect, pulled off the line. Daylight bombing was no longer to be considered an option. In the absence of larger, more powerful aircraft capable of incorporating greater defensive armaments and of a long-range escort fighter, there appeared to be no alternative but to shift to night-time bombing.[24]

As of the summer of 1940, Bomber Command was on the path to becoming a night-time force. This change of approach would eventually lead to the controversy surrounding area bombing. There is still room to dispute the precise catalyst of the area bombing campaign. While Bomber Command was forced to fly at night, the precipitating event almost certainly occurred during the Battle of Britain. As part of preparations for an invasion of Britain, the Luftwaffe began a direct attack on RAF airfields. The object was to achieve air supremacy over the English Channel, a prerequisite for the invasion itself. RAF Fighter Command forced the Luftwaffe to shift to night-time attacks. Eventually, the Luftwaffe switched to attacks on London itself. Churchill then ordered a retaliatory raid. Hitler countered, and the gloves were off. Terraine wrote of this chain of events: "The Luftwaffe had well embarked upon another course of instruction of the British people and their leaders in the nature of total war [the Blitz]; anger and vengance for German bombing raids had become significant motives ... Air policy, Bomber Command policy, the whole course of the strategic offensive were drawn inexorably towards ... area bombing."[25]

Following the Battle of France, the evacuation from Dunkirk, and the Battle of Britain, there was only one means left to carry the war to Germany: Bomber Command. This is an important consideration that is all too easily overlooked when one takes a broad-based view of the war. At the time, there was little prospect of the British Army rebuilding itself to mount an invasion of Europe. Rather, the real issue that underlay most British and Commonwealth deliberations was whether a German invasion could be successfully forestalled. In that light, it became an absolute imperative for Bomber Command to "hold the ring."

The strategic offensive, as we have come to understand it, of large formation raids directed against the Nazi German homeland began in earnest only in July 1941 with a new directive to Bomber Command. It read:

I am directed to inform you that a comprehensive review of the enemy's present political, economic and military situation discloses that the weakest points in his armour lie in the morale of the civil population and in his inland transportation system. The wide expansion of his military activities is placing an ever-increasing strain on the German transportation system and there are many signs that our recent attacks on industrial towns are having great effect on the morale of the civil population.

... I am to request that you will direct the main effort of the bomber force, until further instructions, towards dislocating the German transportation system and to destroying the morale of the civil population as a whole, and of the industrial workers in particular.[26]

In part, this new directive made a virtue of necessity. Bomber Command had attempted to make an impression on German oil production in the preceding months, but to little effect. Bad weather had prevented a sustained offensive against the oil target complex, but in light of what is now known regarding the accuracy of Bomber Command it is unlikely that such an attack would have proven successful.[27] Hence, the directive included a target list of cities in the Ruhr industrial complex and cities along the Rhine. In addition to their importance as industrial and transportation centres, these cities were chosen because their location along the Ruhr and Rhine Rivers provided a distinctive marker for targeting. From that point on, Bomber Command would carry out an unrelenting attack on German cities, an attack that grew with intensity throughout the war.

Bomber Command's new approach was dictated by the lessons learned in the first two phases of its wartime experience. Daylight bombing in the opening months of the war would have decimated Bomber Command in short order had it continued. Night-time attacks against precise targets had proved to be beyond its capability. Thus, it had no alternative but to embark upon a course of area attacks, given that an area was virtually all Bomber Command could be assured of hitting. It was under Air Marshal Sir Arthur Harris, Air-Officer-Commanding, Bomber Command, from 22 February 1942 to the end of the war that the area campaign was prosecuted most vigorously. Harris, however, inherited a force already constrained in the courses of action open to it. Nor did he make the decision to pursue area bombing. That was a decision forced on Bomber Command by the dire circumstances facing it and by the overall British war effort. As Terrain has commented: "It [area bombing] was not [Harris's] brain-child, nor was it his sole responsibility. It was not even the sole responsibility of the Air Staff itself. It was the responsibility of the Chiefs of Staff Committee and later the Combined (British and American) Chiefs of Staff and of the British and American Governments, with, let it be said, the warm approval of the overwhelming majority of their peoples."[28] As Bomber Command grew in numbers and in experience, the weight of the attack began to wreak ever greater havoc on German cities.

The extent of the destruction of the German nation by Bomber Command is well known. By the time the war ended, Bomber Command had flown more than 300,000 sorties and dropped nearly one million tons of bombs. In doing so, almost 9000 Bomber Command aircraft were destroyed or damaged. In terms of aircrew casualties, approximately 60,000 were killed or wounded. To put that figure into perspective, of every one hundred aircrew, fifty would be killed or wounded during operations. A further twenty-six were either killed or wounded on non-operational flights or would be taken prisoner. Only twenty-four would make it through physically unscathed. Against this, the toll of German civilians stood at approximately 800,000 killed.[29] Of particular notoriety were several large raids that resulted in fire-storms. Cologne, Hamburg, and Dresden fell victim to raids of this type (as did numerous other cities), and serve as reminders of the destructive power of modern warfare. They provided the impetus for the moral and legal debate that surrounded the strategic bombing campaign, a debate that continues today. Additionally, doubts regarding the effectiveness of that campaign also emerged in the aftermath of the war. This debate turned on the question of whether the bombing campaign made a contribution to the larger war effort in any way proportional to the resources devoted to Bomber Command.

EFFECTIVENESS OF THE STRATEGIC BOMBING OFFENSIVE

Questions regarding the effectiveness of the strategic bombing offensive continue to bedevil historians. It is perhaps true to say that, apart from the question of morality, no other aspect of the air war has received more attention.[30] In fact, the issue of effectiveness was first raised during the war itself, and the debate over the contribution of the bomber offensive to the larger war effort continued throughout. The scope of this debate was conditioned, in part, by prewar claims that strategic bombing would be the decisive factor in any future war. Unfortunately, the notion of decisiveness eluded precise definition. Hence, it was not always possible to gauge the degree to which strategic bombing was making a meaningful contribution to the overall war effort. In attempting to grapple with this issue, Richard Ovary has neatly encapsulated this dilemma. He wrote: "The difficult question to answer is not whether air power was important, but how important it was. There can be no definite conclusion about how decisive air power was. There was too much inter-dependence between the services and between strategies to produce a list of components that were either more or less decisive ... The only conclusion that the evidence bears is the more negative conclusion that victory for either side could not have been gained without the exercise of air power."[31]

Another difficulty in dealing with the question of decisiveness stems from the fact that, after the entry of the United States into the war, the strategic bombing campaign became a Combined Bomber Offensive (CBO), with Bomber Command continuing its night-time offensive and the United States Army Air Forces (USAAF) and later the United States Strategic Air Forces (USSTAF) conducting daylight operations. It is often impossible to separate and attribute the effects of the bombing campaign to the RAF or the USAAF/USSTAF. Critics of Bomber Command's night-time area campaign have pointed to the United States' efforts to conduct a precision daylight campaign, arguing that the American approach was more likely to produce a decisive effect by knocking out key German industries, thereby undermining the flow of munitions to the German military forces. While there may be some intuitive appeal to that argument, it is difficult if not impossible to prove conclusively that this would have been the result. For instance, it could be argued that, had Bomber Command not continued with its night-time operations, the US daylight campaign would have been made much more difficult. As Malcolm Smith has noted: "The point is that success against a highly organized industrial structure, enjoying a great deal of spare capacity for most of the war, required not simply weight nor accuracy but continuity of attack, and continuity of attack on targets which were important enough to be, by definition, predictable to the defenders would be countered by a German fighter force which simply refused to be ignored."[32] Given Bomber Command's limitations, it could not have pursued a daylight strategic offensive without fighter escorts, something it lacked for the greater part of the war. Hence, to achieve continuity in the Combined Bombing Offensive, Bomber Command was compelled, at least in the eyes of the Air Staff, to continue with its night-time operations.

In an effort to assess the effectiveness of the Combined Bombing Offensive, American and British authorities each established bodies to conduct exhaustive investigations. The better-known and more comprehensive United States Strategic Bombing Survey (USSBS), and the British Bombing Survey Unit (BBSU) gathered data to assess the results of the strategic bombing campaign. Vast quantities of data were collected on virtually every aspect of the German war economy. The objective in each case was to gauge the effects of the bomber offensive on the German war effort. Despite the voluminous reports of the USSBS, and the much more restricted reports of the BBSU, no definitive conclusions regarding the overall effectiveness can be drawn. As a recent article by James Roche and Barry Watts demonstrates, assessment of effectiveness depends to a large degree on the analytical measures employed.[33]

Roche and Watts contrast the interpretations of two members of the USSBS, John Kenneth Galbraith, director of the Overall Economic Effects Division, and his deputy, Burton Klein, regarding the effectiveness of the Combined Bombing Offensive. Galbraith, a vigorous critic of the bombing campaign, argued "that the campaign's effectiveness [should] be judged exclusively on the basis of quantitative production indices for the output of the main types of finished armaments."[34] Using that analytic measure, the results of the Overall Economic Effects Division Report indicate that until very near the end of 1944, German production actually increased. Hence, Galbraith drew the conclusion that the Combined Bombing Offensive had little or no effect on the overall defeat of Germany.

In contrast to Galbraith's approach and conclusions stand those of his deputy, Burton Klein. Employing the same data, but a different analytical measure, Klein drew a markedly different conclusion. He utilized a finer analytic measure, designed to address second-order effects of the bombing campaign.[35] Klein's analysis demonstrates that the bombing campaign had a profound effect by diverting German economic resources and efforts into less productive areas, the first being the production of weapons equipment and aircraft to counter the bombing campaign. Klein's assessment, based on the same raw data as Galbraith's, was that the Combined Bombing Offensive forced the Germans to commit far greater resources to air defence measures than would otherwise have been the case. German production of air defence fighters rose from 35 per cent of total aircraft output in 1942 to 65 per cent in 1944. By June 1944 Klein's analysis reveals that the air defence (aircraft, anti-aircraft artillery, and ammunition) share of overall German armaments production was 33.1 per cent, a considerable increase over the course of the war. In Klein's view, this second order effect was of significant importance and can be attributed largely to the strategic bombing campaign.[36]

Roche and Watts illustrate the problems inherent in measuring the effectiveness of the bombing offensive. They wrote:

A balanced assessment of the CBO cannot be based on one or two course-grained quantitative measures. A wide-range of military as well as economic factors must be taken into account; indirect effects as well as direct; second-order as well as first-order consequences, must be included ... Did the strategic bombing of Germany obviate the need for the Western Allies to land their armies in Northern Europe? Obviously not ... Nevertheless, to argue that the bombing failed to impose disproportionately heavy "costs" on the German wartime economy in relation to resources the Allies devoted to the bombing is not, in our view, credible.[37]

In addition, Richard Ovary made a telling observation when he wrote: "The important consequence of the bombing was not that it failed to stem the increase in arms production, but that it prevented the increase from being very considerably greater than it was. Bombing placed a ceiling on German war production which was well below what Germany, with skilful and more urgent management of the resources, was capable of producing after 1943."[38] There is, moreover, documentary evidence from German archives that the Nazi authorities were aware that the night-time area bombing campaign was having an effect on the morale of the German population. Williamson Murray, writing on this question observed:

In 1943, the heavy bombing caused a dramatic fall in popular morale ... the attacks on Nuremberg, Munich, and Augsburg made the population restive, angry and bitter. The SD (*Sicherheitsdienst*, Secret Police) reports on what the population was saying (reports widely read in the highest level of Nazi leadership) noted that people no longer exchanged the Nazi salute, reviled the party as the author of their trouble, regarded Goebbels as an outright liar and cheat, wore party badges less and less, and were depressed and embittered at the course of the war.[39]

While this is by no means the last word on the question of the effectiveness of the strategic bombing campaign, it does at least put it into a perspective not evident in "Death by Moonlight."

LEGAL AND MORAL QUESTIONS

Before turning to the specific legal and moral considerations surrounding the strategic bombing campaign, a brief discussion of the general concepts of legality and morality as they relate to war is necessary. It is with considerable trepidation that any historian would dare to venture down such a well-trodden but still thorny path. Library shelves groan under the weight of learned treatises on the subject. Yet no matter how voluminous the literature, a satisfactory resolution remains an elusive aim. This stems, in part, from the fact that the subject – war – is ever changing. No war is the same as the last, at least in the eyes of the principals involved. It is, so to speak, a discrete event, in which the aims and objectives are unique. As such, it is possible for the principals involved to claim, rightly or wrongly, that this war is different, and hence falls outside the bounds of any legal regime established to govern the conduct of war in general. Moreover, organized warfare takes place in the realm of sovereign states, where no formal higher authority exists to impose sanction on transgressors. Hence, there is no recourse except that which is available to the victor in imposing a penalty on the vanquished.[40]

Library shelves also hold many treatises on the question of morality and war. It is perhaps only the dilemma of morality and war that exceeds the dilemma of legality and war in opaqueness and tortured logic. This was not always the case, however. During the era dominated by the principle of the divine right of kings, the matter was relatively simple. As the king derived authority from a higher deity, the king's edict carried the weight of that higher being. If the monarch chose to embark upon a course of war, it could only be at the behest of a god. By definition, therefore, the cause was right, the war was just, and hence its conduct moral. Where matters become slightly murky, however, concerns morality *in* the conduct of war, rather than simply the morality of war itself. A god, through an earthly voice – the monarch – may have sought war to further a cause, which was, by definition, just. What was left unclear, though, was the matter of how a war was to be conducted. Was there to be any restraint with respect to the form of fighting or the weapons to be employed?[41] At this point the seemingly separate considerations of legality and morality come together to further confuse the situation. The dilemma is neatly summed up by the following aphorism: "It is a philosophical commonplace that legality and morality are not the same. What is legal may be immoral, and what is moral may be illegal."[42]

Without a doubt the bombing campaign against Nazi Germany exacted a terrible toll in human suffering. During the war itself, there was a degree of protest, muted though it may have been, regarding the legality and morality of such a strategy. Individuals such as Bishop Bell of Chichester, Richard Stokes, and Vera Brittain spoke out against the strategic air offensive at the time. Following the war, there was a move on the part of many British wartime leaders to distance themselves from the grim reality of what Bomber Command had done – so much so that no Bomber Command campaign medal was struck. Some historians, too, have expressed a degree of revulsion at the nature of the strategic bombing campaign. Basil Liddell Hart wrote that the indiscriminate bombing of cities was "the most uncivilised method of warfare the world has known since the Mongol devastations."[43] Later, Geoffrey Best, the eminent scholar of the legal aspects of war, would condemn the practice of area bombing as "the only big blot on Britain's war record."[44] A.J.P. Taylor was moved to remark upon "the readiness, by the British people, to stop at nothing when waging war. Civilised constraints, all considerations of morality, were abandoned."[45]

Conversely, other historians have decried objections to strategic bombing as demonstrating wisdom after the fact, or as not recognizing the needs of the moment. One such claim is advanced by Noble Frankland, one of the authors of the official history. Frankland, himself a Bomber Command navigator, wrote of the moral dilemma:

I think it is between a man and his conscience. It does not trouble my conscience that we struck at the Germans as hard as we could in 1940 and 1941 and until they were beaten. As to whether this had any effect on subsequent policies, I think it would be difficult to sustain. In the interval between wars there are various theories of international legality and morality, but these will become acutely modified in accordance with the crisis which prevails. I think that the big moral question is whether you fight at all. If you will, I think one's proper duty is to win as quickly and cheaply as possible.[46]

Frankland's assertion is based, to a certain extent, upon Lord Kitchener's famous aphorism that "unfortunately we have to make war as we must, and not as we should like to."[47]

This, in essence, captures the dilemma that has coloured the debate over the legal and moral issues surrounding the strategic bombing campaign from the period immediately following the war down to the present. On the one side stand those who condemn it outright as a gross violation of all principles of human decency. On the other, there are those who argue that the cause – the defeat of Nazi Germany – was just, and that any means to that end were themselves justified. How, then, is one to judge the merits of either position? One possible means is to appeal to that body of code and custom known as the Laws of the Conduct of War.[48] The question to be answered is whether a strategic bombing campaign that involved either intentional or accidental area attacks on German cities and civilians could be deemed legitimate in a legal sense. In theory this approach might be expected to provide a clear black or white answer; however, any such answer will only be approximate, since at the time there was no code or treaty that explicitly dealt with air war. Unlike the 1907 Hague Rules that codified the practices of land and naval warfare – even if only imperfectly – aerial warfare was new and, as such, no formal convention governed its conduct. An attempt was made in 1923 to develop just such a set of rules, but in the end the Hague Draft Rules remained unratified.[49]

Given the absence of any explicit laws regarding aerial warfare, one is forced to extrapolate from the laws that did exist governing other forms of warfare, for, in some respects, they provide a means of coming to grips with the question of attacks on civilian targets. In the first instance, one can make reference to the body of convention and code dealing with land warfare, which explicitly prohibited the bombardment of undefended localities. Article 25 of the 1907 Hague Convention on Land War stated that "the attack or bombardment, by whatever means, of towns, villages, dwellings, or buildings which are undefended is prohibited."[50]

While Article 25 may seem quite unequivocal, it is, in reality, far from precise. The root difficulty lies in the interpretation of the word undefended. This may seem to be overly legalistic hair-splitting, but it does raise a basic problem. When is a town, village, dwelling, or building considered undefended? Is it defended only if a military unit or formation is in the town itself? Or is it considered defended if a military unit is merely in the vicinity? If the latter holds true, how proximate must the unit be for the town, village, dwelling, or building to be deemed a defended area? An example from the Great War illustrates just how difficult the problem can be. Taken to its extreme, one could have considered all of Germany to be a defended area, in that the German trench lines in the west extended from the Channel coast in the north, to the Swiss Alps in the south. Hence, every German town and village benefited from a defence. Therefore, from a strictly legal point of view, each German town could be considered defended and, by extension, a legitimate target for attack. In the context of the strategic bombing campaign of the Second World War, the problem of an undefended locality is even more vexatious. Following the Battle of France and the ejection of the British from the Continent, the whole of Europe became an armed fortress, defended, so to speak, by the fighters and anti-aircraft guns of the Luftwaffe. According to the rules of land warfare set out in the Hague Conventions, attacks by strategic air bombardment could be deemed legitimate.

The situation is similarly ambiguous when one refers to the laws of naval war for guidance. In this instance, the relevant treaties, texts, and conventions are contained in the Ninth Hague Convention of

1907. As with the Laws on Land Warfare, these naval rules contained a specific prohibition against the bombardment of undefended towns. Article 1 stated that "the bombardment by naval forces of unde-fended ports, towns, villages, dwellings, or buildings is prohibited."[51] Article 1 of the naval laws is virtually the same as Article 25 of the rules of land warfare. Yet subsequent articles, particularly Article 2, do much to diminish its force. Those articles outline a number of qualifications under which naval bombardment of an undefended locality might be termed legitimate.[52] Article 2 stated:

Military works, military or naval establishments, depots of arms or war materials, workshops or plant which could be utilized for the needs of a hostile fleet or army, and ships of war in the harbour, are not, however, included in this prohibition. The commander of a naval force may destroy them with artillery after a summons followed by a reasonable interval of time, if all other means are impossible, and when the local authorities have not themselves destroyed them within the time fixed.

He incurs no responsibility for any unavoidable damage which may be caused by a bombardment in such circumstances.

If, for military reasons, immediate action is necessary, and no delay can be allowed to the enemy, it is nevertheless understood that the prohibition to bombard the undefended town holds good, as in the case given in the first paragraph, and that the commander shall take all due measures in order that the town shall suffer as little harm as possible.[53]

According to a modern interpretation, Article 2 was designed to take account of a foreseeable problem: navies could not seize and hold territory. For that reason, the drafters gave navies the right to bombard targets of military significance in undefended towns, with or without warning, although this did not extend to the right of general bombardment.[54] The apparent intent of Article 2 was to give some measure of authority to a fleet standing off shore, or transiting through coastal waters. It foresaw that a fleet (or units thereof) could be placed in the invidious position of having to avoid attacking a target of military significance simply because it was located in an undefended town. That military target could, however, pose a serious risk to that fleet if it were left intact.

Article 2 therefore proposed a list of targets that would be considered legitimate. This list is not very precise and addresses the question of just where the line should be drawn. For example, it included "workshops or plant which could be utilized for the needs of a hostile fleet or army." Even at the time of its drafting, that clause left matters open to considerable interpretation and debate. In times of full-scale war, however, virtually every form of industrial plant and workshop might be viewed as being utilized for the needs of the navy, army, or air force. Moreover, Article 2 also stated that the commander bore no responsibility for unavoidable damage caused by such bombardment. The provision whereby navies could bombard targets of military significance in an undefended town raised another problem of ambiguity – that of military significance. This ambiguity would not, and perhaps could not be resolved, opening the way during the emerging era of total war to an expanded notion of what constituted a legitimate target. Within Article 2 it is not difficult to see how this problem arose.

When viewed against the Hague Naval Rules, the strategic area bombing campaign conducted by Bomber Command does not appear to have been an attack against illegitimate targets. As Sir Robert Saundby wrote:

It is generally agreed, for example, that the man who loads or fires a field-gun is a military target. So is the gun itself, and the ammunition dump. So is the truck driver who transports ammunition from the base to the dump ... [But] what about the weapons under construction in the factories, and the men who make them? ... [I]f they are not, where do you draw the line? If they are military targets, are not the industrial areas ... also military targets? Or is it permissible to starve these civilian workers by blockade, or shell them ... but not to bomb them ... ? This is surely a *reductio ad absurdum*.[55]

One may question whether it was proportional to target cities or areas, but, clearly, the body of law that existed at the time did not rule it out. One may also take umbrage with Saundby's characterization of the dilemma that confronted Bomber Command, but his reasoning is not open to serious challenge on either legal or logical grounds.

What, then, can be gained from an examination of the campaign from the point of view of its morality? As noted earlier, that which is legal may not always be moral, and that which is moral may not always be legal. The issue of morality in war is one fraught with many difficulties, not least of which is to establish an appropriate definition as a reasonable point of departure. In *The Concise Oxford English Dictionary*, morality is defined as "moral principles, points of ethics; particular system of morals; degree of conformity to moral principles; moral conduct; moralizing ..." What, then, are the moral principles and code of ethics that may be seen as governing conduct in war? This is a vast and largely open-ended question, for, like the laws of war, principles and ethics are subject to change over time. Of even greater difficulty is the fact that one is entering the realm of philosophical inquiry in which there are no absolutes. Given the potentially vast and amorphous nature of the body of philosophical literature devoted to the treatment of morality in war, it is essential to try to limit the scope of the inquiry. For present purposes, the emphasis will be restricted as far as possible to questions pertaining to the principles of *proportionality*.

It is a "fundamental principle implicit in the laws of war that gratuitous harm ought not to be inflicted."[56] Yet, it is difficult, if not impossible, to arrive at a meaningful and universally acceptable conception of this basic principle. If the laws of war permit, or rather do not rule out the killing of unarmed civilians in certain cases, then it is possible to see how the entire nation can be defined as a legitimate objective. Clearly, however, this is an *reductio ad absurdum*. It can also be viewed, from the military and political points of view, as counter-productive, potentially leading to total, unrestricted warfare, in which the objectives for a war become lost in its very conduct.[57] Hence, there may be every reason to restrict the scope of the definition of the enemy (or target).

The traditional means employed is to apply the principle of proportionality; in other words, it may be permissible to kill unarmed enemy civilians, although the extent to which this may be done should be, in some measure, proportional to the military gain to be achieved. This, however, begs the question of establishing some useful means of establishing the proportional relationship. As Cohen noted, "weighing the harm inflicted against the military gain is not a simple matter of counting heads ... [rather] the principle of proportionality requires us to ask whether the civilian casualties were justified by the military gain."[58]

How then, is one to balance the extent of civilian casualties against the notion of military gain? Is it possible to say that the military gain achieved by Bomber Command's area bombing campaign justified the casualties inflicted on the civilian population in Germany? Cohen admits that this is hard to determine. He makes reference to a claim by Albert Speer that:

Defense against air attacks required the production of thousands of anti-aircraft guns, the stockpiling of tremendous quantities of ammunition all over the country, and holding in readiness hundred of thousands of soldiers, who in addition had to stay in position by their guns, often totally inactive for months at a time.

As far as I can judge from the accounts I have read, no one has yet seen that this was the greatest lost battle on the German side. The losses from the retreats in Russia or from the surrender of Stalingrad were considerably less. Moreover, the nearly 20,000 anti-aircraft guns stationed in the homeland could almost have doubled the anti-tank defenses on the Eastern Front.[59]

Cohen goes on to argue that, since the bombing campaign also had an impact on the war-making potential of Germany through the destruction of manufacturing capability, oil production, and transportation infrastructure, this must constitute some military gain.

So, perhaps the civilian deaths were justified by proportionality. And that is probably enough to justify the bombing campaign. For if we can be unsure whether the civilian losses were justified by the military benefits, then the losses were not wildly out of proportion to the military gain. And how can we hold a belligerent accountable to a more stringent standard (for example, to proving beyond a shadow of a doubt) if the civilian casualties are largely a function of the enemy's defense of legitimate military targets – targets that, if they had been left alone, would undoubtedly have significantly increased the enemy's ability to wage war?[60]

Thus, it would appear that, using the test of proportionality, the area bombing campaign waged by Bomber Command was not immoral. Of course, this conclusion presupposes that the entire war can be viewed as just, although few would dispute that assertion. As Noble Frankland claimed before an audience at the Royal United Services Institute: "The great immorality open to us ... was to lose the war against Hitler's Germany. To have abandoned the only means of direct attack which we had at our disposal would have been a long step in that direction."[61]

CONCLUSIONS: SHADES OF GREY

This brief statement of both the legal and moral considerations that attend the historical debate surrounding Bomber Command's strategic offensive against Nazi Germany, and of the effectiveness question, has placed the debate in a larger context than that presented in "Death by Moonlight." When examined against the legal regimes in effect prior to and during the war, and the prevailing moral principles, the campaign conducted by Bomber Command was neither illegal nor immoral. While one may find oneself aghast at the results of the bombing campaign, this revulsion should not unduly influence the nature of historical inquiry. Moreover, while it may be understandable that some would seek to condemn the bomber offensive on the basis of the result, this can only be at the expense of developing an appreciation of how and why it was conducted in the manner it was. As Horst Boog has written, "it should be borne in mind that the task of historians is not to deliver verdicts, but to analyze and understand – which does not necessarily mean approve of – events as they occurred."[62] Apportioning blame or passing judgment, as "Death by Moonlight" appeared to do, is only incidental, seeking to render in black and white what can only be properly understood by exploring the shades of grey.

NOTES

An earlier version of this article was presented at the 72nd Annual Meeting of the Canadian Historical Association at Carleton University, Ottawa, 5–8 June 1993. I would like to acknowledge the comments of David Hall, Stephen Harris, Michael Hennessy, Lieutenant Command Colin Plows, Chris Tucker, and the editors, Syd Wise and David Bercuson. Mary-Gay Morrison gave freely of her time to improve my oft-times tortured prose. I alone, however, bear responsibility for the views presented.

1 For a capsule of this exchange see Anne Collins, "The Battle over 'The Valour and the Horror,'" *Saturday Night*, May 1993, 45–9, 72–9.

2 David MacIsaac, "Voices from the Central Blue," in Peter Paret, ed., *Makers of Modern Strategy* (Oxford: Clarendon Press 1986), 636–7.

3 Noble Frankland, cited in MacIsaac, "Voices," 636.

4 Robin Higham, "New Research on the Royal Air Force: Retrospect and Prospect with Emphasis upon World War II," unpublished manuscript, no date.

5 John Terraine, *A Time for Courage: The Royal Air Force in the European War 1939–1945* (New York: Macmillan 1985). Published in the United Kingdom as *The Right of the Line*.

6 Richard Ovary, *The Air War, 1939–1945* (London: Stein and Day 1980).

7 Martin Middlebrook and Chris Everitt, *The Bomber Command War Diaries* (London: Penguin 1985).

8 For a relatively recent bibliographic essay on the RAF, see Stephen Harris and Norman Hillmer, "The Development of the Royal Air Force, 1909–1945," and on the RCAF, see Ronald Haycock, "The Dominion Services: Canada." Both essays appear in Gerald Jordan, ed., *British Military History: A Supplement to Robin Higham's Guide to the Sources* (New York: Garland Publishing 1988).

9 Stephen Harris and Brereton Greenhous, "British Commonwealth Air Forces," *Aerospace Historian* 31, 1 (March 1984): 51.

10 MacIsaac, "Voices," 624–47.

11 Horst Boog, ed., *The Conduct of the Air War in the Second World War* (Oxford: Berg Publishers 1992). Of particular note is the fact that this was an

international conference, and as such it provides an Axis and an Allied perspective.

12 Michael S. Sherry, *The Rise of American Air Power: The Creation of Armageddon* (New Haven: Yale University Press 1987); Conrad C. Crane, *Bombs, Cities and Civilians* (Lawrence: University Press of Kansas 1993); Alan J. Levine, *The Strategic Bombing of Germany, 1940–1945* (Westport, CT: Praeger 1992).

13 The official history of the British air services in the Great War provides a detailed account of the "strategic" bombing campaign. See Sir Walter Raleigh and H.A. Jones, *The War in the Air*, 6 vols. (Oxford: Clarendon Press 1922–37). A more recent treatment can be found in the official history of the RCAF, vol. 1. See S.F. Wise, *Canadian Airmen and the First World War* (Toronto: University of Toronto Press 1981), Part III: Strategic Air Power, 234–333.

14 For a full discussion, see Malcolm Cooper, *The Birth of Independent Air Power* (London: Allen and Unwin 1986).

15 Barry Powers, *Strategy without Slide-Rule* (London: Croom Helm 1976), 110.

16 Malcolm Smith, *British Air Strategy between the Wars* (London: Clarendon Press 1984), 1.

17 Uri Bialer, *The Shadow of the Bomber* (London: Royal Historical Society 1980).

18 The historical literature on the interwar RAF and its development of the theory of strategic air war is vast and still growing. For a synopsis see Scot Robertson, "Hugh Trenchard: Making the Unorthodox Orthodox," in B.J.C. McKercher and Hamish Ion, eds., *Military Heretics* (New York: Praeger, forthcoming). A more comprehensive account is Malcolm Smith, *British Air Strategy* (Oxford: Oxford University Press 1984).

19 Max Hastings, *Bomber Command* (London: Pan Books 1981).

20 Ibid., 17.

21 Ibid., 17.

22 The Western Air PLans are set out in CAB 53/49, COS Paper No. 915(JP) dated 13 June 1939.

23 Winston Churchill, cited in Terraine, *A Time for Courage*, 288.

24 There was another problem with Bomber Command, although at the time it was not so readily obvious, masked as it was by the more serious one of loss rate. That problem was accuracy in delivery. The bomber aircraft was only the platform. Its real weapon was the bomb. The bomb needed to be delivered accurately on the target, and once on the target, it had to produce a significant effect. All too often, accuracy was poor. Moreover, bomb design was a problem. The explosive-to-weight ratio was too low, and fuses proved unreliable. So, in many instances, a raid produced little or no effect despite a high loss rate.

25 Terraine, *A Time for Courage*, 262.

26 Directive from the Air Ministry to commander-in-chief, Bomber Command, 9 July 1941, cited in Sir Charles Webster and Noble Frankland, *The Strategic Air Offensive against Germany*, vol. 4 (London: HMSO 1961), 135–6.

27 The accuracy problem was not, however, well known at that point. It was not until the completion of the Butt report in the autumn of 1941 that the full scope of the problem was laid bare. At the instigation of Lord Cherwell, scientific adviser to the prime minister, D.M.B. Butt of the War Cabinet Secretariat was tasked to carry out a statistical study of the results of Bomber Command's efforts during the months of June and July. The conclusions were depressing. Butt concluded that "1) Of those aircraft recorded as attacking their target, only one in three got within five miles. 2) ... over Germany as a whole the proportion was one in four; over the Ruhr it was only one in ten." Cited ibid., 205.

28 John Terraine, "Theory and Practice of Air War: The RAF," in Boog, ed., *The Conduct of the Air War*, 488. Harris was, however, a very single-minded and energetic proponent of the area offensive, perhaps to a fault. On taking over as air officer commanding, Bomber Command, Harris pursued the area offensive to the virtual exclusion of all other forms of air warfare. He complained bitterly when the Air Staff directed Bomber Command to attack targets that he deemed "panaceas" and diversions from what he held as the single most important objective – enemy "morale."

29 These statistics are drawn from Middlebrook and Everitt, *Bomber Command War Diaries*, 707–8, and Charles Messenger, *"Bomber" Harris and the Strategic Bombing Offensive, 1939–1945* (London: Arms and Armour Press 1984), 191–214. There will never be a definitive count of German deaths. The figure of 800,000 is only an estimate. In contrast, approximately 60,000 British civilians died in the German bombing attacks against the United Kingdom.

30 The opening salvo in this ongoing debate was fired by Sir Arthur Harris with the publication of his *Bomber Offensive* (London: Collins 1947). Harris's account amounted to a vigorous defence of Bomber Comand's activities. The debate has continued for nearly fifty years. Some of the major contributions to this debate include H.R. Allen, *The Legacy of Lord Trenchard* (London: Cassell 1972); Gerald Dickens, *Bombing and Strategy: The Fallacy of Total War* (London: Low 1947); David Divine, *The Blunted Sword* (London: Hutchinson 1964); Max Hastings, *Bomber Command* (London: Pan 1981); Neville Jones, *The Origins of Strategic Bombing* (London: Kimber 1973); Lee Kennett, *A History of Strategic Bombing* (New York: Scribner's 1982); R.A. Mason, *War in the Third Dimension* (London: Brassey's 1986); Charles Messenger, *Bomber Harris and the Strategic Bombing Offensive, 1939–1945* (London: Arms and Armour Press 1984); Dudley Saward, *Bomber Harris* (London: Sphere 1984); Anthony Verrier, *The Bomber Offensive* (London: Macmillan 1968); and Sir Charles Webster and Noble Frankland, *The*

Strategic Air Offensive against Germany, 4 vols. (London: HMSO 1961). These are but a few of the contributions to this debate, which has been rekindled again in the aftermath of the Gulf War of 1991.

31 Ovary, *The Air War*, 205–6.

32 Malcolm Smith, "Harris's Offensive in Historical Perspective," *Journal of the Royal United Services Institute* 130, 2 (June 1985): 64.

33 James Roche and Barry Watts, "Choosing Analytic Measures," *Journal of Strategic Studies* 14, 2 (June 1991): 165–209.

34 Ibid., 175.

35 Ibid., 179.

36 Klein, cited ibid., 179–83.

37 Roche and Watts, "Choosing Analytic Measures," 183.

38 Ovary, *The Air War*, 123.

39 Williamson Murray, *Luftwaffe* (Baltimore: Nautical and Aviation Publishing 1985), 283. What is sometimes difficult to ascertain from observations such as these is the effect that the diminution of morale had on the overall German war effort. The problem of translating this general effect to some form of quantitative measure leads to a reliance on economic and production figures.

40 The *post facto* imposition of a legal sanction against the vanquished is not, in itself, an efficacious measure, given that no party resorting to war sets out with the intention of losing. Hence, the "fear" of a *post facto* sanction is hardly foremost in the planning prior to the declaration of war.

41 There is a vast literature dealing with restraints imposed on the actual conduct of war. One of the most comprehensive and readable treatments of this subject is Geoffrey Best, *Humanity in Warfare: The Modern History of the International Law of Armed Conflicts* (London: Weidenfeld & Nicolson 1980). Best deals with the question of restraints in war throughout, but particularly in chapter 4.

42 Cited in Sheldon M. Cohen, *Arms and Judgement: Law Morality and the Conduct of War in the Twentieth Century* (Boulder: Westview 1989), 7.

43 Cited in Larry Bidinian, *The Combined Allied Bombing Offensive against the German Civilian, 1942–1945* (Lawrence, KS: Coronado Press 1976), 160. This comment by Liddell Hart is somewhat curious in that he was one of the interwar years' most vocal advocates of the air force and the employment of what he termed the "indirect approach" to strategy. While he applied this conception mostly to "grand strategy," it is also true to say that he foresaw strategic and operational benefits accruing from an indirect approach. Liddell Hart's conception of the indirect approach derived from his experience as a young officer in the British Army during the First World War. Repelled by the horrors of trench warfare, Liddell Hart believed that such an experience could be avoided in future by seeking to go around (or over) an enemy force and attacking in unexpected places. It

could be argued that Bomber Command was pursuing a variant of the indirect approach.

44 Best, *Humanity in War*, 284.

45 A.J.P. Taylor, *From Sarajevo to Potsdam: The Years 1914–1945* (London: Thames and Hudson 1974), 178.

46 Noble Frankland, *Journal of the Royal United Services Institute*, May 1962, 108–9.

47 Cited in Winston Churchill, *The World Crisis*, vol. 2 (New York: Scribners 1923), 490.

48 A superb treatment of the evolution of modern Laws of War can be found in Best, *Humanity of War*, chap. 3, 128–215.

49 For a brief but excellent discussion of the difficulties that plagued the efforts to draw up rules governing air war at the 1922–23 Hague meetings, see W. Hays Parks, "Air War and the Laws of War," in Boog, ed., *The Conduct of the Air War*, 310–72, in particular 332–44.

50 Cited in Cohen, *Arms and Judgement*, 34. The full text of the 1907 Hague Conventions can be found in A.P. Higgins, *The Hague Peace Conferences and Other International Conferences Concerning the Laws and Usages of War: Texts of Conventions with Commentaries* (Cambridge: Cambridge University Press 1909).

51 The text can be found in Higgins, *The Hague Peace Conferences*.

52 For the purposes of this discussion, it is to be assumed that the difficulty attached to defining the term "undefended" in the context of the land rules applies equally to the naval rules.

53 Hague Convention (IX), "Bombardment by Naval Forces," Higgins, *The Hague Peace Conferences*, 347–8.

54 Cohen, *Arms and Judgement*, 118.

55 Sir Robert Saundby, "The Ethics of Bombing," *RAF Quarterly* (summer 1967): 97.

56 Cohen, *Arms and Judgement*, 124.

57 This is, of course, the difficulty identified by Clausewitz and others, and the problem that plagues the modern world with weapons of mass destruction.

58 Cohen, *Arms and Judgement*, 127.

59 Excerpt from Albert Speer, *Spandau: The Secret Diaries*, cited ibid., 129. It has been intimated by some that Speer was being disingenuous in his statements, perhaps telling his captors what they wanted to hear. There is other evidence available from other German sources that bears out Speer's comment. For instance, von Mellenthin observed, "during the last months of the war communications were entirely disrupted so that it was impossible for any replacement to reach its destination ... Even though the necessary equipment was available in Germany, it could not always reach the front line – at least in sufficient quantities." F.W. von Mellenthin,

Panzer Battles (New York: Ballantine 1971), 433–4, cited in Levine, *The Strategic Bombing of Germany*, 192–3.

60 Cohen, *Arms and Judgement*, 130.
61 Noble Frankland, cited in Terraine, *A Time for Courage*, 683. It would perhaps be appropriate to modify Frankland's statement to read, "to have abandoned [one of the] only means of direct attack."
62 Boog, ed., *The Conduct of the Air War*, 4.

The Valour and the Horror Controversy and the Official History of the Royal Canadian Air Force, Volume 3

The publication of volume 3 of the *Official History of the Royal Canadian Air Force* by Brereton Greenhous, Stephen J. Harris, William C. Johnston, and William G.P. Rawling (University of Toronto Press 1994) reawakened the media controversy over *The Valour and the Horror*, particularly that related to the "Death by Moonlight" episode. Although there are certain similarities in approach between the official history and the film, some of them superficial and some not, the differences are far more significant than the similarities. Volume 3 is in fact a comprehensive and well-documented history of the RCAF's overseas operations in the Second World War; the RCAF's role in the bombing offensive occupies 344 of 909 pages of text. Though much of this section is taken up with the origins and history of No. 6 (RCAF) Group, the authors also examine the origins of the RAF's bombing philosophy in the 1919–39 period and trace the evolution and execution of RAF bombing policy during the war.

The merits of this volume of the RCAF history were not what caught the attention of the media (which, by contrast, had all but ignored the first two volumes of the history). Rather, the authors appeared to be arguing that Sir Arthur Harris's accession to the leadership of Bomber Command in 1942 brought a decided shift to "area" bombing aimed at destroying German morale by killing, wounding, and "de-housing" as many German city dwellers as possible, especially in industrial cities. Such a conjuncture was precisely the argument of *The Valour and the Horror*. Unlike the film, however, the authors of volume 3 show that the decision to stress area bombing was a decision of the higher command, including the British War Cabinet, and that it came about because of several factors, including long-held theories about the potential impact of bombing on enemy morale; the inability of the RAF to make precision attacks at night; the strongly held desire of the British (and Canadians, if poll results presented in the book are a valid measure) to pay the Germans back for their own area bombing of London, Coventry, and other centres; and the necessity of making some important contribution to the war in the west while the forces of the Soviet Union were fighting and dying in large numbers in the east. In short, while the official history offers a complex – and surely valid – explanation of the onset of area bombing, *The Valour and the Horror* did not, preferring to account for the strategy in its depiction of the devil-figure Arthur Harris.

Yet there is a sense in which the two accounts of the bomber offensive coincide. Both volume 3 of the official history and 'Death by Moonlight' elaborate a common central point: that British and Canadian aircrews were deliberately sent out, night after night, to kill innocent Germans, with little benefit to the war effort. At its crudest, the argument of both is that the RAF and RCAF killed Germans just for the sake of killing Germans. The impact of this contention is perhaps stronger in volume 3 of the official history because it is, after all, an elaborately researched and documented official history. The melancholy conclusion its team of authors reach in assessing the bombing role is that "the Combined Bomber Offensive (by both the RAF/RCAF and the United States Army Air Force) against Germany did not begin to meet its objectives – the progressive, if not sudden, decline in enemy war production and, later, civilian morale – until the last months of 1944, four full years after it began in earnest" (865–7). It should be noted that although the authors assert in the sentence quoted here that the strategic bombing offensive began in 1940, it was 1942 that was the true beginning of the offensive, according to the authors themselves. It was this contention – the combination of frightfulness and pointless sacrifice – that attracted the media and appeared to offer vindication for the position taken by the McKennas in *The Valour and the Horror.*

We believe it is precisely here that volume 3 of the official history is most open to criticism. But before taking up that point we should state that this book has many real strengths. It is well written and almost invariably interesting. Divided into sections on Air Policy, The Fighter War, The Maritime Air War, The Bomber War, and Air Transport, it gives a remarkably complete overview of the massive and varied Canadian air effort in overseas theatres during the Second World War. The Bomber War section is especially valuable for the technical detail it supplies on bombing operations, aircraft, and the course of actual missions. An outstanding merit of the section is the analysis of the war of electronic measures and countermeasures, a major feature of the night-bombing campaign. The description of this aspect of the bomber war is probably the best short account that has appeared in print.

Yet there are problems with volume 3 of the official history, particularly in its treatment of the strategic bombing offensive. The authors are almost obsessively concerned to establish that Harris's sole aim in the offensive was to destroy German cities and kill German civilians. But this is contested by no credible historian; it has long been well established that the German population and the morale of the German people were prime targets of Bomber Command. The real puzzle was why the air staff believed so firmly in the fragility of civilian morale, yet this question is never raised in volume 3 of the official history. (The roots of this belief are to be found in the RAF staff in 1917–18, and may in part be connected with an upper-class perception of the emotional volatility of the industrial working classes – a mistaken assumption if ever there was one.)

The assault on German civilians and their morale was by no means the only endeavour engaged in by Bomber Command, which in fact waged a multifaceted campaign against industrial targets, rail and communication systems, aircraft manufacturing plants and other war material industries, oil refineries, and so on. All this is carefully detailed in volume 3 of the official history, at the same time as the authorial team condemns Harris for being so single-minded about area bombing. Sometimes Harris selected targets other than cities of his own volition, and sometimes at the suggestion of his seniors, such as Portal and Eisenhower. This contradiction, which runs through the bombing section of volume 3, suggests that the authors took literally Harris's bombastic rhetoric, as in his letter to the undersecretary of state for air of 25 October 1943 in which he declared that the aim of RAF bombing was, quite simply, "the destruction of German cities, the killing of German workers and the disruption of civilised community life throughout Germany" (724–5). If Harris was so rigidly committed to these objectives, as the authors believe, then why the varied missions mounted by Bomber Command?

The likely answer is that Harris shared the inconsistencies that overtake all of us, including senior commanders. He made compromises, he was susceptible to pressures from others, and occasionally he changed his mind or was ready to try new approaches. Moreover, Harris was not Bomber Command, only its air officer commanding in chief. Volume 3 of the official history reduces Bomber Command to a one-man show. It is to be regretted that the kind of sophisticated analysis of the many factors making up American bombing policy (and its many contradictions) to be found in Conrad

C. Crane's *Bombs, Cities, and Civilians: American Airpower Strategy in World War II* (Lawrence: University Press of Kansas 1993) are missing in this volume.

In another respect the approach taken by the authors of this volume of the official history intersects with that of the producers of *The Valour and the Horror*. Both conclude that the bomber offensive did not achieve the objectives of its proponents. In two or three paragraphs tacked on to the end of the Bomber War section, a series of considerations are listed which attest to the importance of the bombing offensive, whether establishing a "Second Front" when no other means was available to do so or diverting substantial German manpower and war material to air defence at the cost of German armies in the field. But given the weight of the narrative, these paragraphs are perfunctory and appear almost as afterthoughts.

What grounds do the authors have for their conclusions about the effectiveness of the Combined Bomber Offensive? There is no scholarly assessment of the United States share of that offensive, nor is there any discussion of the differing views that exist on the overall offensive. Nearly half a century after the compilation of the British and American strategic bombing surveys, the authors of volume 3 accepted the view of some authorities on the meaning of that body of evidence – authorities well known for their opinion that the campaign was a failure – and ignore the evidence brought forward by other authorities of a different view. Neither Williamson Murray nor Richard Overy, for example, are cited, yet their research pointed to the conclusion that the RAF offensive had a significant impact on the course of the war. There is, in sum, a remarkable contrast between the quality of the analysis made by the authors on bombing operations and German defensive measures, and the lack of analysis in assessing the value of the campaign of which these operations were a part. The jury is still out on the actual impact of the bombing offensive on Germany and on the outcome of the war itself; it cannot be said that volume 3 of the official history has contributed much to the matter.

It would be hard to say whether the stance taken by the authors on the bombing offensive derives in part from a moral revulsion against the form that offensive took. At one point (843) the authors refer to the "moral ambiguity" of area bombing against German cities, but nowhere in their section on the Bomber War is there either a moral or a legal discussion of the issues raised by an air war levied against civilian populations. Scot Robertson, in his essay on the strategic bombing offensive in this book, confronts these questions directly. Indeed, the authors of volume 3 at the very least do not contend that German cities were "open" and "undefended"; their discussion of Lutfwaffe defensive measures is admirably thorough, and heavy Canadian aircrew losses are a testimony to the effectiveness of the German air defence system.

In the concluding pages of the Bomber War section, the authors quote from an editorial of the *Globe and Mail* of 23 March 1945 (864). The editorial, after asserting that the bomber offensive had crippled the German economy, contended that "the real victory of Allied air power" was "a thing of the mind – a lesson so terrible as never to be forgotten ... The German people will not need the presence of Allied armies to persuade them that they lost this war. The storm which is sweeping them from the air ... is convincing them that they have suffered the most terrible defeat ever inflicted on a people in all history." Out of this, the *Globe* hoped, would come a resolve by the people of Germany to live "constructively and compatibly alongside [their] neighbours."

The comment by the authors of this official history is deeply revealing of their interpretive position. "If that were the case," they wrote, "then the long casualty lists the *Globe* had published over the last five years would have some meaning." The whole thrust of volume 3 of the official history is that the bomber offensive was a misguided failure and that the deaths of 9919 Canadians in Bomber Command were essentially meaningless in the total picture of the war.

But surely the *Globe* editorial was fundamentally correct. No event other than the final surge of the Red Army into Berlin brought the war home more crushingly to the German people than the long-sustained bomber offensive with its terrible casualties and immense damage. They knew, and their postwar, post-Nazi leaders knew, that Germany could not suffer another war as terrible as the Second World War and that the German state would have to take a new path. Out of this realization came the Schuman Plan of 1950, the European Economic Community of 1957, and the European Community of today. Out of it also came the emergence of a democratic and responsible Germany in full partnership and alliance with the states that once had bombed it.

Contributors

DAVID J. BERCUSON is a professor of history and dean of graduate studies at the University of Calgary; he is also a Fellow of the Royal Society of Canada.

JOHN FERRIS is an associate professor in history at the University of Calgary.

BILL McANDREW is a historian at the Director General History, National Defence Headquarters, Ottawa.

SCOT ROBERTSON is a historian at the Directorate of Force Concepts, National Defence Headquarters, Ottawa.

S.F. WISE is a professor of history and former dean of graduate studies and research at Carleton University; he is also a Member of the Order of Canada and a Fellow of the Royal Society of Canada.